x 45

11

Gaúcho Politics in Brazil

Gaúcho Politics in Brazil

The Politics of
Rio Grande do Sul, 1930-1964

Carlos E. Cortés

UNIVERSITY OF
NEW MEXICO PRESS

Albuquerque

Photographs courtesy Atelier O. Dutra,
Pôrto Alegre, and *Revista do Globo,*
Pôrto Alegre.

For Murielle
My Parents
My Grandparents
and the Gaúchos

Preface

There is not sufficient space to thank all of the many people and organizations who helped me with this project. However, I would like to give special acknowledgement to certain groups and individuals.

The Foreign Area Fellowship Program provided a grant so that my wife and I could live in Brazil from April 1966 through October 1967, during which time I did the basic research for this book. In addition, a series of intramural research grants from the University of California, Riverside, and a Humanities Institute grant from the University of California enabled me to complete my research and writing.

Government officials in both Brazil and the United States substantially expedited my work. Moreover, I would like to thank the Instituto Histórico e Geográfico do Rio Grande do Sul for its hospitality in making available to me its unique collection, including the Antônio Augusto Borges de Medeiros archive.

I want to express my deep gratitude to the families of Joaquim Francisco de Assis Brasil, Francisco Antunes Maciel Junior, Lindolfo Collor, Getúlio Vargas, and Oswaldo Aranha, who graciously permitted me to use the papers of these Gaúcho leaders. In addition, I offer my thanks to Sinval Saldanha and Rony Lopes de Almeida for allowing me to work in their personal archives.

I would like to acknowledge my indebtedness to the more than seventy Brazilian politicians, historians, and other analysts who devoted countless hours to interviews and conversations and made their libraries available to me. Six native and "naturalized"

Gaúchos who gave me special insights into the Rio Grande phenomenon—José Fernando Carneiro, José Antônio Aranha, Erico Verissimo, Maurício Rosenblatt, Moysés Vellinho, and Leônidas Xausa—have my particular gratitude for both their friendship and their help.

I would like to thank my typist, Clara Dean, and those who generously commented on my manuscript—Troy Floyd, Martin Needler, Eul-Soo Pang, Joseph Love, and Susan Philips. To Edwin Lieuwen, whose advice and encouragement have been invaluable, I owe a special debt of gratitude.

But most important has been my wife, Murielle. Whether commenting on my manuscript, assisting me in archives, aiding me with her insight into Brazil, or helping to make our stay in Brazil an unforgettable one, she has been a constant source of strength and inspiration. Without her intelligence, understanding, and devotion, this book might not have been.

Contents

MAPS

Abbreviations Used

ADP   Popular Democratic Action (Ação Democrática Popular)
AL   Liberator Action (Ação Libertadora)
ARENA National Renovation Alliance (Aliança Renovadora Nacional)
ARS   Socialist Republican Alliance (Aliança Republicana Socialista)
FD   Democratic Front (Frente Democrática)
FU   United Front (Frente Única)
LEC   Catholic Electoral League (Liga Eleitoral Católica)
MDB   Brazilian Democratic Movement (Movimento Democrático Brasileiro)
MTR   Labor Renovation Movement (Movimento Trabalhista Renovador)
PCB   Brazilian Communist Party (Partido Comunista do Brasil; Partido Comunista Brasileiro)
PDC   Christian Democratic Party (Partido Democrata Cristão)
PDP   Paulista Democratic Party (Partido Democrático Paulista)
PL   Liberator Party (Partido Libertador)
PR   Republican Party (Partido Republicano)
PRC   Castilhist Republican Party (Partido Republicano Castilhista)
PRL   Liberal Republican Party (Partido Republicano Liberal)
PRP   Paulista Republican Party (Partido Republicano Paulista—chapters two through five)
     Popular Representation Party (Partido da Representação Popular—chapters six through eleven)
PRR   Riograndense Republican Party (Partido Republicano Riograndense)
PSB   Brazilian Socialist Party (Partido Socialista Brasileiro)
PSD   Social Democratic Party (Partido Social Democrático)
PSDA   Autonomous Social Democratic Party (Partido Social Democrático Autônomo)

PSP	Social Progressive Party (Partido Social Progressista)
PTB	Brazilian Labor Party (Partido Trabalhista Brasileiro)
UDB	Brazilian Democratic Union (União Democrática Brasileira)
UDN	National Democratic Union (União Democrática Nacional)
USB	Brazilian Social Union (União Social Brasileira)

**Brazil and Neighboring Countries, Showing States
and Territories of Brazil and Their Capitals**

Rio Grande do Sul in the Old Republic

Santa Catarina

Marcelino Ramos ○

Passo Fundo ○

Vacaria ○

São Borja ○

Soledade ○

Tupanciretã ○

Encantado ○   Caxias ○

São Pedro ○

Santa Maria ○   Novo Hamburgo ○
São Leopoldo ○

Uruguaiana ○

Cachoeira ○   Pôrto Alegre ◎

A R G E N T I N A

U R U G U A Y

Livramento ○
Rivera ○

Pelotas ○

Rio Grande ○

DUCK LAKE

ATLANTIC OCEAN

N

0   40   80   120
Kilometers

Rio Grande do Sul

PART ONE

Prologue

1

A Military Heritage

In 1930, leaders of the Brazilian state of Rio Grande do Sul spearheaded a revolution* which toppled the country's forty-one-year-old First Republic and installed the governor of Rio Grande as Brazilian chief of state. In 1964, a military revolt toppled the nineteen-year-old Third Republic and forced the president, also from Rio Grande do Sul, to flee into exile in Uruguay. These two events provided the opening and closing curtains for an era marked by a major Rio Grande presence in Brazilian politics.

During this turbulent period, Riograndenses often attempted, sometimes with success, to establish national political hegemony. For twenty-two of those thirty-four years Rio Grande furnished Brazil's presidents. In addition, an extraordinary number of the nation's political and military leaders came from this unique state. During that same era, Rio Grande continually mounted military challenges to the central government—twice imposing a Rio-grandense in the national presidency and often determining Brazil's internal military balance of power.

Rio Grande do Sul has had a consistently powerful impact on Brazilian political history that is far out of proportion to the state's geographical size (3 percent of Brazil's land area) or its population (generally about 8 percent of the national head count). To a considerable degree, Rio Grande's strong influence on Brazilian politics reflects the state's intense heritage of violence and military conflict. Geography helped set the stage for Rio

---

Revolution will be used throughout to mean the overthrow or attempted overthrow of a government.

1

Grande's special militaristic evolution. The state lies at the southern coastal tip of Brazil. Mountains stretch across the northern
part of Rio Grande, forming a natural barricade which isolates the
state from the rest of the country and turns it into a de facto
island.

In contrast to the enervating tropics of most of the nation,
Rio Grande enjoys a vigorous, four-season climate. Combined with
the state's varied, fertile land, this climate has helped the development of a diversified agriculture, earning for Rio Grande the nickname of "the food basket of Brazil." Added to this has been the
emergence of a small and medium-sized artisan industry and a
considerable national and, at times, international trade. Although
the state has suffered economic problems (often in relation to the
nation's political-economic heartland, the south-central triangle of
Rio de Janeiro, São Paulo, and Minas Gerais), Rio Grande has
enjoyed relative prosperity in comparison with most other Brazilian states.

Shaped like an overinflated football, Rio Grande can be divided into three major geopolitical zones—the frontier zone, the
colonial zone, and the *litoral*.[1] The frontier zone consists of
sprawling plains and rolling hills which slash a giant arc through
the southern and western regions of the state along the Uruguayan
and Argentine borders. Reminiscent of the southwestern United
States, this zone is characterized by pastoral latifundia—great
cattle and sheep ranches *(estâncias)*—and the rugged Rio Grande
cowboy. Until the 1940s the Luso-Brazilian ranching families of
this zone dominated state politics and furnished most of the
state's political leaders.

In contrast to the open plains and rolling hills of the frontier
zone stand the forested mountains, valleys, and plateaus of the
state's north-northeast. This region has become known as the colonial zone because it has been the focus of the state's immigrant
colonization, predominantly Italian and German. Characterized by
small farms instead of huge ranches, by agricultural rather than
pastoral pursuits, the colonial zone has become noted economically for lumber, hogs, grapes, wine, wheat, corn, beans, and a
variety of industrial consumer products.

Finally, there is the litoral, the southeastern strip of land
which lies along the Atlantic Ocean. The state's commercial and
industrial center, the litoral includes Rio Grande's two largest

cities, Pelotas and Pôrto Alegre, the state capital. Politically the litoral has been the focus of governmental activity, with Pôrto Alegre the residence of most state political leaders. Traditionally these politicians were members or allies of the powerful frontier-zone ranching families. But in the past three decades, much political power has shifted to the German and Italian colonial-zone families and their Pôrto Alegre relatives and compatriots.

The land of Rio Grande has been fertile not only for pastoral and agricultural pursuits. It has also proven fertile for conflict and violence, which have racked Rio Grande constantly for more than three centuries.

International rivalry initiated the state's tradition of strife, violence, and war. In the early seventeenth century the area later known as Rio Grande do Sul became a focus of conflict between Spain and Portugal. Spanish Jesuits made the first European efforts to colonize the area, founding Indian missions in western Rio Grande in 1626. A decade later this concentration of Indians attracted slave-hunting expeditions from the Brazilian province of São Paulo, which forced the Jesuits to withdraw. However, the priests returned in 1687 to establish a flourishing Jesuit-Indian civilization which became known as the Seven Missions.[2]

In 1725 the Portuguese established their first settlement in the region and proceeded to convert the area into a military fortress. Portuguese settlers had two major roles: they were to block Spanish and Indian expansion from the west, and they were to provide logistical support for Colônia do Sacramento, the southernmost Portuguese settlement, which had been established in 1680 on the Banda Oriental ("East Bank" of the Rio de la Plata—modern Uruguay) across the estuary from Buenos Aires.

Into the Rio Grande do Sul agricultural paradise came hardy settlers from other Brazilian states—primarily São Paulo, Minas Gerais, Rio de Janeiro, and Santa Catarina—and vigorous, independent immigrants from the Azores Islands. They were accompanied by a flow of soldiers from around Brazil to man the forts of this statewide armed camp. Established as a military buffer zone, Rio Grande remained in a state of constant military preparedness. Settlers doubled as soldiers, with every man a part-time warrior, ready to fight at a moment's notice.

From 1754 until 1828, Rio Grande served as the site of actual fighting or the source of troops for a series of international wars. Under the Treaty of Madrid of 1750, Portugal agreed to exchange the Banda Oriental for Spanish territory, including the Jesuit missions on Rio Grande's western frontier. When the Indians resisted, Portuguese and Spanish troops fought them in the War of the Seven Missions (1754-56). This was followed by struggles between Portugal and Spain in 1762, in 1767, and from 1774 to 1776, terminated by the Treaty of San Ildefonso of 1777, which secured the Banda Oriental for Spain.

Beginning in 1776, Rio Grande basked in thirty-five years of peace, broken only by a short conflict between Portugal and Spain in 1801. Riograndenses took advantage of that brief struggle to disband finally the Jesuit Seven Missions. Benefitting from these years of general calm, Rio Grande experienced rapid economic and population growth.[3]

In 1811 Regent João VI of Portugal shattered Rio Grande's peace when he tried to profit from the Spanish-American wars of independence by annexing the Banda Oriental. This venture initiated seventeen years of nearly continuous fighting, with Rio Grande once again bearing much of the burden, Finally, in 1828, with British urging, Argentina (then the United Provinces of the Rio de la Plata) and Brazil (which had obtained its independence from Portugal in 1822) allowed the disputed area to become the Republic of Uruguay. But by then the prolonged struggle had terminated an era of Rio Grande progress, exhausted the state's public treasury, destroyed many of its cities, and decimated its population.[4] Furthermore, the Gaúchos* (Riograndenses—persons from Rio Grande do Sul) charged that the central government's economic discrimination and neglect of the state's problems were strangling its economy and turning Rio Grande into the "slum of the Empire."

Tired of being used as military and economic sacrificial lambs, the Gaúchos revolted in 1835 and established an independent Riograndense Republic. Whether the Gaúchos wanted to create a permanent separate republic, force better central government treatment of Rio Grande, or "republicanize" monarchical Brazil is still a matter of historical controversy. For ten years the

---

*"Gaúcho" has two meanings. In a restricted sense it means cowboy (used for cowboys of Rio Grande do Sul)—roughly synonymous with the Spanish word, "gaucho," cowboy of Uruguay or Argentina. However, throughout the book Gaúcho will be used in its more generic sense to identify *all* Riograndenses (persons from Rio Grande do Sul).

rebels fought the rest of Brazil in a civil war known as the Far-roupilha War (War of the Ragamuffins). Finally, when Argentine dictator Juan Manuel de Rosas invited the hard-pressed Gaúchos to join the United Provinces of Argentina, they vigorously rejected him and rejoined the Brazilian Empire in 1845.[5]

Reincorporation into the Empire did not bring lasting peace to the war-torn state. Uruguayan civil wars forced the Gaúchos to defend constantly against pillaging and cattle rustling on the southern border. In addition, although Rio Grande had less than 5 percent of the Brazilian population, Gaúchos composed three-fourths of the Brazilian force that helped defeat Rosas at the Battle of Monte Caseros in 1852. In the War of the Triple Alliance against Paraguayan dictator Francisco Solano López from 1865 to 1870, Rio Grande furnished 24 percent of the Brazilian troops, as well as most of the generals and corps commanders. During that war Paraguayan troops ravaged the Gaúcho frontier cities of Uruguaiana and São Borja.[6]

Climaxed by the Paraguayan War, the more than a century of strife had an enduring effect on the Gaúcho psyche and on future Gaúcho political behavior. These years of immense human and economic sacrifice made the Gaúcho intensely proud of and defensive about his state and its history. He came to believe that his suffering and bloodshed in his country's behalf, and his decision to be Brazilian rather than Argentine, had made him a better citizen than his "involuntary Brazilian" fellow countrymen.

Moreover, this turbulent century had inculcated in the Gaúcho the conviction that non-Gaúchos continually drained Rio Grande's lifeblood, neglected Rio Grande's needs, and sought to prevent Rio Grande from obtaining its rightful place in the national structure. These not entirely unjustified perceptions—which would be reinforced in future years—led to an almost instinctive rejection of impositions from the national level, whether by the national government or by national political organizations.

Gaúchos also became convinced that their state's history had earned for Rio Grande a special, autonomous status. In a general sense, this attitude would emerge as Gaúcho defense of constitutional federalism and state autonomy and opposition to centralism and federal intervention in the states. In a specific sense, it would mean frequent recourse to violent defense against encroachments on Gaúcho autonomy, pride, or interests.

It was a short step from this defensive position to an offensive one—the imposition of Gaúcho domination, beliefs, or interests on the rest of Brazil. As they had attempted to do in the 1835-45 Farroupilha War, Gaúchos would sometimes resort to force in an effort to impose their will nationally.* In these efforts to assert national power through force, future Gaúchos would benefit from the state's powerful military base.

The Rio Grande state military brigade, formed in 1892, would grow to fifteen thousand men by 1965. Yet this represented only a minor part of total Gaúcho military strength. Proud of his heritage of strife, the civilian Gaúcho could be counted on to answer the alarum bell of state mobilization. Thousands of men could be raised in a matter of hours in the form of provisional corps, a type of unofficial civilian ready reserve.

Gaúchos generally made up an estimated one-third of the Brazilian army. Moreover, they formed an even greater part of the powerful, Rio Grande-based Brazilian Third Army,† which composed between one-fourth and one-third of the national force.** As Gaúchos in the Brazilian army often remained primarily loyal to Rio Grande rather than to Brazil and at critical moments allied themselves with Gaúcho state forces, Rio Grande ultimately posed a military threat far beyond that of its brigade and civilian volunteers.

However, before Gaúchos could transform their military potential into an effective force on the national scene, the state would undergo decades of internal conflict. In particular, Gaúcho national military effectiveness would await the political restructuring of the state.

---

*Francisco Ferraz, a young Rio Grande political scientist, has developed the theory of Gaúcho "tutorship" over the rest of Brazil. According to Ferraz, Rio Grande do Sul has revolted at various times in its history in order to educate Brazil politically, such as in 1835, 1930, and 1961. Author's interview with Francisco Ferraz, Pôrto Alegre, March 28, 1967.

† The Brazilian army is composed of four commands—the First Army with headquarters in Rio de Janeiro, Second Army in São Paulo, Third Army in Pôrto Alegre, and Fourth Army in Recife. Rio Grande's strategic location on the Argentine and Uruguayan borders has meant consistently heavy troop concentrations in the state.

**One recent study indicated that Gaúchos made up nearly 20 percent of the active duty army generals in 1964, and even this represented a decline (from 36 percent in 1935, for example). The study also reported that Gaúchos made up all of the draftees, 95 percent of the career corporals, 70 to 80 percent of the sergeants, and 50 to 60 percent of the officers of the Third Army units in Rio Grande. See Alfred Stepan, *The Military in Politics. Changing Patterns in Brazil* (Princeton, N. J.: Princeton University Press, 1971), pp. 14,40.

Such restructuring began even while the Paraguayan War raged, with the emergence of a new republican movement in Rio Grande do Sul. Since the collapse of the Riograndense Republic, the state had been divided between the Conservative and Liberal parties, the two national political organizations. Gaúcho republicanism developed in conjunction with its growth throughout Brazil; in 1882 a state convention launched the Riograndense Republican Party (PRR–Partido Republicano Riograndense).[7]

At that time Gaspar da Silveira Martins, chief of the state Liberal Party, was the paramount Gaúcho political leader and a major figure in the Brazilian Imperial government.[8] In the latter years of the Empire he constructed the strongest state Liberal Party in Brazil. It was a powerful political machine based on an alliance of regional *coroneis*,* particularly wealthy ranchers (*estancieiros*) of the frontier zone. As the Liberal Party increased its domination over Gaúcho politics, many disillusioned Conservative leaders defected from their withering organization and joined the aggressive Republican Party. By the end of the Empire, the PRR had replaced the Conservative Party as the second-strongest political unit in Rio Grande.

A military coup toppled Emperor Pedro II in 1889 and paved the way for Brazil's First Republic. Marshal Deodoro da Fonseca, who led the revolt, became chief of state and later president. As one of his early acts, he exiled Silveira Martins, who had been a bulwark of the Empire.

On the Rio Grande do Sul level, the revolution led to the ascension to state power of the PRR under its brilliant, determined, autocratic chief, Júlio de Castilhos. Throughout four turbulent years of intraparty struggle, during which the state government changed Republican hands eighteen times, Castilhos constructed a hierarchical, militant organization. In it he united his Republican supporters with Conservative defectors. Once in power as governor, Castilhos removed Liberal officials and public

---

*The *coronel* (plural–*coroneis*) is the traditional Brazilian county political chieftain. He is usually a wealthy landowner or another representative of the socioeconomic elite, and his principal task is to deliver votes by any means necessary, including pressure, threats, and the seduction of governmental favors. Brazilian county-level politics, particularly in the interior, has historically been a struggle between opposing coroneis, although the secret ballot and other recent political and socioeconomic changes have severely modified the power of the coronel. See Victor Nunes Leal, *Coronelismo, Enxada e Voto. O Município e o Regime Representativo no Brasil* (Rio de Janeiro: Revista Forense, 1948), pp. 10,24.

functionaries, demolished the Liberal electoral machine, formed a civic guard as the military base of his regime, and prepared for the inevitable struggle against the forces of Silveira Martins.[9]

To institutionalize his control Castilhos wrote the Rio Grande do Sul constitution of 1891, establishing a republican dictatorship.[10] The constitution reflected both Castilhos' doctrinary commitment to the positivism of Auguste Comte and his practical commitment to liquidating an opposition which had both economic power and social prestige. The document gave the governor (officially the state "president" during the First Republic) almost dictatorial powers, such as that of promulgating all legislation, while it restricted the state assembly to budgetary and tax functions. It also permitted indefinite gubernatorial reelection.

Elections throughout Brazil during the First Republic were characterized by fraud, corruption, threats, and violence. The secret ballot did not exist, and the party in power generally won elections. In Rio Grande do Sul the national system of public voting was even more highly refined to assure Republican control. Voters were required to sign their ballots publicly, and electoral officials could not stop anyone with a voter's card from voting, even if the card were of a person of the opposite sex.

Returning from exile in 1892, Silveira Martins formed the Federalist Party (Partido Federalista), composed of former Liberals, anti-Castilhos Conservatives, and dissident Republicans who had rebelled against Castilhos' dictatorialness. The Federalists championed parliamentarism and liberalism against the Republicans' presidentialism and authoritarianism. However, this doctrinary confrontation merely provided verbal camouflage for the power struggle between the followers of Castilhos and Silveira Martins, with violence rather than words the primary political weapon. Suffering rigorous government persecution and realizing the futility of electoral competition with the government-based Republican machine, Federalists emigrated en masse to Uruguay and Argentina. There they began preparations to overthrow the Castilhos government.[11]

In alliance with naval officers then rebelling in Rio de Janeiro against the new Brazilian president, Floriano Peixoto, the Federalists (also known as Maragatos because they imported Uruguayan mercenaries from the Maragato region of Uruguay) launched a combined invasion and statewide insurrection in 1893. The Gasparist local chiefs and powerful ranchers, particularly from the frontier zone, raised private armies. Castilhos countered with his newly created state military brigade and with civilian provisional corps.[12] These were volunteer units of one or more contiguous counties, generally organized and commanded by local ranchers, mayors, or political bosses. They could be mobilized by the state government with striking rapidity due to the Gaúcho's fight-loving nature, the tradition of obedience to the local political boss, and the personal dynamism of corps commanders.

Both sides resolved to destroy their opposition, no matter what the cost, and the revolution turned into a savage two-year civil war, with ten to twelve thousand casualties in this state of one million persons.[13] Mass throat-cutting of enemy prisoners became the order of the day, and severed heads hanging from trees served as testaments to violence. With support from the central government, Castilhos crushed the Federalists in 1895. By his devastating victory, he erased the immediate possibility of an effective opposition movement and consolidated the Republican hold on Rio Grande, which lasted until 1932.

This most brutal of conflicts in Gaúcho annals had a profound impact on the state's future, establishing political patterns which continue to the present. It divided Rio Grande into two irreconcilable camps and left a permanent scar of political hatred. It intensified and gave substance to a number of Gaúcho political characteristics that had been developing as a result of the state's extended military tradition.[14]

Out of this long military heritage emerged a unitary view of war and politics as one and the same. This conviction was further dramatized with violence and solidified with blood by the Federalist revolution. Gaúchos considered politics, like war, to be a two-sided struggle between "we and they." Third positions were rejected, compromise was abhorred, and neutrality was viewed as weakness. Castilhos established the Gaúcho yardstick with his motto, "Whoever is not a friend is an enemy." This rigid political polarity was reflected in the state's persistent two-party structure. With only brief interruptions, the state remained divided into two political camps from 1889 to 1964. This contrasted sharply with the national political scene both from 1889 to 1945, when there was no continuous national party system, and from 1945 to 1964, when a national multiparty system existed.

Since politics was warfare, victory at any cost was condoned. Force, violence, and even war became legitimized as methods for resolving political problems. Once again Castilhos set the standard with his admonition, "Do not spare an enemy, neither his life nor his possessions."

To meet the demands of the violent political milieu, parties were organized along military lines as rigid, hierarchical structures, headed by the party chief. Members of the Republican Party were even referred to as party soldiers. Rio Grande's long military hero tradition reinforced the chieftain system and gave a highly personal stamp to Gaúcho politics, with state divisions polarizing around dominant personalities. Absolute obedience to higher authorities became a fundamental element of party catechism, with ultimate power in the hands of the party chief. The classic parable of Gaúcho party obedience concerns a Republican meeting at which one member started to give an opinion, using the words "I think. . . ." At that point party chief Antônio Augusto Borges de Medeiros cut him off sharply, admonishing him, "You only think that you think. I am the one who thinks."

Party loyalty became sanctified. Switching parties was interpreted as treason and considered acceptable only in brief periods of transition and party instability. To those who committed the sin of party-switching, Gaúchos applied the terms "turncoat" (*vira-casaca*) or "watermelon" (*melancia*)—he who is one color on the outside but another on the inside.

By the end of the Federalist revolution, Rio Grande's vibrant military heritage had become fully integrated into the Gaúcho political structure, process, and personality. Júlio de Castilhos' rise to power had culminated the formative era of Gaúcho politics. Rio Grande would not enter its national political heyday until 1930, but by the end of the nineteenth century much of the political-military base had been built.

2

The Old Republic

His governmental ideas enshrined in the 1891 Gaúcho constitution and his opposition shattered during the Federalist revolution, Júlio de Castilhos solidified his hold on Rio Grande. As in the deceased Liberal and dying Federalist parties, Republican leadership came primarily from the rural aristocracy. But Castilhos broadened the PRR's socioeconomic base by uniting these rancher-lawyers with the state's nascent urban middle class, principally small merchants, professional people, public functionaries, and military brigade officers.

To maintain Republican hegemony, Castilhos developed a new type of political leader—the bureaucratic coronel, a middle-class county* boss who derived his power solely from state government support rather than from personal land, wealth, or social prestige.[1] Through the traditional landed coroneis and these new bureaucratic coroneis, the PRR used force, fraud, bribery, and threats to control elections. This was common throughout Brazil under an electoral system in which there was no secret vote and each party distributed its own ballots. Republican officials handed out their ballots "at the mouth of the ballot box" so that they could record individual voter behavior for inevitable government rewards or retribution. [2]

Having built a powerful machine, Castilhos retired as governor in 1898. He chose Antônio Augusto Borges de Medeiros

---

*Brazilian states are subdivided into small administrative units known as *municípios*. A município is composed of a city or town and the surrounding area, both with the same name. In this book the term "county" will be used for município, with the executive head of the county government referred to as "mayor."

11

as his successor, although the Republican boss continued to run the state. When Castilhos died in 1903, Borges de Medeiros also became PRR chief and ruled absolutely over state politics until 1928. He served as governor for twenty-five of the thirty years between 1898 and 1928 and as party chief from 1903 to 1937, when the PRR was extinguished.[3]

While Borges reigned in Rio Grande, Senator José Gomes Pinheiro Machado represented the state in the nation's capital. An intelligent, ruthless, intrepid tyrant, Pinheiro Machado was a kind of national political boss. He dominated congress and, in league with lesser political bosses in the smaller states, controlled elections throughout the country. In 1910 he broke the sixteen-year presidential stranglehold of the two largest, most powerful states, São Paulo and Minas Gerais, by masterminding the successful candidacy of Rio Grande-born minister of war Marshal Hermes da Fonseca. Having made countless enemies, both for himself and for Rio Grande do Sul, Pinheiro Machado met a bloody fate in 1915, when he was stabbed in the back in a Rio de Janeiro hotel lobby.[4]

Pinheiro Machado's death created a vacuum of Gaúcho political power at the federal level. In 1922 Borges de Medeiros, who previously had restricted his activities to state politics, tried to pick up the national reins where the slain Gaúcho senator had dropped them. In league with the states of Rio de Janeiro, Bahia, and Pernambuco, he organized the Republican Resistance and launched the presidential candidacy of former President Nilo Peçanha (1909-10) of Rio de Janeiro State. Peçanha and the Republican Resistance opposed Minas Gerais governor Arthur da Silva Bernardes, candidate of the São Paulo-Minas Gerais axis. Borges' first major venture into national politics ended in failure, as the São Paulo-Minas forces elected Bernardes.[5]

A small group of anti-Bernardes army officers decided to block the inauguration by overthrowing the federal government. The ill-planned, ill-coordinated revolution broke out in Rio de Janeiro on July 5, 1922, but was quickly crushed. Potential supporting revolts in other states collapsed at the starting line. The most dramatic moment occurred on July 6, when seventeen army rebels and one overly enthusiastic Gaúcho civil engineer marched down Rio's Copacabana Beach against massed government troops, who killed sixteen men and seriously wounded the other two.[6]

This famous march of the "Eighteen of Copacabana" signaled the opening of Brazil's revolutionary era. It also created a pantheon of martyrs and gave birth to a generation of middle-class military revolutionaries. Known as *tenentes* (lieutenants), they had a messianic belief in their mission to provide Brazil with political, economic, and social reform and regeneration.[7]

Upon learning of the revolt, Borges issued a manifesto entitled "For Order," in which he vehemently condemned the revolt and placed himself on the side of law and order.[8] But the damage had been done. By electorally opposing Bernardes, Borges had opened a breach in the political armor of his Rio Grande fortress.

In the years since the Federalist revolution, sporadic Gaúcho opposition movements had been consistently ineffective and ephemeral. But Borges' authoritarianism and the Republicans' repressive methods had reinforced Castilhos' legacy of political bitterness. When Borges entered the national political arena in support of Peçanha, some of the opposition Gaúchos had supported Bernardes. Now, with the vindictive Mineiro at the nation's helm, the opposition decided to make its first major bid to unseat the eternal governor, who was seeking his fifth term. Federalists, liberal democrats, and dissident Republicans united as the Liberation Alliance. These Liberators selected as their candidate a venerable former Republican, Joaquim Francisco de Assis Brasil.

A brother-in-law of Júlio de Castilhos, Assis Brasil had been the only Republican deputy in the Rio Grande do Sul provincial assembly during the Empire. Later he served as part of a triumvirate which governed Rio Grande for a brief period in the early days of the Republic, but he broke with Castilhos in 1892 and quit the Republican Party. During the ensuing years Assis had carried out his triple role as Gaúcho rancher, Brazilian diplomat, and political leader. Through his books and speeches, the articulate Assis had become renowned as a defender of liberal constitutional democracy and one of the nation's leading political theorists.

The bitterly fought 1922 Gaúcho gubernatorial election reverberated with more than the customary amount of violence, as Republicans faced the rare reality of a strong opposition challenge. Even the state constitution, drawn up by Republican patriarch Júlio de Castilhos, complicated matters for the Borgists. To compensate for the provision permitting eternal reelection, the Castilhos constitution provided that an incumbent governor had to receive three-fourths of the votes to be reelected. In normal times this was meaningless, since the Republican machine could deliver as many votes as necessary. But the 1922 election was abnormal, and the opposition landholders, with their ranch hands and gangs of gunmen, provided a serious challenge to the Republican system of controlled elections.

The spectre of Republican defeat loomed even larger on election day, as it appeared that Assis Brasil might have blocked Borges' attempt to obtain the three-fourths of the votes necessary for reelection. The state assembly, which held final electoral jurisdiction, selected a three-member all-Republican legislative committee to validate the votes. It was headed by Getúlio Vargas, a young assemblyman from the frontier county of São Borja, where his father, a prominent rancher, had long been the Republican coronel. The Vargas committee did its job in the prescribed Republican Party tradition, declaring Borges the victor.

Today many ex-Republicans "admit" that Borges may have actually lost the election. According to the popular story, the Vargas committee went to inform the governor of the disaster of his defeat, but before they could speak, Borges effusively thanked them for coming in person to congratulate him on his victory. Borges' "instructions" did not go unheeded. The three Republicans "recounted" the ballots and quickly discovered their egregious mathematical error.

Charging that the election was fraudulent, the opposition decided to try to amend the results by force. On the day of Borges' inauguration in January 1923, a rebellion exploded throughout the state. Revenge-minded Federalists, idealistic democrats, and civil libertarians united with a common goal—to end the long reign of Borges de Medeiros and destroy the Castilhos constitution.

Faced with the well-armed thirty-five-hundred-man Gaúcho military brigade, eighty-five hundred Republican provisional corps volunteers, and five hundred Uruguayan mercenaries, the rebels formed five mobile guerrilla columns totaling some six thousand men. With little hope of overthrowing the Borges government directly, the poorly armed rebels sought to create sufficient havoc throughout the state to demonstrate that Borges did not really control Rio Grande and prompt Bernardes to replace him with a compromise governor. The desire to dethrone Borges had overcome love of state autonomy.

The heart of the rebel strategy lay in the immediate establishment of a revolutionary capital under Assis Brasil in Uruguaiana, a cattle town on Rio Grande's western frontier. Rebel forces led by the able *caudilho*, Honório Lemes, descended rapidly on Uruguaiana. But the mayor, an audacious rancher named José Antônio Flôres da Cunha, mobilized Republican loyalists and repulsed Lemes' attack. Gathering Republicans from neighboring counties, including a unit led by another young rancher, Oswaldo Aranha, and incorporating a state brigade regiment, Flôres da Cunha set out after the Lemes Column. Warfare raged throughout the state, yet the drama of Flôres' bloody, relentless ten-month pursuit of Lemes quickly became the focus of public attention. Although Flôres never captured the wily Lemes, he forestalled the establishment of a revolutionary capital, broke the back of the critical rebel offensive, and saved Borges' government.[9] Moreover, Flôres projected himself into political prominence.

The white-neckerchiefed Republicans failed to defeat the red-neckerchiefed Liberators, but they prevented them from creating the desired havoc. Finally, in late 1923, the federal government stepped in to bring peace. It did not remove Borges as the rebels had hoped, but instead mediated and arranged the Peace of Pedras Altas. According to its terms, Borges retained his governorship. However, the pact made basic changes in the state constitution—banning gubernatorial reelection, providing for an elected vice-governor, and guaranteeing the election of at least one opposition state and federal deputy from each state district.[10]

Although the Peace of Pedras Altas also provided full amnesty for the rebels, it brought only brief respite to Rio Grande do Sul. Learning that the Chimangos,* as the Republicans became known, were planning to assassinate him, Assis Brasil fled with his family into exile in Uruguay. Political persecution increased, and periodic conflicts erupted between Republicans and Liberators.

---

*A chimango is a vulturelike bird found in Rio Grande do Sul—a symbol of cowardliness in Gaúcho lore. One brilliant, embittered Republican, Ramiro Barcellos, wrote a lengthy satirical poem entitled *Antônio Chimango*, which caricatured Borges de Medeiros as a chimango. The poem caused such a sensation that the opposition began to label all Republicans as Chimangos and Borges as the Old Chimango.

Rio Grande do Sul had returned to the era of the armed camp. Gaúchos remained in a state of constant military readiness, with civilian volunteer units prepared for rapid mobilization.

External events, as well as internal dissension, provoked state turmoil. On July 5, 1924, reform-minded military men (tenentes) in the states of São Paulo, Amazonas, and Sergipe revolted against the federal government. When the Sergipe and Amazonas revolts collapsed, the São Paulo rebels were left isolated. On July 27 the thirty-five-hundred-man revolutionary army withdrew from São Paulo into western Paraná.[11]

On the night of October 28-29, tenentes led an uprising in northwestern Rio Grande in conjunction with an invasion by Liberator veterans of the 1923 civil war, including Honório Lemes. Federal and state forces quickly converged on the rebel region, where Flôres da Cunha defeated Lemes and drove his twenty-five-hundred-man column into Argentina. Gaúcho tenente Luis Carlos Prestes, the revolutionary commander, led his two-thousand-man column out of Rio Grande and north toward Paraná to join the Paulista troops despite close pursuit by Gaúcho forces.[12]

By the time the rebel units met in March 1925, only about sixteen hundred men remained in the combined revolutionary army. For more than two years the Prestes Column, as the rebel force became known, fought its way over fourteen thousand miles of the Brazilian interior. Finally, with few more than six hundred men, Prestes went into exile in Bolivia in February 1927. The saga of the Prestes Column contributed immeasurably to the nation's revolutionary climate and turned the little Gaúcho into a mystical figure as Brazil's "Cavalier of Hope."[13]

While Prestes was receiving most attention, sporadic short-lived supporting revolts occurred periodically throughout Brazil, particularly in Rio Grande do Sul. The never-say-die Honório Lemes invaded the state again in September 1925, but his third strike meant an out, as the persistent Flôres da Cunha cornered and captured him.[14] In November 1926, two brothers, army lieutenants Alcides and Nelson Etchegoyen, led a revolt in the strategic Gaúcho railroad center of Santa Maria in an attempt to relieve the pressure on Prestes. Once again Liberator exiles slashed into Rio Grande in a series of "lightning columns." Ostensibly in support of Prestes and the Etchegoyens, these Liberators were more intent on revenge against Borges and the Republicans. But battle-hardened Gaúcho forces, led by Flôres da Cunha and his fellow Republican caudilhos, quickly drove the rebels back into exile in January 1927.[15]

The defeat of the "lightning campaign" and the disbandment of the Prestes Column brought relative peace. In the 1926 presidential election the weary opposition did not even present a candidate. Governor Washington Luis Pereira de Souza of São Paulo won in accordance with the 1921 agreement between São Paulo and Minas Gerais to take turns in the Brazilian presidency, the politics of "coffee with milk." This expression referred to the alliance of São Paulo, the coffee state, with Minas Gerais, the dairy state.

It appeared to be the dawn of a new era, with everybody behind Washington Luis. Even Rio Grande do Sul made peace with its historical São Paulo and Minas Gerais rivals. In return, the president selected Congressman Getúlio Vargas, leader of the Gaúcho delegation in the federal chamber of deputies, to be his finance minister.

In practice Washington Luis steered his own economic ship. He used London and New York loans to finance his monetary reform, highway construction, and currency stabilization policies. But beneath them ran the eternal strength and essential weakness of the Brazilian economy—coffee. With the nation's heavy dependence on coffee, which provided more than 70 percent of Brazil's income during the 1920s, the country had to rise and fall with that product's fortunes.

A new national opposition began to coalesce. In 1927 the Gaúcho Liberation Alliance united with the small Paulista Democratic Party (PDP—Partido Democrático Paulista) to form the National Democratic Party under the presidency of Assis Brasil, but it had little impact outside of these two states. The following year the Liberation Alliance was transformed into the Liberator Party (PL—Partido Libertador), with Assis Brasil as president. Most Federalists entered the PL, and one of the Federalist leaders, Pôrto Alegre physician Raul Pilla, became vice-president of the new party. Assis Brasil drew up a classical liberal program calling for the secret ballot, proportional representation, independent electoral courts, and civil liberties. Since the new party contained both Assis-led adherents of presidentialism and Pilla-led believers in the Federalist doctrine of parliamentarism, the program begged the divisive issue by adopting neither political philosophy as a party tenet. Instead, that decision was left a matter of individual choice. [16]

The Peace of Pedras Altas had terminated Borges' reign by prohibiting his reelection. Faced with the heartbreaking task of relinquishing his governorship, Borges selected his successor—Getúlio Vargas, the young man who had "elected" him in 1923 and later had served Rio Grande well as congressman and federal finance minister. A genius at the art of compromise, Vargas even had Liberator friends, a mortal sin by old Republican commandments. Delighted to be rid of Borges and to have him replaced by a moderate like Vargas, the Liberators did not even contest the gubernatorial election, which they realized they could not win anyway. [17]

When Borges first became govenor, Júlio de Castilhos had continued to run the state, with Borges little more than a puppet until the Republican chieftain's death. Borges believed Vargas would play the same role for him, but he soon discovered his error. Quietly, firmly, Vargas established his gubernatorial independence.

He rejected Borges' recommended conservative secretariat (cabinet) and chose his own men, headed by reformist Oswaldo Aranha as secretary of justice and the interior.[18] He turned his back on Borges' Calvin Coolidge-type mania for budgetary balance, which had created a full state treasury but had delayed vital public works. Moreover, he extended the peace pipe to the Liberators—making them welcome for the first time in the governor's palace, permitting them to win some municipal elections, and including them in the benefits of his economic reforms, such as loans from the Vargas-created Bank of Rio Grande do Sul. Through his good relations with President Washington Luis, Vargas also obtained significant federal economic concessions and put Rio Grande on the receiving end of the federal-state money flow. [19] But the presidential election of 1930 and the world depression of 1929-30 were to shatter this halcyon era for Brazil and Rio Grande.

According to the 1921 "coffee with milk" pact, 1930 was Minas Gerais' year to win the presidency. But President Washington Luis was less than enamored of Minas governor Antônio Carlos de Andrada, who had been experimenting with the secret ballot in his state and had criticized the president's monetary stabilization program. [20] The president made it clear that Paulista governor Júlio Prestes would be his successor.

The furious Mineiro governor decided that if Washington Luis denied him the throne, he would block Prestes, the president's crown prince. Electoral mathematics showed Antônio Carlos that to defeat Washington Luis, who controlled São Paulo and had a nationwide alliance with the governors and political bosses of the other states, he would need the support of Brazil's third largest electorate—Rio Grande do Sul. Actually, Rio Grande ranked fourth in population behind Minas Gerais, São Paulo, and Bahia, but since it had the highest literacy rate (about 40 percent) in Brazil and only literates could vote, the Gaúcho electorate was third behind Minas and São Paulo.

As there was no reason for Gaúchos to support Antônio Carlos in preference to the "official" presidential candidate, the Minas governor tempted Rio Grande by offering Mineiro support for either Borges de Medeiros or Getúlio Vargas. Borges approved the idea but declined the candidacy. Victory was impossible without a united Rio Grande, and the Liberators still bore too many Borgist scars to support the Republican chieftain. Vargas was another matter. Assis Brasil convinced the PL to accept the Vargas candidacy, although Raul Pilla and the bulk of the Liberators did so unenthusiastically due to the continuation of Republican persecution in the Rio Grande interior. [21]

Throughout his rich political career Vargas showed a decided preference for compromise, negotiation, and manipulation rather than open battle. However, Borges' acceptance of the Minas proposal left the Gaúcho governor little choice but to run, and the Vargas and Prestes candidacies became realities. Behind Vargas stood a united Rio Grande do Sul, a somewhat divided Minas Gerais, and the little northeastern state of Paraíba, whose governor, João Pessoa, became Vargas' running mate. Behind Júlio Prestes stood President Washington Luis, São Paulo, and the other sixteen states.

The pro-Vargas coalition, which also included the small Paulista Democratic Party and opposition groups in other states, became known as the Liberal Alliance. Lindolfo Collor, a brilliant young Gaúcho Republican journalist, drew up the Alliance platform, containing not only the standard Liberator-Democratic demands for electoral reform and civil liberties but also a section on social reform. [22] Although such concepts as the secret ballot reversed the sanctified Castilhist doctrine of public ballot and supervised elections, politics was war, anything went, and fervent Castilhists became equally fervent constitutional democrats overnight. Ancient enemy Republicans and Liberators linked arms as the United Front (FU—Frente Única), an alliance so startling it was called "the miracle of Rio Grande."

A campaign characterized by flaming oratory, unrelieved violence, and political killings led to a March 1, 1930, election with notable fraud on both sides. In Rio Grande do Sul, Vargas obtained 287,321 votes to a ridiculous 789 which the United Front allotted Prestes. But Washington Luis controlled more states and therefore more ballot boxes, so Prestes won nationally with 1,097,379 votes to 744,674 for Vargas.

These results came as no real surprise. Expecting this defeat, Rio Grande interior secretary Oswaldo Aranha and some of the more radical young Gaúchos had begun in September 1929 to make plans to reverse the election militarily. The conspirators got an assist from the world depression, which caused Brazilian coffee prices to fall by more than 50 percent. When President Washington Luis refused to shelve his own programs in favor of using federal money to support the coffee market, he alienated the Paulista planters and created a fearsome adversary known as "General Coffee." In Rio Grande do Sul farmers and ranchers began to default on mortgage payments, leading to a state banking crisis. [23] Gaúchos hungrily eyed federal power, funds, and jobs as the source of state economic salvation.

Taking advantage of these tense conditions, the daring, energetic Oswaldo Aranha created a bizarre revolutionary accord between Liberal Alliance politicians and exiled tenentes. Despite their scorn for politicians and the democratic process, which the Liberal Alliance championed, the tenentes were eager to try their hand at revolution again and maybe gain an opportunity to implement their hazy reformist ideas.

Aranha's trump card, however, was a united Rio Grande. Vargas had paved the way with his pacification policy; the Liberal Alliance campaign had brought a comrade-in-arms unity of purpose. Washington Luis further strengthened Gaúcho resolve with his "election" of Júlio Prestes and a series of high-handed, postelection acts of vengeance against the opposition states. Even though Minas Gerais and Paraíba bore the brunt of Washington Luis' vindictiveness—Rio Grande being saved by Vargas' success in reestablishing good relations with the president—central government persecution of Rio Grande's allies incensed autonomy-minded Gaúchos. Revolution-prone Liberators quickly joined Aranha, as did combative Republican "Young Turks" like Flôres da Cunha, Lindolfo Collor, and João Neves da Fontoura.

Three major obstacles remained. Minas governor Antônio Carlos, a wily politicians' politician but no revolutionary, infuriated Aranha with his vacillation. The conservative Borges de Medeiros opposed the revolution, and to attempt a revolution in Rio Grande without Borges' support would have been suicidal, since the state military brigade and thousands of Republicans accepted his word as law. Finally, Vargas himself displayed recalcitrance, and revolution without the movement's "presidental candidate" would be ridiculous. Irate over these frustrations, Aranha resigned as interior secretary in June 1930. The revolution appeared dead.

But the political fates came to Aranha's rescue. A personal squabble involving some published love letters resulted in the assassination of Paraíba governor João Pessoa, Vargas' vice-presidential running mate.[24] The revolutionaries had the martyr they needed. Ignoring the amorous aspects of the Pessoa murder, they accused Washington Luis, who less than secretly had been supporting an anti-Pessoa rebellion in the Paraíba interior. Most important, Aranha now had the emotional ammunition to convince Borges of Rio Grande's moral obligation to overthrow the Washington Luis government. With Borges came most of the more conservative Republicans and the military brigade.[25] Vargas, too, definitively entered the revolutionary fold. The new Minas Gerais governor, the elderly Olegário Maciel, completed the revolutionary cast when he pledged his state's cooperation.

After several postponements the revolution erupted on October 3 in Rio Grande do Sul and Minas Gerais and on the following day in the northeast. Rio Grande fell to the rebels within forty-eight hours, with only twenty dying in the fighting in Pôrto Alegre. Throughout Rio Grande the army put up only minimal resistance, as conspirators had successfully subverted the local military.[26] Most army units surrendered without a struggle, many joining the revolutionary forces. The rebels had been helped by the fact that about one-third of the army was composed of Gaúchos, whose love for Rio Grande and familial ties with state politicians compromised their loyalty to the federal government. Furthermore, few non-Gaúcho soldiers felt like sacrificing their lives in the unequal struggle.

The movement also went well in Minas Gerais and in the northeast, where rebel troops in both regions soon began to advance against the federal forces. But the key to the revolution lay in the south. There the state government mobilized sixty thousand troops within a few days as Gaúchos responded ecstatically to Vargas' manifesto calling for "Rio Grande, on your feet for Brazil."

Army Lieutenant Colonel Pedro Aurélio de Góes Monteiro, rebel commander in the south, planned a blitzkrieg from Rio Grande to the north. By October 6, Gaúcho troops had crossed the neighboring states of Santa Catarina and Paraná, which joined the revolution. By October 10 nearly thirty thousand rebels had reached the federal stronghold of Itararé, a Paulista town straddling the railroad to the north. Here federal troops and the Paulista public force had constructed massive fortifications and prepared for their major stand.

A two-week stalemate set in, brought about by the powerful federal defensive installations, federal arms superiority, and inclement weather. Finally Góes Monteiro ordered a major assault on Itararé, but before this could occur, a group of generals and admirals in Rio de Janeiro took matters into their own hands. Believing that Washington Luis had outlived his usefulness to Brazil and did not merit continued bloodshed, they publicly called for the president to resign. After a few hours of futile stubbornness, the dignified Paulista accepted the inevitable and on October 24 surrendered himself for immediate deportation.

The fall of Washington Luis brought a cancellation of the Itararé attack, but for a few days it appeared as if fighting might be resumed. For three days the self-proclaimed three-man military junta which replaced Washington Luis gave indications that it might not surrender the government to the revolutionaries. However, having come this far, Vargas, Aranha, and Góes refused to be thwarted. A series of telegrams made the situation brutally clear to the junta—turn over the government to Vargas or the war would continue. The junta capitulated.

On October 31, three thousand Rio Grande troops rode into the nation's capital, where a group led by Flôres da Cunha's sons fulfilled a Gaúcho revolutionary promise by tethering their horses to the obelisk monument on Rio's main street. [27] On November 3, Vargas became chief of the revolutionary government. Nearly one hundred years after the Farroupilha Revolution of 1835, Rio Grande do Sul apparently had avenged what it considered to be years of persecution and had asserted its domination over the federal government. [28]

The 1930 revolution inaugurated the seven-year Rio Grande do Sul era in Brazilian politics, during which Gaúchos dominated the political scene. The old party patriarchs, Borges de Medeiros and Assis Brasil, were still around. Virtually unchallenged in their party leadersip during the First Republic, their power declined following the revolution as the younger Gaúchos took control. The 1920s had given birth to a new generation of Gaúcho leaders, matured and toughened by the strife and turmoil of the violent years leading up to the 1930 revolution. Never before or since has a single Brazilian state produced an array of dynamic leaders comparable to this Gaúcho "Generation of 1930."

Out of the Republican ranks came such men as Lindolfo Collor, João Neves da Fontoura, and Maurício Cardoso. Collor, a splendid journalist of German ancestry and the social conscience of the 1930 revolution, became Brazil's first labor minister and the architect of the Brazilian labor system which continues to the present. Neves, an oratorical giant in the body of a mite, shone as one of the most brilliant representatives of this brilliant generation. Cardoso, a brooding, taciturn constitutional expert and political organizer, lacked both Neves' explosive brilliance and Collor's visionary genius. However, he partially compensated with a stoic resoluteness which enabled him to lead the Republican Party through its period of deepest despair.

The Liberator Party contributed men like Raul Pilla, Francisco Antunes Maciel Junior, and João Baptista Luzardo. Pilla, a bespectacled skeleton, became legendary for his honesty and principles in a milieu of political opportunism and deceit. The Brazilian true believer, he dedicated his life to the crusade for parliamentarism as the necessary condition for national salvation.

Maciel, a fierce little man of exceptional political skill, stood out for his calm leadership and unsurpassed personal loyalty in time of crisis. Baptista Luzardo, whose bravery on the battlefield was matched only by his volubility behind a podium, was the classic Liberator fighter, bringing ferocity and dynamism to his every struggle.

During the seven years of the Rio Grande do Sul era, three Gaúchos towered above their compatriots—José Antônio Flôres da Cunha, Oswaldo Aranha, and Getúlio Vargas. The story of these three ranchers from the Rio Grande frontier embodies the essential drama of the 1930-37 period.

If ever there were a typical Gaúcho, it would have to be Flôres da Cunha, the Republican military hero of the 1920s. Handsome, dashing, brave, intemperate, explosive, vindictive, unpredictable, visionary, undisciplined, passionate—he personified most of the virtues and weaknesses of Rio Grande do Sul. An eloquent orator, a warrior of almost suicidal bravery, a daring military commander, and an iron-willed caudilho, he was equally at home riding over the Gaúcho prairie or reciting Racine, grappling with his political enemies or courting French actresses. So emotional he would sob at the least provocation—the appearance of a close friend or the sight of the state flag—he earned the title of "Big Crybaby."

Yet Flôres' very picturesqueness obscured the fact that he may have been the finest governor in Gaúcho history. With the same gambling instinct he exhibited on the battlefield, at the horse races, or in his perennial card games, he carved out an imaginative, progressive state administration from 1930 to 1937, marred only by the injurious effects of constant political strife. A defender of state autonomy, he also sought to become a second Pinheiro Machado by using his personal dynamism and Gaúcho military might to assert pressure and intervene in politics throughout Brazil. Although, like most leading politicians, he eyed the presidency, Rio Grande do Sul's "last caudilho" was content to be kingmaker, not king.

Such was not the case with Oswaldo Aranha, who wanted desperately to become president.[29] After masterminding the 1930 revolution, Aranha shifted his base of operations from Pôrto Alegre to Rio de Janeiro, his orientation from state to national politics. Often Vargas' right-hand man, eager to be his successor,

Aranha became one of Brazil's most controversial figures. Like Flôres he was handsome, brave, brilliant, daring, imaginative, administratively skillful, and politically astute. Only slightly less colorful than Flôres, he had considerably more self-control than his explosive fellow Gaúcho. Although they were old friends and comrades-in-arms, an inevitable rivalry soon developed between these two pretenders to Brazil's number-two position of power behind Vargas.

On top, of course, was that singular phenomenon, Getúlio Vargas. A quiet, contemplative, introspective, cigar-smoking stump of a man, Vargas lacked the brilliance, eloquence, or glamour of some of his fellow Gaúchos, but he dwarfed them all with political skill unequaled in Brazilian history.

In some respects Vargas was a genuine product of Gaúcho Republicanism, a national-level Borges de Medeiros. He loved being president as much as Borges had loved being governor. Neither gave up his post willingly, both being forced out militarily in traumatic circumstances. Borges held on for twenty-five years; although Vargas did not match his predecessor's record, it was not through lack of effort. The retention or recapture of their beloved offices furnished the primary motivating force behind the political actions of both men. According to Alzira Vargas do Amaral Peixoto, daughter of the late president, there is a saying that as long as the "Portuguese" run the government, everything goes fairly smoothly, but once those "Spaniards" from Rio Grande move in, you never get them out. [30]

Both Borges and Vargas abhorred legislative bodies. In Rio Grande do Sul during the Old Republic the governor issued all legislation. Vargas liked this system, felt that legislative bodies merely interfered with the proper function of government, preferred to decree laws without congressional obstruction, and, quite naturally, consistently maneuvered to rid himself of these obstacles.

Like Borges, Vargas took pride in his governmental honesty, although both devoted an unreasonable amount of time to administrative minutiae. [31] Unfortunately, like Borges, Vargas suffered from administrative myopia. His naïve trust in the honesty of his associates permitted governmental irregularities and corruption. Also, like Borges', Vargas' administrative morality was not paralleled by political ethics. Both gladly used any means possible for political victory.

Vargas federalized Borges' policy of governmental centralism. Where Borges centralized state control from Pôrto Alegre, Vargas centralized national control from Rio. A former defender of state autonomy, Vargas became a resolute centralist as president, even when it meant the destruction of Gaúcho autonomy.

In other respects Vargas differed sharply from the Republican patriarch. He rejected Borges' fixation on balanced budgets in favor of government investment for modernization and development. He also diverged from the Castilhos-Borges party tradition by which anyone who was not a friend was an enemy to be persecuted implacably. Instead he favored a policy of maintaining equilibrium of political forces so that none would have the independent strength to threaten his control.

Rejecting the traditional Gaúcho politics of confrontation for his own politics of compromise, Vargas had the great ability to wait. His faith in the benevolent effect of time was reflected in his motto, "Leave it as it is and see how it turns out." He had the patience and self-control to maintain his composure during critical periods and the perceptiveness to act at the proper moment.[32] As Vargas described himself, "I am not an opportunist, but one who takes advantage of opportunities." It was this political skill that epitomized the genius of Getúlio Vargas and enabled him to govern Brazil for nearly nineteen of the twenty-four years between 1930 and 1954.

PART TWO

The First Vargas Era

3

Revolution to Revolution

One week after being installed as national chief executive, Vargas established by decree the ground rules for his provisional government. Suspending constitutional rights and dissolving all legislative bodies, Vargas arrogated dictatorial powers for himself.[1] He also replaced the deposed governors with interventors, state-level dictators who in turn selected the county mayors. The only exception was Olegário Maciel in Minas Gerais, who remained governor as a reward for having supported the revolution.

The victorious Gaúchos and Mineiros figured prominently in Vargas' cabinet. Rio Grande do Sul received three of the seven nonmilitary ministries, with Justice Minister Oswaldo Aranha, Agriculture Minister Assis Brasil, and Labor Minister Lindolfo Collor. Vargas named other Gaúchos to key posts, such as Baptista Luzardo as police chief for the Federal District, João Neves da Fontoura as legal counsel for the Bank of Brazil, and Annibal de Barros Cassal as director of the National Government Press. Flôres da Cunha, who had led one of the Gaúcho columns in the October campaign, became interventor in Rio Grande do Sul. In addition, Vargas passed out southern state interventorships to other trusted Gaúchos, such as Ptolomeu de Assis Brasil in Santa Catarina and Plínio Casado in Rio de Janeiro State.

Invading Gaúchos created a scandal by gobbling up coveted notarial offices and thousands of other government jobs in Rio, São Paulo, and elsewhere. According to one popular anecdote, the statue of Christ atop Rio's Corcovado (Hunchback) Mountain stretched forth its arms and implored, "Enough Gaúchos."[2]

Most controversial of the new ministerial appointments was Labor Minister Collor, author of the Liberal Alliance platform and an eager reformer. Prior to the revolution there had been no labor ministry; as Washington Luis aptly put it, "The social problem is a police problem." Following the revolution, businessmen and industrialists pressured Vargas and tried to bribe Collor to prevent the establishment of the ministry. The worried Vargas offered Collor other ministerial posts in lieu of its creation, but the Gaúcho journalist remained adamant.[3] On November 27, Vargas reluctantly established the Ministry of Labor, Industry, and Commerce. According to Gaúcho historian Moysés Vellinho, Vargas succinctly summed up his misgivings with the comment, "I hope that German doesn't cause any trouble."[4]

He did. In the fifteen months of his ministry Collor conducted his own social revolution with a flood of labor laws. He established a government-supported union structure, a series of labor courts and employer-employee conciliation commissions, a set of government social security institutes, a collective bargaining process, and a minimum wage system. Collor's reforms had such an emotional impact on the laboring class that when he toured northern Brazil in November 1931, he encountered tumultuous receptions at every stop. Observing Collor's triumphal junket, the perspicacious Vargas began to contemplate labor as an untapped source of political power. Yet Collor's and later Vargas' reforms applied only to urban labor. The revolution never reached the rural workers, including those belonging to Vargas and his fellow Gaúcho ranchers.

While Collor methodically revolutionized the Brazilian labor system, Vargas grappled with the nation's imposing economic and political problems. The world depression, the collapse of coffee prices, Brazil's unpayable foreign debt, a severe northeastern drought, and requests for aid from revolutionaries throughout the country necessitated huge sums of money, which the government did not have.

No economist himself, Vargas was deluged by conflicting advice, particularly from conservative Finance Minister José Maria Whitaker of São Paulo and the more daring Justice Minister Aranha. After nearly a year of vacillation, Vargas handed the nation's economic direction to Aranha, who succeeded Whitaker as finance minister. Aranha engineered such acts as burning excess coffee stocks and obtaining a suspension of payments on Brazil's foreign debt, but despite a plethora of schemes, Brazil's economic crisis continued.

This was paralleled by equally severe political turmoil. The revolution had always lacked cohesion, its motley ranks embracing everything from old conservatives like Arthur Bernardes and Borges de Medeiros to military radicals like the tenentes. Once the Washington Luis government had been disposed of, two major revolutionary camps developed—the constitutionalists and the authoritarian reformers.

The Liberal Alliance leaders, including most of the principal Gaúchos, formed the heart of the elite-based constitutionalist movement. They viewed the Vargas dictatorship as an unpleasant journey to be completed as quickly as possible en route to the rapid political reformation of Brazil via a new electoral law and a classically liberal constitution. These men believed that the secret ballot, judicial independence, and civil liberties would resolve Brazil's problems.[5]

The authoritarian reformers included the young, middle-class tenentes and such civilian allies as Oswaldo Aranha. They saw these constitutionalist goals as not merely inconsequential but actually dysfunctional to Brazilian progress. They opposed rapid reconstitutionalization as nothing more than a return to electoral domination by the traditional elites and state machines, believing only an extended dictatorship could destroy the old machines, rid Brazil of corrupt politicians, replace the country's "anarchic" federalism with a powerful centralized governmental system, spiritually regenerate the nation, and bring socioeconomic modernization.[6] Led by Aranha and Góes Monteiro, the tenente leaders in Rio formed the October Third Club as the movement's supreme directory, while tenentes in the north and northeast organized the Revolutionary Legion.

Vargas refused to align himself definitively with either contending camp. Since the Octobrists supported the continuation of his dictatorship, Vargas was naturally inclined to them. He named tenente João Alberto Lins de Barros as São Paulo interventor and tenente Juarez Távora as "Viceroy of the North" to supervise all interventors north of Rio State. However, Vargas felt neither faith nor confidence in the Octobrists as a political base since the volatile tenentes might overthrow him if they became too strong.

With consummate skill he permitted the Octobrists to delay reconstitutionalization, while simultaneously placing limits on their power.

As tension mounted, Vargas patiently relied on his politics of compromise and equilibrium. Letting others talk, he reveled in his dictatorship and quietly impeded reconstitutionalization. Not until February 1931, more than three months after he had taken office, did Vargas establish a subcommission, headed by Assis Brasil, to draft an electoral law. Two weeks later he sent Assis to Buenos Aires on a diplomatic mission, seriously hindering work on the law.

The tenente-constitutionalist struggle reverberated throughout Brazil. In Rio Grande do Sul, where the two traditional parties dominated, the tenentes had little success and the constitutionalist movement flourished, championed ardently by Liberator vice-president Raul Pilla. Always distrustful of Vargas, Pilla had consistently opposed the revolutionary installation of the Gaúcho governor as national chief executive. Instead, even before Vargas had left Pôrto Alegre in October 1930, Pilla had argued in a Liberator directory meeting that the PL should insist on the formation of a national governing junta to prepare for rapid, honest elections and a constituent assembly. But party chief Assis Brasil had greater confidence in Vargas and convinced the directory to accept him as provisional president.[7]

Once Assis Brasil had gone to Rio to become agriculture minister, Pilla assumed de facto control of the PL. Within a month he began to write editorials in the Liberator newspaper, *O Estado do Rio Grande,* criticizing Vargas and Aranha for their relations with the tenentes and their recalcitrance toward reconstitutionalization.[8] Nor did the state government please the Liberator leader, who accused Interventor Flôres da Cunha of conducting a partisan, pro-Republican administration.[9]

The focus of Pilla's attention was São Paulo, which had become the major battlefield of the tenente-constitutionalist struggle. There the conflict over reconstitutionalization was exacerbated by the question of the state's interventor, particularly since Vargas had given him control over the São Paulo Coffee Institute.[10]

Aranha and his tenente allies had prevailed upon Vargas to ignore the Paulista Democratic Party, a participant in the Liberal

Alliance, and name Pernambucan tenente João Alberto Lins de Barros as interventor. Paulistas soon became frightened by João Alberto's socioeconomic reform program and antagonized by the many tenentes in the state government. In April 1931, the PDP broke openly with João Alberto, launching a campaign for a Paulista civilian interventor.[11]

To support his Paulista allies, Pilla assembled a PL congress in Pôrto Alegre that same month. Following Pilla's vigorous denunciation of the provisional government's errors, the congress passed a pair of sharply worded motions supporting the PDP and the quickest possible reconstitutionalization.[12] Some Liberators, including state finance secretary Francisco Antunes Maciel Junior, criticized Pilla's aggressive antigovernment activities. A founder of the PL, a close friend of Assis Brasil, and a dedicated supporter of the government, Maciel even refused to attend the congress.

Interventor Flôres da Cunha also rejected Pilla's hard-line reconstitutionalization position, taking instead the moderate view that the dictatorship should last no more than a year and a half.[13] But Flôres, too, was angry at Vargas, feeling he had neglected Rio Grande financially since becoming dictator.

Flôres had taken over a state in economic decline, aggravated by the world depression. The inadequate state transportation system had led to the economic stagnation of certain regions, particularly the northern Italian zone. Rio Grande's vital dried-beef industry had declined sharply as a result of the product's loss of popularity and the growth of producers in states closer to the major national markets. This, in turn, had made ranchers increasingly dependent on the state's foreign-owned slaughterhouses which, according to Gaúchos, offered ridiculously low prices.

The 1930 revolution had taken its special toll. In making requisitions for the war effort, the state government had incurred heavy debts and had issued twenty thousand *contos* worth of a temporary state currency, which had to be redeemed. The Rio Grande treasury lacked funds to pay state employees; the state Bank of Rio Grande do Sul was nearly insolvent. Although wealthy in mortgages and real estate of defaulting landowners, the state's leading private bank, the Pelotense Bank, was critically short of cash.[14]

Gaúchos had hoped that their 1930 military victory would bring a shower of federal funds and economic benefits on Rio

Grande, but they had been sorely disappointed. Vargas quickly made it clear that he was not planning to govern in favor of his home state. When asked why he did not do more for Rio Grande, Vargas responded, "I am not the president of the Riograndenses, but the president of all Brazilians."[15] Although Gaúchos received plenty of political positions, Vargas had given the finance ministry to São Paulo and the Bank of Brazil to Minas Gerais. Despite appeals from Flôres, state finance secretary Antunes Maciel, and Bank of Brazil legal counsel João Neves da Fontoura, Vargas had refused to rescue the Pelotense Bank, forcing Flôres to liquidate it.[16] Flôres publicly and privately lamented Vargas' neglect of Gaúcho needs.[17] In a letter to João Neves, Maciel pleaded, "How can we lead Rio Grande down the right road if they abandon us this way?"[18]

Despite these frustrations, Flôres and Maciel maintained their distance from the Pilla-led campaign for immediate reconstitutionalization. But in July 1931, Pilla received support which more than compensated for the few Liberator defections. After months of relative silence, Borges de Medeiros spoke out strongly in favor of rapid return to democratic government.[19] His statements reestablished PRR-PL solidarity, this time in favor of terminating the provisional government. The northern interventors responded by forming the Northern Bloc in opposition to the Gaúcho demands and in favor of radical reforms.[20] Both sides had put their prestige on the line; the first real reconstitutionalization crisis had developed.

For the first time Flôres da Cunha assumed his self-proclaimed role as national political boss in the tradition of former Gaúcho senator Pinheiro Machado. Flying to Rio, he convinced Vargas to resolve the crisis by taking a major step toward constitutionalism—the publication of Assis Brasil's electoral registration law draft—which Vargas did on September 11, 1931. The compromise worked, easing tensions and increasing Flôres' national prestige by demonstrating that he could be a statesman as well as a soldier.[21]

Events in São Paulo soon shattered the truce. PDP and national constitutionalist pressure had brought about the resignation of tenente interventor João Alberto and the appointment of a Paulista civilian interventor, Laudo de Camargo. When the tenentes retaliated by forcing Camargo out of office in November

1931, the Gaúcho United Front reacted, this time with Flôres' support.

Two days after Camargo's resignation, Flôres, Borges, Pilla, and João Neves met at Neves' home in the city of Cachoeira do Sul, near Borges' modest Irapuasinho Ranch. It was a historic occasion, the first meeting of the heads of the state's two traditional opposing parties since Júlio de Castilhos and Gaspar da Silveira Martins had met prior to the 1893 revolution. This hiatus reflected the historical intensity of the Gaúcho political struggle; the conference also marked the first meeting ever of archenemies Borges and Pilla. Out of this first Cachoeira conference came a joint Borges-Pilla note to Vargas with Flôres' tacit support, calling for voter registration and a new Paulista civilian interventor. [22]

Surrendering to FU pressure, Vargas switched Octobrist Oswaldo Aranha to the empty finance ministry and appointed Gaúcho Republican constitutionalist Maurício Cardoso as justice minister. Despite this setback, Vargas hoped—and expected—that electoral reform would still be distant. But Cardoso had other ideas. Immediately assembling the electoral law commission, he tirelessly drove his associates, and on January 26, 1932, Cardoso delivered the completed electoral law to the dismayed Vargas, who had not counted on such rapidity.

The completion of the electoral law coincided with a veritable revolution in São Paulo. Anti-Gaúcho feeling had been running high in that state since the 1930 revolution. Bitter Paulistas referred to the mass removal of state functionaries in favor of friends and relatives of the rebels as the "Gaúchoization of São Paulo." [23] Vargas' use of tenentes in the state government and his game of interventional musical chairs also had angered the independent Paulistas.

On January 15, 1932, the PDP broke officially with Vargas and the provisional government. To vent their wrath against Vargas and the Gaúchoization of their state, Paulistas stoned the Gaúcho center in São Paulo and ripped down the Rio Grande state shield. Taking advantage of the chaos, the Paulista Republican Party (PRP—Partido Republicano Paulista) came out of political hibernation and united with the PDP to form the Paulista United Front.* Together they demanded rapid reconstitutionalization and

---

*Hereafter the Paulista United Front will be referred to as such and the Gaúcho United Front will be referred to as the United Front or FU (Frente Única).

restoration of state autonomy. In an attempt to mollify the new alliance, Vargas selected an aging retired Paulista diplomat named Pedro de Toledo as interventor, but by then pacification was impossible. United, angry, with a renewed sense of power, the proud Paulistas were determined to continue challenging the government and, if necessary, to bring it down by force.

His relations with São Paulo in shambles, Vargas also had to contend with Cardoso's electoral law. He adopted his normal procrastination, but the Liberator directory, supported by Borges de Medeiros, threatened to break with Vargas if he did not sign the law immediately. Not wanting Rio Grande to follow the Paulista example, Vargas signed the law on February 24, setting off celebration rallies throughout Rio Grande and São Paulo. The signing also set off angry tenentes, who sacked the offices of Rio's *Diário Carioca,* an outspoken proconstitutionalist newspaper. When Vargas appeared unwilling to punish the attackers, prominent Gaúcho constitutionalists like Cardoso, Collor, Luzardo, Neves, and Barros Cassal resigned their posts in protest and returned to Rio Grande.

Gaúcho leaders converged on Pôrto Alegre for a Rio Grande summit conference; even Borges de Medeiros made a rare trip from his ranch for the meeting. The Paulistas, who had already begun planning a revolution, sent two representatives. Major Gaúcho absentees were Aranha, who rejected Flôres' invitation, and Vargas, who asked Agriculture Minister Assis Brasil, then in Buenos Aires, to be his peace ambassador to the United Front.[24]

By the time Assis Brasil arrived in Pôrto Alegre, the FU had prepared a vitriolic ultimatum for Vargas, which became known as the "shrapnel." Demands included a Supreme Court investigation into the *Diário Carioca* affair, immediate restoration of 1891 constitutional rights, press freedom, a constitutional commission, electoral registration, elections before the end of 1932, federal assumption of state foreign debts, and the formation of an economic-financial advisory council.

Attending his first meeting, at which he and Borges renewed personal relations after a forty-year hiatus, Assis Brasil convinced his impassioned companions to soften their ultimatum.[25] Although Vargas did not submit to the demands, he answered in a friendly manner, even asking Maurício Cardoso to return as justice minister to work out a compromise.[26] Tired of Vargas' stalling tactics, Borges and Pilla responded with the original "shrapnel" and a circular telegram informing all ministers and interventors of their action.[27] Unwilling to allow the FU to dictate to him, Vargas rejected the new ultimatum.[28] On this basis, the more radical Gaúchos, led by Pilla, Collor, and Luzardo, pledged Riograndense support for the Paulistas if revolutionary military action were to become necessary.[29]

The exchange of messages widened the breach between the FU and Vargas, now detached from party influence and regional restrictions. Vargas and Aranha had determined to maintain federal power and prestige, in conflict with the FU's attempt to impose its domination over the national government. Between the two intransigent blocs stood José Antônio Flôres da Cunha.

The undeclared Gaúcho civil war had created a schizophrenic condition for the emotional interventor. Flôres' duty to Vargas as his official representative in Rio Grande do Sul was reinforced by the interventor's friendship with both Vargas and Aranha. At the same time, Flôres felt deep loyalty to the Republican Party and particularly to Borges de Medeiros, the tiny party chief whose very presence would bring tears to the eyes of the strapping caudilho. Because of Flôres' official position, political prestige, military genius, and command of the Gaúcho military machine, he became the final arbiter, the balance between the two antagonistic forces. Throughout the coming months both sides unceasingly courted Flôres, who was inexorably forced into the unhappy position of having to make a final commitment.[30]

As the state's chief executive, Flôres was more than a political participant; he was also the guide of Rio Grande's economy. Although frustrated by the lack of federal support, Flôres had instituted overdue reforms and an imaginative recovery program. He had rejected the conservative economic policies of other interventors, who generally had increased taxes in an attempt to balance their budgets. Instead Flôres had stimulated Gaúcho commerce by reducing export taxes and establishing state subsidies for agricultural products. To finance his public works program and such innovations as the establishment of a state welfare institute for public functionaries, he had issued more paper money in May 1931.[31]

The Gaúcho economy had received an additional boost by the ministerial shake-up of November 1931. In addition to

Oswaldo Aranha's appointment as finance minister, Gaúcho banker Arthur da Souza Costa had become Bank of Brazil president. This Gaúcho financial tandem had arranged for the payment of 50 percent of the 1930 revolutionary requisitions from Rio Grande, for the construction of state railroad and telegraph lines, and for the reduction of landowners' bank debts by 50 percent.[32]

When the FU broke with the central government in March 1932, Vargas suddenly became quite solicitous toward Flôres. He personally fulfilled a number of long-ignored requests in an attempt to keep the interventor from allying with the FU against him. He granted fifty thousand contos in Bank of Brazil loans to Gaúcho ranchers, paid twenty thousand contos in channel taxes that had been withheld from Rio Grande since 1928, and expropriated the Brazil Great Southern Railroad, turning its operation over to the Gaúcho government.[33] Tempted and pressured from both sides, Flôres wavered agonizingly between the central government and the FU.

Despite its failure to obtain an unconditional commitment from the interventor, the FU pressed its position. In late April it sent João Neves da Fontoura to Rio as FU ambassador to work for fulfillment of Gaúcho demands, particularly the establishment of an election date and the solution of the Paulista question. Two weeks after Neves' arrival in Rio, Vargas met the first demand by scheduling the constituent assembly election for May 3, 1933.

The São Paulo question was another matter. The establishment in early May of a unity pact between the Gaúcho and Paulista United Fronts had strengthened the constitutionalist position.[34] Backed by the Gaúchos, the Paulista United Front increased its protests against tenente influence in the state. When Vargas sent the protenente Oswaldo Aranha to São Paulo on May 22 to resolve the crisis, Paulista constitutionalists viewed it as a new attempt to undermine their position, and Aranha's arrival ignited two days of riots in the state. Taking matters into their own hands, interventor Pedro de Toledo and the Paulista United Front, without Vargas' placet, threw the tenentes out of the state government.

Gaúchos joined Paulistas in celebrating the São Paulo triumph. Taking advantage of the momentum from the May victory, the United Fronts' joint ambassador, João Neves, began to line up support from other states for a national constitutionalist party.[35] He also initiated negotiations with Vargas on the possible formation of a new national ministry to be dominated by Gaúcho, Paulista, and Mineiro constitutionalists.

One of Neves' prime targets was War Minister General Leite de Castro, who had strong ties with the October Third Club. As the constitutionalists wanted, Vargas did remove Leite de Castro. However, ignoring the United Fronts' favorite generals, Vargas unexpectedly replaced him with General Augusto Inácio de Espírito Santo Cardoso, candidate of tenente João Alberto. Furious because Vargas had not consulted with him, Neves broke off negotiations.[36] The Paulistas immediately accelerated their military preparations, and, in early July, Gaúcho FU leaders pledged Rio Grande support for the revolution.[37] But they did not inform Flôres da Cunha.

The interventor was Brazil's major question mark. The FU relied on Flôres as the Gaúcho military leader, but from the conspiracy's beginning he had been perplexingly inconsistent. As Vargas' delegate and Aranha's friend, he had labored to reconcile the FU with the central government and to calm the revolutionary spirits of the more rabid Gaúchos. However, as a loyal Republican and Gaúcho, Flôres simultaneously had planned Riograndense military strategy. He had distributed three thousand rifles throughout the interior for potential provisional corps and had built eleven strategic railroad bypasses. Furthermore, he had transferred a state cavalry regiment to the town of Marcelino Ramos at the head of the Gaúcho railway network on the Santa Catarina border, from where it could proceed north at once.

According to Flôres' requirements, which the FU had accepted, if the FU wanted him to lead Rio Grande in a revolt, São Paulo would have to give him sufficient warning prior to any action so that he could resign as interventor and take command of the revolutionary forces. He also established four *casi belli* for his participation—federal modification of the Paulista secretariat or the removal of Flôres, Third Military Region Commander General Andrade Neves, or General Bertoldo Klinger, army commander in the state of Mato Grosso. Any one of these would bring Flôres into the revolution.[38]

The Pôrto Alegre conspirators, led by Pilla, Collor, and Luzardo, became the victims of self-mystification. Because they lacked confidence in the vacillating interventor, they began to exclude him from their meetings in June 1932. Yet they made no alternative military preparations, confident that at the critical moment Borges could convince the emotional Flôres to lead the revolution out of state and party loyalty. The Paulistas agreed to give the Gaúchos sufficient warning of the revolution date so that Borges could weave his spell over the interventor.[39]

But the Paulistas precipitated the revolt without giving Borges enough time to reach the Gaúcho capital. In early July, General Klinger, a key figure in the conspiracy, sent a bristling letter to the new war minister, rejecting his authority. The latter had no choice but to remove the Mato Grosso commander, uncovering the Paulista western flank. Forced to act before Klinger surrendered his command, the Paulistas revolted on the night of July 9.

Army troops in São Paulo united with the Paulista public force in support of the revolution; on July 10 Paulista troops began to march toward Rio. The Paulistas could have forced an immediate showdown by risking a lightning strike on Rio. Instead, relying on their pact with the Gaúchos, they soon dug in to wait for reinforcements from Rio Grande. Expecting the Gaúchos to carry Santa Catarina and Paraná into the rebel camp to create a powerful southern phalanx, the rebels were justifiably confident that this southern alliance could sweep into Rio, possibly with little bloodshed.[40] It was problematical if army troops in Rio would even oppose the southern forces.[41] In addition, conspirators in the capital had prepared a subsidiary movement to begin once the Gaúchos and Paulistas had declared their alliance.[42]

By precipitating the revolution, Klinger and the Paulistas had upset the FU timetable. Aware that he could not reach Pôrto Alegre before the revolt, Borges telegraphed Flôres da Cunha:

> Evoking our agreements of honor and your incomparable patriotism and edifying Republican fidelity, let your old and dedicated friend suggest to you, in this grave hour, that between the Dictatorship and the fate of the Republic and Rio Grande, it is not licit to hesitate. If the worn and irritated patience of the Brazilians should express itself in

armed protest to revindicate their confiscated liberties, I have faith that you will not hesitate to assume the only attitude compatible with your past and glory. Stay with Rio Grande and be its gallant leader in the new redemptive crusade.[43]

With Borges' telegram, Flôres' moment of truth had arrived. The interventor rejected Klinger's removal as sufficient justification for supporting the revolution, since Klinger had intentionally provoked disciplinary action. Racked by months of agonizing indecision and irritated by his recent ostracism from the conspiracy, Flôres now had to choose between his sentimental loyalty to Borges and the PRR and his friendship with and official loyalty to Vargas. Seeking an escape, he sent anguished telegrams to both Borges and Vargas, resigning his post.[44]

Vargas, like the conspirators, realized that Flôres would decide the provisional government's fate. The interventor's resignation would permit the FU to take control of Rio Grande and throw the state's military might behind São Paulo. Vargas' hope for survival rested on his ability to convince Flôres to remain at the Gaúcho helm. In desperation, like Borges, Vargas appealed to Flôres as a friend:

> I can not accept your resignation. There is no better guarantor of Rio Grande honor than my dear friend at a moment when we are victims of a treachery which seeks to stab us in the back in a clearly reactionary movement. I have elements to resist and am ready to do so until I succumb as a soldier of the revolution in defense of the ideals which led us to it.[45]

After a final moment of soul-searching, Flôres committed himself to Vargas, answering, "I will maintain order or die."[46]

By supporting Vargas in opposition to most other Gaúcho leaders, Flôres had turned the governor's palace into an oasis in a desert of anti-Vargas feeling. He ordered some trusted followers, like his brother, Francisco, and Getúlio's youngest brother, Benjamin, to form provisional corps in the interior. Calling on some forty dedicated supporters to join him in the palace for what might be a suicide defense, Flôres prepared to resist as long as possible.[47]

But the interventor did more than maintain the order he had promised Vargas. In conjunction with the army regional commander, Flôres immediately dispatched Gaúcho troops north toward São Paulo along with army forces, without informing the Gaúchos why or against whom they were advancing.[48] When the brigade commander objected out of solidarity with Borges, Flôres removed him.

Flôres had a dual strategic aim: he wanted to move the maximum number of troops to the front while he still controlled the government and also remove the threat of the military brigade, whose officers were still largely loyal to Borges and therefore were a potential conspiratorial source. By July 15 three of the brigade's five infantry battalions and two of its three cavalry regiments had left Rio Grande, to be followed soon by two of the three remaining units.[49]

Flôres audaciously gambled on the inability of the United Front to mobilize immediately. The FU fulfilled Flôres' hopes, remaining despondently inert until Borges arrived in Pôrto Alegre. One can only conjecture whether Borges could have converted Flôres to the revolution had he been in Pôrto Alegre when the movement began. By the time the little Republican chief saw the interventor on July 11, Flôres was already committed to Vargas. He rejected Borges' appeal to side with São Paulo or at least to recall Gaúcho troops, making Rio Grande a benevolent neutral whose military strength could be used to force a cease-fire.[50]

The refusal shocked the FU leaders out of their dreamworld of blind confidence in Borges' domination of Flôres. They telegraphed São Paulo suggesting a cease in hostilities, but the Paulistas feared Vargas' retribution if they withdrew from the struggle.[51] Having failed in their first war and peace efforts, the United Frontists began to plot against Flôres.

As a revolutionary leader, Borges proved an albatross to the FU. In war as in politics, Republicans remained inflexibly dependent on the decisions of the conservative, rigid Borges, who could not become an instant revolutionary. His indecision handcuffed his followers and, by extension, the Liberators.

The FU spread the word for a series of simultaneous revolts throughout the interior on July 19, after which rebel forces would converge on Pôrto Alegre and overthrow Flôres. But before the movement could erupt, Flôres invited Maurício Cardoso to go to Rio and São Paulo as his peace envoy to try to arrange an armistice.[52] Clutching at this hope for a peaceful termination of the bloody war, already being waged bitterly at various points along the Paulista frontier, Borges sent with Cardoso his suggested bases for national pacification. [53] At the same time he ordered the rebel leaders to postpone the revolt.

The postponement order never reached Baptista Luzardo, who had gone to Vacaria, a strategic city on the road running north from Pôrto Alegre to Santa Catarina. He led a revolt in cooperation with former mayor Octacílio Fernandes, who had received arms from Flôres to form two provisional corps. When Flôres quickly encircled the small rebel force with four thousand troops, Borges intervened to avert the imminent slaughter. [54] A three-man commission representing Flôres, Borges, and Pilla went to Vacaria and arranged a peace treaty, terminating the five-day movement with amnesty for the rebels. [55]

Cardoso made little progress in his pacification efforts. Neither side would accept an unfavorable armistice. Vargas looked askance at Flôres' peace initiative, since the Paulistas had lost their opportunity for a quick victory when they decided to wait for the Gaúchos before attacking Rio. With loyalist troops besieging São Paulo, the confident Vargas decided that the Paulistas would have to come begging for peace. [56]

For their part, the Paulistas still believed in victory, despite the shock of Flôres' decision. They counted on Mineiro support, a trust which ultimately would be shattered when loyalist forces crushed an abortive uprising led by former president Arthur Bernardes. They also were buoyed by the arrival in São Paulo of João Neves da Fontoura, who had escaped from Rio. Confident that Borges and Pilla would rally Rio Grande against Flôres, Neves assured the Paulistas that the interventor would succumb by early August and Gaúcho troops would switch to the Paulista cause. [57]

Although Cardoso's mission dragged on for two months, Borges soon lost faith in it. At the urging of his FU cohorts, the Republican chief committed himself irrevocably to revolution. Neves wrote a fervent appeal to Borges to save Rio Grande's honor, severely damaged by Flôres' "treachery." He assured Borges that "if Rio Grande acts without delay, the game will still be won and won well." [58]

But acting without delay was not Borges' forte. He continued to hamper his followers. A group of young FU politicians and members of the military brigade's palace guard prepared a plot to capture and depose the interventor in the palace. But, in a display of anachronistic Gaúcho chivalry, Borges vetoed the plan. Certain that Flôres would resist to the death, the Republican chief would not consent to a plan which quite likely would bring death to his old friend, who had defended Borges valiantly during the civil wars of the 1920s.[59] By that sentimental decision, Borges cost the FU victory in Rio Grande and, by logical extension, made São Paulo's defeat a certainty.

Instead Borges returned to the plan of simultaneous interior revolts. Yet, although the new conspiracy began in late July and time was of the essence for beleaguered São Paulo, the careful Borges scheduled the Gaúcho revolt for a distant August 20. On that date rebel units from around the state, which were to take the field in the preceding days, would converge on the city of Santa Maria. This vital railroad crossroads in the heart of Rio Grande would then become the revolutionary state capital.[60]

Conspirators in Santa Maria moved more rapidly. They made plans to take over the city in early August, set up a three-man revolutionary junta to function until Borges' arrival, and stop all trains. This immediate paralysis of railroad traffic would be the signal for revolts throughout the region. But on the day of the proposed uprising the conspirators received word from Borges to await his orders, since he was still coordinating his plot. By the time the Santa Maria plotters protested and received Borges' permission to move at will, Flôres had discovered the conspiracy and already had begun to arrest conspirators, transfer Borgist brigade officers, and reinforce his control of the city with provisional troops.

The remaining Santa Maria plotters decided to follow Borges' plan: stage revolts in surrounding cities on August 19 and lay siege to Santa Maria on August 20 with the Republican chief. However, conspirators in other cities now refused, having conditioned their participation on the prior revolution in Santa Maria.[61] In that region only Colonel Marcial Terra in Tupanciretã and Colonel Turíbio Gomes in São Pedro brought rebel troops into the field.

In spite of his age and the bitter, wet Gaúcho winter, the frail sixty-eight-year-old Borges insisted on taking the field with the revolutionary forces to pay his debt of honor to São Paulo. That he reached Santa Maria at all was a minor miracle. Flôres had turned Rio Grande into a police state, with imprisonments, rigid censorship of the press, radio, mail, and telegraph, and close surveillance of roads and railroads. His investigators filled Pôrto Alegre, trailing the FU leaders day and night. Despite this, in a novelistic episode, Borges and Luzardo eluded the police and slipped out of Pôrto Alegre in the bottom of a launch. After crossing the river, they rode to Santa Maria, first by horse and later by car, arriving on August 20.[62]

Expecting thousands of supporters, Borges was cruelly disappointed to find only about twenty men in the revolutionary camp. They soon were joined by a few brigade sergeants who had escaped from Santa Maria and by Raul Pilla, who had evaded detection following a visit to Assis Brasil in Pedras Altas. Attempting to inspire supporting revolts, the rebel leaders issued a revolutionary proclamation, but Flôres' stranglehold on the state effectively limited its distribution.[63]

Motivated by a combination of love for his old chieftain, concern for Borges' health, and fear of his inspirational revolutionary potential, Flôres appealed to the rebels to lay down their arms. In return he promised full amnesty, freedom of movement, and the release of all political prisoners. Flôres also promised Borges that if he returned home, he could conspire without restriction, and even offered to fly the rebels to São Paulo so they could aid the Paulistas without bringing unnecessary death and destruction to Rio Grande. Buoyed by the news that São Paulo would supply money for arms and ammunition, Borges rejected Flôres' appeal, saying that Rio Grande's honor was at stake. The following day Pilla left for Buenos Aires to secure arms, but he did not have time to return, since Flôres crushed the rebellion within a month.[64]

Throughout the state's northeastern quadrant, a series of small pro-Borges uprisings occurred in various counties. The people of Encantado selected and proclaimed a revolutionary mayor, while Soledade raised an eight-hundred-man revolutionary army. However, Flôres quickly isolated and destroyed these movements. The climactic battle took place on September 13, when military brigade and provisional corps troops engaged the Soledade rebels in a three-and-one-half-hour clash at the Fão River.[65]

Northwest of Santa Maria, the São Pedro and Tupanciretã rebel groups united to form the eight-hundred-man Marcial Terra

Column, but Flôres quickly erected a military screen between it and the Borges encampment southeast of Santa Maria. Forced to proceed northwest, the Terra Column, which included Lindolfo Collor, fought its way through eight counties in a vain search for arms, ammunition, and promised rebel adhesions. Surrounded by eight thousand government troops and having received no news from Borges for nearly two weeks, Terra finally surrendered on September 6. Protesting Terra's decision, Turíbio Gomes and his three hundred men from São Pedro slipped through the encircle-ment. After trying for two weeks to pierce Flôres' screen and reach the Borges Column, Gomes dissolved his force and went into exile in Uruguay.[66]

One of Terra's unaccomplished goals had been to reach the western frontier city of Uruguaiana, where army units had promised to join his column. On the night of September 22, a few soldiers there staged a barracks revolt but surrendered the follow-ing morning.[67] A more serious movement developed among brigade units fighting on São Paulo's southern border, since many officers were still loyal to Borges. Learning that Borges supported São Paulo and bombarded by leaflets from João Neves da Fontoura inciting them to defect, they contemplated leading their units back to Rio Grande to fight for the Republican chief. However, the plot ultimately collapsed due to defections, the dispersal of brigade units among army troops and provisional corps, and the falsification of a telegram from Borges, declaring his support of Vargas.[68]

There were a number of reasons for the FU's failure to obtain greater revolutionary support. Despite their 1930 experience, Re-publicans found it difficult to oppose the state government after years of defending legality. Most rank-and-file Republicans be-longed to the party because of personal loyalties or the benefits of being in the government party. With party leadership now divided, many Republicans, particularly the younger generation, felt greater loyalty to Vargas, Aranha, and particularly Flôres da Cunha than to the old guard. Moreover, most Republicans who agreed to revolt did so conditionally—if there were already a large rebel army in the field with good prospects for victory.

The experienced Liberators were more revolution-prone than their Republican allies, but the PL was also divided. Pilla's authori-tarian leadership had split the PL, driving away many Liberators.

These included followers of Assis Brasil, who opposed the revolution as unnecessary bloodshed, and Antunes Maciel, whom Pilla had expelled from the party in June because of his support of Vargas. [69]

Most important, Flôres da Cunha checkmated the FU's revolutionary attempts. His tight control of transportation and communications prevented revolutionary coordination and dissemination of propaganda, his spy system uncovered most plots before the slow-moving United Frontists could turn talk into action, and his continuous, unpredictable movement of men and units impeded conspiracies. Also, his isolating of revolutionary pockets demoralized the rebels, while his relentless pursuit of rebel columns forced them to concentrate on escape and survival rather than on the search for support.

Flôres' main concern was removing Borges from the field without harming his old friend. After Borges rejected four peace proposals, Flôres intensified his pressure. Unaware of the FU failures throughout the state, the Borges Column moved southeast in a dual effort to evade its pursuers and obtain human and material reinforcements. [70]

The showdown came on September 20 at the Battle of Cêrro Alegre Ranch in southeastern Rio Grande, where eight hundred of Flôres' troops, mainly provisionals, engaged the two-hundred-man Borges Column. Taken by surprise, the revolutionary line collapsed after two hours of fighting. Most of the rebels, including Baptista Luzardo, escaped on horseback in small groups. With only three horses left, the honor-bound Borges refused to abandon his fourteen remaining companions and chose to fight alongside them to the finish. After resisting for two more hours in the ranch house until their last round was fired, they surrendered. [71] The battle, which effectively ended Rio Grande's last civil war, occurred on the ninety-seventh anniversary of the beginning of the state's greatest civil war, the Farroupilha War of 1835-45, and within a few miles of the site where the Riograndense Republic's constitution had been proclaimed.

According to one eyewitness, when Flôres learned that Borges had been captured unharmed, he burst into tears, exclaiming, "Blessed Be Our Lord Jesus Christ!" [72] Fearing a reaction if he brought Borges to Pôrto Alegre as a prisoner, Flôres sent him by sea to Rio. It was Borges' first visit to the capital since the 1891 Constitutional Assembly.

The collapse of the Gaúcho revolution ended the Paulistas' last hope for victory. On October 2 they surrendered, ending the unequal struggle. After the failure of the revolt, the revolutionaries gave Flôres the title "The Savior of Getúlio Vargas and His Government."

4

Uneasy Alliance

The 1932 revolution shattered the Gaúcho political structure, decimated United Front leadership, and exacerbated state political hatreds. With the conflict ended, Flôres da Cunha immediately sought to reconstruct political Rio Grande and pacify his enemies.

He lifted censorship. He called for amnesty and rapid reconstitutionalization. When the FU informed Flôres that it would participate in the May 3, 1933, election, he offered to name Maurício Cardoso, the acting FU leader, as transitional state interior secretary to insure proper voter registration and a free electoral campaign. But blood still flowed from FU wounds; the embittered exiles, busy conspiring with Paulista exiles to invade Brazil, rejected Flôres' proposal.[1]

The revolutionary upheaval had inaugurated one of those rare periods in Gaúcho history when politicians could change parties without suffering severe political consequences. Taking advantage of the FU's momentary disarray, Flôres created the Liberal Republican Party (PRL—Partido Republicano Liberal) to combat his enemies.

Into the PRL flocked the bulk of Republican coroneis and minor political leaders. Their belief in Castilhist ideology and loyalty to Borges de Medeiros had disappeared conveniently in favor of their remaining in power by switching to the new government party. The PL, accustomed by history to being the out-party, suffered a less dramatic exodus. This loss consisted primarily of Antunes Maciel and that minority of Liberators who had sided with Flôres during the revolution. The many farmers, businessmen, industrialists, and merchants who were more concerned with stability and government favors than with the game of politics also backed the interventor's party.

In addition, the PRL attracted a new element–young Gaúchos who had tired of the socioeconomic conservatism of the FU parties. The PRL appealed to them with a platform that grappled with the political and economic problems of the era. Rejecting presidentialist and parliamentarist theorizing, it advocated elements of both systems. In addition to political reforms, it also recommended greater state involvement in such areas as economic development, social welfare, and education.[2]

However, for all of the idealistic words in its program, the essence of the PRL was power, not ideology. It was the political army of the dominant Gaúcho triumvirate–Vargas, Flôres, and Aranha–the institutionalization of the uneasy alliance between these three Gaúchos, united by their opposition to the FU but divided by personal ambition, ideological conflict, and mutual distrust.

Although freely admitting that Flôres had saved him, Vargas felt little confidence in the Gaúcho interventor. Flôres had plotted against him and might have supported the Paulistas had Borges been in Pôrto Alegre when the revolution began. Two years later Flôres told the press:

> If I had been warned four or five days in advance (of the 1932 revolution), I would have abandoned the government and retired to my ranch or emigrated. But Borges did not do this and appealed to me at the last minute without taking into consideration my personality and honor. When they (the FU) invited me to join the revolution, it already had exploded.[3]

Vargas revealed his distrust of the Gaúcho interventor by reneging on his promise to make Flôres his new justice minister and ordering Flôres to deliver to the army all arms and ammunition captured from the Paulistas.[4]

In turn, Flôres had reservations about Getúlio's willingness to terminate his dictatorship and, aided by Aranha, led the campaign for reconstitutionalization. Under mounting constitutionalist pressure, Vargas asked Flôres to name the new justice minister. His choice was Antunes Maciel, his trusted finance secretary and former law school roommate. With Maciel, Finance Minister Aranha, and Labor Minister Joaquim Pedro Salgado Filho, the

Gaúchos once again held three of the seven civilian ministries, despite the resignation of Assis Brasil as agriculture minister.

Maciel's selection was celebrated nationally as a constitutionalist victory. Upon taking office on November 7, the new justice minister announced that reconstitutionalization would be his main job. He immediately convoked a commission to draw up the preliminary draft of the constitution. Many tenentes, particularly the northern interventors, moved to postpone the May 1933 election, and there were rumors that Vargas planned to delay the election for six months. But Flôres, Maciel, and Aranha, who had loosened his ties with the tenentes and vowed to resign if the election were postponed, united with other constitutionalist leaders to repel these threats.

Having maintained the May 3 election date, Flôres turned to Rio Grande to make sure that his Rio victory would not become the pyrrhic variety. By recruiting most Republican and many Liberator county bosses, Flôres had appropriated much of the grass-roots organization of the two traditional parties and made the PRL formidable despite its infancy.

In contrast the FU faced a painful rebuilding process. Although many Republicans and Liberators remained faithful to their parties, the 1932 struggle had depleted much of the FU membership and destroyed the structure which had been its strength. The revolution also had created a leadership vacuum, with Pilla, Collor, Neves, Luzardo, and many others in Uruguayan-Argentine exile. Vargas had considered deporting Borges to Europe, but Flôres had interceded, fearing that Borges would return to Uruguay and join the conspirators there.[5] Instead the government had "exiled" the Republican chief to Pernambuco, where he was free to wander throughout the state on his promise not to escape.

However, despite its numerical and organizational weaknesses, the FU emerged from the 1932 conflict with one new strength—a greater PRR-PL unity without the mistrust that previously had characterized the alliance. The appearance of a common state-level enemy—the PRL of Vargas, Aranha, and the "traitor," Flôres—had overcome years of personal and ideological enmity. Under Maurício Cardoso, interim chief in Pôrto Alegre, the FU began to function almost as a single political unit with joint central and county directorates, presenting itself for the first time as a single ticket. The classic PRR-PL struggle had given way to a PRL-FU confrontation, but the state's tradition of a two-camp division remained intact.

Both political camps received pressure from a nonparty force–the Catholic Electoral League (LEC–Liga Eleitoral Católica). A branch of the national league, the Gaúcho LEC conducted intensive electoral registration, particularly in the Italian zone, and influenced Catholic voters. It also asked the Gaúcho parties and individual candidates to agree formally to support the Catholic constitutional program, which called for facultative religious instruction in the public schools, facultative religious assistance in the armed forces, state recognition of church ceremonies, and no divorce. Since the PRL supported the program most vigorously, the LEC state junta published a declaration in favor of the Liberal Party candidates. It also stated that Catholics could vote for United Frontists who individually accepted the program.[6]

Flôres da Cunha found himself in a dilemma. Although a national champion of electoral reform, he was conditioned to the violent, controlled elections of the Old Republic. He could not reconcile himself to playing the democratic game by its new rules and giving the FU a chance to win.

Flôres mitigated the potentially dangerous impact of the secret ballot by impeding the opposition's registration drive and electoral campaign. He reinstituted press censorship, refused to permit FU public rallies, restricted the travel of FU leaders, and even imprisoned some United Frontists. Flôres' supporters, particularly in the interior, sometimes resorted to threats and beatings.[7]

In late April, Flôres surprised the FU by requesting and obtaining the abrogation of the political rights of four FU candidates on the grounds of having participated in the 1932 conspiracy. The electoral law stated that a vote cast for an illegal candidate would invalidate all names on that ballot. As a result the already-distributed FU ballots, which listed all candidates, became worthless.* Coming almost on election eve, Flôres' coup forced

---

*Each party printed its own ballots with the names of all of its candidates. The voter had the option of voting for the entire party slate, in which case both the party and each individual candidate received one vote, or of striking out certain names, in which case the party did not receive a vote and only the undeleted candidates received votes. Party vote

the FU leaders to work around the clock to print and distribute new ballots.

But Flôres had a final trick. He had the PRL ballots printed on light cardboard, in contrast to the FU's paper ballots. Although voters entered secret booths to place their ballots in the official envelopes, they deposited their envelopes in public ballot boxes. Party inspectors easily determined the party vote by the bend of the envelope.[8] These acts helped insure a PRL victory, but they also marred Flôres' national image as a champion of democracy.

Considering the tradition of Gaúcho election day violence, May 3 passed calmly. There was only one death, a Liberal police deputy murdered by United Frontists. Aided by the cardboard ballot detection device, Interior Secretary João Carlos Machado announced the PRL victory on May 5, although the "secret" ballot boxes had not yet arrived in Pôrto Alegre to be opened. Rio Grande was not unique. Other interventors, having done their best to control their states' elections, rushed to proclaim triumphs.

Flôres claimed victory prematurely but not incorrectly. The PRL slate received 132,056 votes to 37,400 for the FU. It elected thirteen of the state's sixteen constituent assembly delegates. Through selective voting the Catholic Electoral League influenced the final ranking of the candidates and assured the election of two of its leaders.[9] The PRL victory typified the triumphs of most prointerventor parties throughout Brazil.

A major exception occurred in São Paulo, where Democrats and Republicans won as the United Ticket, although Vargas had been courting the state since his 1932 military triumph. Aware of the difficulty of governing effectively without São Paulo's support, Vargas had been following a pro-Paulista coffee policy and had instructed the Bank of Brazil to redeem 1932 Paulista war bonds. This incensed Flôres da Cunha and the Gaúchos since Vargas had refused to redeem Rio Grande's equivalent 1930 revolutionary currency.[10] Following the United Ticket's electoral victory, Getúlio appointed a Paulista civilian interventor, a popular young engineer named Armando de Salles Oliveira.

Minas Gerais also presented Vargas with a serious problem— the struggle for power within the governing Progressive Party. The

totals were used to establish the proportion of deputies elected by each party; the seats awarded to each party were then filled on the basis of the individual vote totals of that party's candidates.

death of Minas governor Olegário Maciel on September 15, 1933, complicated the problem by raising the critical question of his successor. Vargas did not commit himself immediately to making this thankless selection but instead followed his time-hallowed formula, "Leave it as it is and see how it turns out." He ordered the next man in the state governmental hierarchy, Interior Secretary Gustavo Capanema, to serve as interim interventor until he could make a permanent choice.

Flôres da Cunha and Oswaldo Aranha did nothing to ease the Minas crisis. Since the 1932 revolution, the Flôres-Aranha rivalry for the number-two power slot behind Vargas had been growing. Aranha hungered to be Vargas' successor. In contrast, although Flôres would not have refused the presidency, he was more concerned with establishing himself as the new national political boss à la Pinheiro Machado. Flôres did not insist on becoming president; he merely wanted to run the country.

Minas Gerais became the battleground for the two Gaúcho adversaries, with the interventorship the coveted prize. Aranha supported the candidacy of his close friend, Virgílio de Melo Franco, a young reformer also backed by the tenentes. Rather than lose by default, Flôres proclaimed himself the champion of Gustavo Capanema.[11]

After three months of procrastination, Vargas drew up a decree naming Virgílio. The furious Flôres threatened that if Virgílio's selection became official, he would see to it that the constituent assembly did not elect Getúlio president.[12] Vargas countered by naming instead an unknown party regular named Benedito Valadares, a brilliant example of Vargas' strategy of waiting out a problem. He had allowed the powerful politicians to create a stalemate and had then named his own man, who would be dependent on Vargas for his strength.

For Flôres the selection of Valadares was a partial victory, since the Gaúcho interventor had supported Capanema merely to block Aranha and Virgílio. For Aranha it was a major defeat, which derailed the finance secretary's political express. Following the completion of the 1934 Brazilian constitution, Aranha went into temporary political exile as ambassador to the United States in order to heal his wounds.

When the constituent assembly opened in November 1933, the ideological conflict between Vargas and Flôres became apparent.[13] What Júlio de Castilhos and Borges de Medeiros had done for Rio Grande do Sul, Vargas wanted to do for Brazil—institute a strongly centralistic constitution, reduce the strength of the component territorial units, and increase the power of the central government and its chief executive. In this quest he received vital support from General Góes Monteiro, whom he named war minister in January 1934. Góes fervently believed in the necessity of unifying Brazil, restructuring the army to make it a source of national strength, and reducing the power of or absorbing state militias and provisional corps.

In contrast Flôres proposed a "Federation-Unity" formula, a variation of the historical Republican motto, "Centralization—Dismemberment; Decentralization—Unity."[14] Flôres' formula meant resistance to such concepts as concentration of power in the national government, federalization of state militias, and tax redistribution to increase central government revenues at the expense of the states and counties. Instead he favored state autonomy and the federal system of the 1891 constitution. Flôres also opposed the indirect election to congress of class representatives of labor, business, the professions, and government functionaries. There were forty such deputies in the 254-seat constituent assembly.

As the constituent assembly lumbered along, both Vargas and Flôres—each in his characteristic manner—attempted to influence its proceedings and outcome. Quietly, subtly, Vargas made his wishes known through various progovernment leaders and delegates. When it became evident that the assembly would not accept his "guidance," Vargas withdrew from the battlefield.[15]

Predictably, Flôres took a more direct tack with speeches, interviews, declarations, and even threats in the Pinheiro Machado style. He urged the assembly to finish its work as rapidly as possible and defended the successful idea of block voting for large sections of the constitution rather than article-by-article voting. However, Flôres' primary contribution was his strong defense of the assembly, enabling it to complete its work in the face of periodic threats that a military coup might dissolve it.

In a direct challenge to the tenentes and particularly War Minister Góes Monteiro, prime author of these threats, Flôres placed his personal prestige and Rio Grande's military might behind the assembly. On April 2, 1934, the decaying October

Third Club issued a manifesto condemning liberal democracy and the current draft of the constitution. Sharing Vargas' disdain for legislative bodies and preference for dictatorship over democracy, Góes Monteiro rattled his saber louder through continuous interviews threatening army dissolution of the assembly. Flôres threw down the gauntlet. On April 22 he delivered a speech stating:

> I hope and pray to God that I will not again have to carry out an act as sad as that of combating my brothers to preserve order and maintain intact the traditions of Rio Grande. However, whether they like it or not, I will say to the enemies of order, inside and outside of the state, that to maintain it, I am duly prepared.[16]

When the Rio newspapers publicized Flôres' remarks as a challenge to the army, he tried to soften the impact by issuing an official note declaring "the army has no better friend than I." But in the same note he also commented, "I am prepared, it is true, to maintain order within my state and even outside its frontiers. . . . Order will be maintained in this country, no matter what the cost, no matter what may happen."[17] Rumors spread that to implement his "paz Floresca" the Gaúcho interventor was mobilizing provisional corps and deploying state troops to isolate federal garrisons as in 1930.[18]

Despite continued talk of Góes' military coup conspiracy and Flôres' antiarmy maneuvers, neither did the war minister bring down the assembly with his threatened grenadiers nor did the Gaúcho interventor have to prove whether he could maintain order inside and outside of Rio Grande. But the crisis underscored the question of Brazil's military balance of power. In particular it accentuated the clash between the Pinheiro Machadism of Flôres da Cunha and the Bonapartism of Góes Monteiro and made the war minister more determined than ever to strengthen the army and crush state forces in the name of a centralized, unified Brazil.

Its life guaranteed by Flôres' military machine, the constituent assembly began to vote on the constitution. Led by a "coordinating committee" of the Rio Grande, Minas Gerais, Bahia, Pernambuco, and Rio de Janeiro delegations, each responsible to its respective interventor, the majority steamroller accelerated the proceedings. Despite fierce opposition protest, it set time limits on the heated debates and voted on large blocks of articles.

In addition to approving the substantive constitutional material, the assembly rammed through a number of important transitory provisions. These included articles making Vargas eligible for the presidency, declaring interventors eligible for the governorships, and extending the assembly until the end of 1934. The assembly also approved in block all federal, state, and county government acts since the 1930 revolution but, to Vargas' chagrin, it denied the new president the right to continue issuing decree laws.

On July 16 the assembly promulgated the 1934 constitution as the supreme document of the Second Republic. It was a sad day for Vargas. Not only did he have to surrender his dictatorial powers, but he also found himself trammeled by a constitution which fell far short of his hopes and expectations.

It was a curious document. It included the civil libertarian and electoral demands of the constitutionalists and such socioeconomic reforms as constitutionalization of the Collor labor program and affirmation of government responsibility in social and economic sectors. The inclusion of fifty class representatives in the three-hundred-seat chamber of deputies fulfilled a tenente wish. Although more centralistic than its 1891 predecessor, the 1934 constitution did not approach satisfying Vargas' desires. Through the efforts of the large states, including Rio Grande do Sul, federalism and states' rights had triumphed. Furthermore, the constitution restricted presidential powers and followed the 1891 pattern of limiting the president to a four-year term with no reelection.

Upon receiving news of the proclamation of the constitution, Vargas slammed shut his desk drawer and muttered to a visitor in his office, "I believe that I will be the first to revise the constitution."[19] But he could take some solace in being the odds-on favorite in the presidential election the following day in the assembly. Even Flôres da Cunha, who had defeated Vargas on the federalism-centralism issue, vigorously supported his fellow Gaúcho.

The opposition had encountered continual frustration in its search for a presidential candidate. It had contemplated three names—former foreign minister Afrânio de Melo Franco, Oswaldo Aranha, and Góes Monteiro—but all three projects had collapsed. The Paulistas rejected Melo Franco and did not like Aranha.[20]

The Gaúcho exiles rebelled at the thought of the finance minister, whom they considered Rio Grande's prime turncoat next to Flôres.[21]

With his army-tenente backing, Góes Monteiro appeared the most promising candidate. The opposition even brought Góes a manifesto of support with the signatures of 128 of the 254 assembly delegates.[22] However, after lengthy contemplation, Góes refused the candidacy. The reasons for his refusal are unclear: possibly the careful, suspicious Góes feared the defection of some of the "pledged" delegates or perhaps he intentionally deceived the opposition into believing he would be its candidate in order to withdraw at the last minute, leaving the opposition without a contender.

Unable to find a viable candidate, the opposition instead chose a symbolic one—Borges de Medeiros. In exile in Pernambuco since shortly after the 1932 revolution, Borges had undergone a major ideological transformation, publishing his new ideas in a book entitled *O Poder Moderador na República Presidencial (The Moderative Power in the Presidential Republic)*. In this Brazilian equivalent of Luther's theses, Borges rejected his lifetime of Castilhist, positivist presidentialism in favor of a modified parliamentarism.[23]

The exiled Republican chief reluctantly accepted the invitation, becoming an official candidate only one day before the election. Few oppositionists actually believed Borges could defeat Vargas. A notable exception was the self-deluded Maurício Cardoso, who had launched the Borges candidacy.[24] Borges himself admitted that he would not receive more than 80 votes. Even this turned out to be too optimistic, as Vargas crushed his former patron by a 175-to-59 vote in the July 17 election. The irate, exiled João Neves da Fontoura termed the election the "arrival of the Third Emperor."[25]

Sworn in as president on July 20, Vargas immediately sought to detach himself from the unpredictable Flôres. As retribution for Flôres' campaigns for reconstitutionalization and a federalist constitution, Vargas selected only one Gaúcho for his new ministry—Bank of Brazil president and Vargas crony Arthur da Souza Costa as finance minister. Rio Grande lost both the justice and labor ministries. As he loosened his ties with Flôres and Rio Grande, Vargas strengthened his position with São Paulo and

Minas Gerais by awarding each two ministries, with São Paulo receiving the politically powerful justice ministry, monopolized since 1930 by Rio Grande.

While detaching himself from Flôres in national politics, Vargas still relied on the interventor in the crucial state-level struggle. Within the PRL only Flôres had sufficient prestige to oppose Borges and Pilla as they led their followers back from exile and into the long-awaited confrontation with the Liberals.[26]

This FU desire for revenge had begun with the 1932 revolution and had grown in intensity during two years of political and economic deprivation. When the 1932 revolution had ended, some FU leaders, like Pilla and Collor, were in Uruguay, attempting to raise an army to invade Rio Grande.[27] After São Paulo surrendered, the exiles continued preparing for an invasion to occur simultaneously with proposed revolts within Brazil. With Paulista money the exiles obtained arms, including U.S. airplanes, and plotted with supporters throughout Brazil.[28] But the passage of time, progress toward reconstitutionalization, and an enervating struggle among the exile leaders for control of the proposed movement ultimately eroded revolutionary zeal. As it became clear to all but the most uncompromising conspirators that a successful revolution-invasion was no more than a pipe dream, the exiles redirected their efforts toward the presidential election and plans for returning to Brazil.[29]

Although some Gaúcho exiles settled in Buenos Aires and Montevideo, most chose Rivera, a small Uruguayan border town adjoining the Rio Grande cattle center of Sant'Anna do Livramento, home of the Flôres da Cunha family. The interventor's older brother, Francisco, was Livramento's political boss. Because of its convenient location, Rivera became the site of FU conferences attended by both exiles and United Frontists still in Rio Grande. It also provided the most notorious incident of the exile era—the murder of Waldemar Ripoll.

The most dedicated revolutionary among the Gaúcho exiles, Liberator Ripoll led the dwindling invasion-at-all-costs bloc. The twenty-seven-year-old journalist also discovered a smuggling racket run by a Brazilian customs official who, coincidentally, was foreman of Francisco Flôres da Cunha's ranch. To keep the racket from being exposed, the official had a ranch worker hack the sleeping Ripoll to death with a machete in January 1934.[30]

The murder stirred Rio Grande. The arrival of Ripoll's body set off a mass demonstration in Pôrto Alegre, where FU orators turned his burial into a Julius Caesar-like affair, with attacks on Flôres' government. Francisco Flôres, who had nothing to do with the murder, came to the defense of his foreman. Out of brotherly affection the interventor halted the investigation of the case, although the identities of the guilty parties were a matter of public knowledge.[31] That fraternal but politically unwise decision gave the FU a martyr for the 1934 electoral campaign for congress and the state assembly.

With the proclamation of the constitution the exiles returned, ready for battle. Some, like Pilla, felt that continued agitation would further convulse strife-torn Rio Grande and suggested that the campaign be conducted on an ideological level. But FU passions were high, and many United Frontists, like Neves and Luzardo, wanted the election to be a settling of accounts with Flôres. They returned to Rio Grande breathing fire or, in Flôres' words, "like barbarians in a barbaric land."[32]

Although the Liberal-FU struggle provided the heart of the 1934 Gaúcho election, the contest also marked the electoral debut of Brazilian Integralist Action (Ação Integralista Brasileira). This fascist organization had arisen in São Paulo in October 1932, in the backwash of the Constitutionalist revolution. Led by Paulista Plínio Salgado, a self-styled Brazilian Führer, Integralism had spread rapidly, benefiting from the increased belief in the need for a radical solution to Brazil's problems.[33] In Rio Grande do Sul, the movement had particular success in the German and Italian zones.[34]

As in 1933, the central figure in the 1934 election was Flôres da Cunha. Using his extensive governmental powers, he had strengthened the PRL organization since the 1933 election. He also had proven himself a progressive, imaginative administrator. He had expanded the state public works program, built the first intermunicipal paved roads, and created a series of official commercial cartels, known as institutes, which were responsible for the marketing of Rio Grande's basic products. Moreover, he had begun negotiations for the establishment of a state commercial fleet to relieve Gaúcho economic dependence on the inadequate national merchant marine.

On the other hand, Flôres bore the political handicaps of

some of his past activities. The FU hammered at the old accusation of treachery in the 1932 revolution and the new theme of Flôres' refusal to punish the well-known killers of Waldemar Ripoll. In addition, in order to raise the capital necessary for Gaúcho economic programs, Flôres had made bargains with and had given excessive benefits to certain groups, particularly a number of commercial combines. This led to considerable criticism and the "Lard Scandal" of 1934.

The latter—a complex, controversial international financial manipulation involving the Gaúcho government and the Rio Grande Lard Syndicate—brought handsome profits to the state. However, a number of individuals profited even more from the transaction. The ensuing criticism led to the emergence of a new, sardonic nickname for the Gaúcho interventor—Flôres da Banha (the Portuguese word for "lard").

In contrast to the relatively peaceful 1933 election, violence characterized the 1934 campaign. Flôres responded to the FU's campaign of hatred with his own campaign of terror, implemented by his mayors, police, local political bosses, military brigade officers, and National Resistance Action, a pro-Flôres civil-military militant organization with the Castilhos-like motto "Whoever is not for us is against us."[35] They resorted to many types of coercion—arrest and exile of FU chiefs; harassment of opposition newspapers and journalists; enforced "retirement" or transfer of public functionaries, railroad workers, and brigade officers who refused to sign pro-Flôres manifestoes; intimidation, violence, and even murder to prevent United Frontists from campaigning and voting.[36] The FU protested to the federal government, but United Frontists also retaliated with their own violence, including murder and assaults on PRL rallies.

Out of this turbulent campaign came a hollow Liberal victory in the October 14 election. Although the PRL slate received 130,000 votes, about the same as in 1933, the FU vote doubled from 37,000 in 1933 to over 75,000 in 1934.[37] The Integralist slate received only 2,266 votes, not enough to elect a single legislator. This failure was to become status quo for third forces in the two-camp Gaúcho political struggle.

The FU was elated; Flôres was enraged. He lashed out with his famous caudilho's fury. He summarily dismissed mayors who had failed to deliver Liberal majorities, removed public functionaries he felt had voted for the FU, and forced the firing of pro-FU employees from companies heavily dependent on government favors. Even more vindictively, he mutilated selected counties which had voted for the FU, using the dismembered areas to form new counties. One of these ironically received the name of Getúlio Vargas.[38]

Flôres had still one more electoral gambit. Because of irregularities, the Regional Electoral Tribunal nullified the votes in certain districts and scheduled supplementary elections for December 17. Aware that the October 14 election had guaranteed a certain number of FU seats, Flôres decided to determine which United Frontists would fill those seats. He distributed a number of combination ballots which, in addition to listing some Liberals, contained the names of selected FU candidates.

With their vote totals padded by these combination ballots, Flôres' hand-picked "candidates" captured four of the six FU congressional seats and seven of the eleven FU state assembly seats, blocking the election of such men as João Neves da Fontoura and Lindolfo Collor.[39] The FU leadership partially rectified these results by convincing all but three of the Flôres-elected United Frontists to resign their seats in favor of those who would have won if there had been no Liberal vote padding.

Vargas noted the decline of Flôres' political power and decided to reduce even further his dependence on the interventor. Returning to Pôrto Alegre in November 1934 for the first time since the 1930 revolution, Vargas maintained a discreet reserve toward Flôres. He even refused Flôres' invitation to be a guest in the governor's palace, nearly a public insult. Speaking at a banquet in the president's honor, Vargas dwelled on the revolution's accomplishments in his speech but, except for one passing reference, pointedly ignored Flôres.[40]

Faced with the erosion of Vargas' support, Flôres increased his efforts to rebuild his strength at home by pacifying and uniting Rio Grande. The interventor had begun his pacification campaign immediately after the 1932 revolution, continuing it steadily, even during the violent 1934 electoral campaign. Wary of the potential hypertrophy of Flôres' national power should he pacify and unite Rio Grande behind him, Vargas and Góes Monteiro impeded Gaúcho peace negotiations. They dangled the bait of possible FU participation in the national government if it rejected a regional agreement with Flôres.

At first the FU insisted that Flôres resign and agree not to be a candidate for governor if there were to be pacification. But as it became clear that neither Flôres nor the PRL would accept such conditions, the FU softened its stand. At Flôres' request, FU leaders in Pôrto Alegre drew up a series of administrative norms which, if implemented by the state government, could lead to gradual pacification. These included full freedom of party and electoral activities, removal of violent and arbitrary police officials, and restoration of public functionaries who had been removed or transferred for political reasons.[41]

When the state constituent assembly began in April 1935, the FU delegation took a further step toward pacification. It dedicated itself to constitutional issues, refusing to transform the assembly into an arena for a vendetta against Flôres. This disappointed both Vargas and revenge-minded FU leaders in the interior, who were engaged in their own bitter local contests with the PRL.

As the loyal opposition, the FU had little power. With a twenty-one-to-eleven majority, further augmented by seven class deputies chosen by state government "coordination," the PRL did what it pleased. It elected Flôres as governor and two Liberals as senators. It wrote the 1935 state constitution. Like the 1934 federal constitution and in line with the PRL program, the state document gave the government greater socioeconomic powers and responsibilities, which the FU generally opposed.[42] When the constituent assembly became the regular state assembly, the FU deputies continued their laudable conduct. This contrasted with the João Neves-led FU congressional delegation, which launched violent personal attacks on Flôres.

With relative peace at home, Flôres could concentrate on his national policies and strategies. More than ever he engaged in unrestrained Pinheiro Machadism, asserting his influence in congress, in intrastate conflicts, and within the military. As his political activities expanded, he found himself in conflict with Vargas, Góes Monteiro, and São Paulo's governing Constitutionalist Party, an increasingly powerful force in national politics.

Flôres and Góes were fated to be prime antagonists as champions of incompatible philosophies. Flôres personified state autonomy, defending it with words, political manipulations, and military threats. His strength rested on the six-thousand-man Gaúcho military brigade, the state's twenty-thousand-man civilian militia provisional corps, and his many allies within the heavily Gaúchoized army. Góes embodied the quest for strong central government, a powerful obedient army, and weak states without independent military power.

Since the 1930 revolution, Flôres and Góes had clashed with increasing frequency over such matters as reconstitutionalization, the constituent assembly, and Gaúcho pacification. As war minister, Góes insisted that Vargas request a military pay increase in early 1935, threatening a military revolution if congress refused to approve the raise. In opposition to this agitation, Flôres again mobilized his forces and demanded that Vargas remove Góes.[43]

With Flôres' backing, a group of army officers in Rio Grande's Cachoeira garrison sent Góes a widely publicized telegram protesting against the war minister's "moral misery" in agitating for the pay raise. When Góes tried to punish them, they refused to accept his authority and demanded his resignation. Flôres seconded the ultimatum.[44] To further trammel Góes, Flôres' congressional delegation presented an economically ludicrous substitute bill raising salaries for civilian functionaries as well as military men. Congress passed it overwhelmingly. His bill a shambles and military discipline a farce, Góes resigned, accusing Flôres of corrupting the army and blaming his removal on the "finger of the giant."[45] Vargas ultimately vetoed the civilian pay increase, a veto upheld by congress. The PRL supported Vargas' veto, since by then Flôres had achieved his goal—the removal of Góes Monteiro as war minister.

Flôres suggested two generals as Góes' replacement. But, in line with his campaign to reduce Flôres' power, Vargas rejected the suggestions, telling Góes, "He will pay for what he did."[46] Vargas began at once to make Flôres pay. Continuing his pro-São Paulo strategy, Vargas accepted Paulista governor Armando de Salles Oliveira's recommendation of General João Gomes for war minister. The president also blocked Flôres' cherished expropriation of the São Paulo-Rio Grande Railroad and refused federal financial support for his proposed Riograndense Fleet.

Flôres' most galling reversals came in the state gubernatorial struggles. These were critical, since the new governors would be in power during the 1938 presidential election. Although this was three years away, politicians already were forming battle lines. Flôres announced that Rio Grande should not accept the presidency again after eight years in power. However, he insisted that Rio Grande do Sul would be heard on the presidential succession, "no matter what difficulties might arise."[47] In raw terms this meant that although Flôres did not intend to be king, like Pinheiro Machado, he planned to select and crown him.

The most likely presidential candidate was São Paulo governor Salles Oliveira. It also appeared as if Vargas would support Salles, having lavished economic benefits on São Paulo and having made Paulista Vicente Ráo his justice minister, the government's political coordinator. To defeat the potential Vargas-Salles axis, Flôres decided on Antônio Carlos de Andrada, the old Mineiro political fox, as his candidate. Flôres envisioned a grand alliance including Rio Grande do Sul, Minas Gerais, the Paulista Republican Party, which opposed Salles' Constitutionalist Party, and key political leaders in the other states. Some of the gubernatorial contests provided a preliminary test of strength between Flôres and Salles, represented by Justice Minister Ráo. In these confrontations, Ráo generally triumphed.[48]

For military reasons, Flôres' major concern lay with the elections in the states of Santa Catarina and Rio de Janeiro. Resting on the Gaúcho northern border, Santa Catarina provided both a defensive buffer and the route for any Gaúcho offensive thrust. Flôres' closest Catarinense ally, Interventor Aristiliano Ramos, failed to control the elections and found himself with an assembly minority. Despite the efforts of Flôres and his Rio agent, former justice minister Antunes Maciel, the Santa Catarina assembly elected Aristiliano's cousin and enemy, Nereu Ramos.

More important was the gubernatorial struggle in the state of Rio de Janeiro, whose capital, Niterói, sat imposingly across Guanabara Bay from the nation's capital.* In case of military action, control of the Rio de Janeiro government could be decisive. Flôres' candidate, Colonel Christóvão Barcellos, con-

---

*The state of Rio de Janeiro is not to be confused with the city of Rio de Janeiro in the old Federal District, later the state of Guanabara.

trolled twenty-two deputies. Although divided, the other twenty-three deputies finally compromised on Navy Minister Admiral Protógenes Guimarães, who had Vargas' support. Justice Minister Ráo blatantly aided the opposition; to keep votes in line, he dispatched two hundred police investigators to "keep order" in the Rio assembly during the election.

A long and complex affair, the Rio state election was not completed officially until November 1935. However, the decisive events occurred in late September while Vargas was in Pôrto Alegre for the inauguration of the Farroupilha Centennial. This gigantic three-month exposition was staged by Flôres da Cunha in honor of the hundredth anniversary of the 1835-45 Farroupilha War. When Vargas arrived in Pôrto Alegre for the opening, he and Flôres were still cautious, distrustful friends. When he left a week later, the two Gaúchos had become undeclared enemies.

At the exposition's inaugural ceremony, Vargas became upset at his tepid public reception. In comparison, Flôres received an enthusiastic popular manifestation.[49] Moreover, while publicly participating in centennial activities, the two Gaúchos telegraphically made their final moves in the Rio contest. The angry Flôres considered Vargas' opposition to his candidate to be the last straw in the president's rejection of Rio Grande and favoritism for São Paulo. Already disturbed by Flôres' crusade to dominate Brazil, Vargas became even more disgusted when Flôres pilfered some of his telegrams and sent a ringing public pledge of support to the Christóvão Barcellos faction, intimating that Vargas was betraying his old friends.[50] Despite Flôres' efforts, the Vargas-Ráo axis triumphed, securing the election of Guimarães.

Vargas felt hostility toward Flôres, but he felt even more bitterness toward congress. Unaccustomed to sharing power, the frustrated Vargas decided to recapture his lost dictatorial powers rather than try to work with what he considered a verbose, obstructionist congress. He gave Flôres a final test.

Going to Flôres' palace bedroom, the president proposed a new Vargas-Flôres revolution, making him dictator again and securing Flôres' absolute control over Rio Grande. An avowed constitutionalist, Flôres angrily rejected Vargas' proposal.[51] This incident made it clear to Vargas that the key step toward restoration of his dictatorship would have to be the liquidation of Flôres.

Tension over the Rio case and Flôres' rejection of Vargas' coup proposal irreversibly ended their tenuous alliance. Vargas' last days in Pôrto Alegre became notable for the frigidity of the two Gaúchos' public relationship. Flôres treated Vargas with no more courtesy than demanded by protocol; Vargas even lost his eternal smile.[52] After Vargas flew back to Rio, Flôres made his stand public:

> . . . . Rio Grande will do everything to normalize the country's political life and to remove from certain heads the thought of implanting another dictatorship, whatever its coloration. If such should happen, I believe that Rio Grande would arise as one man to protest with arms against the terrible adventure. Let the nation know that I would struggle until the last drop of blood.[53]

The uneasy alliance had ended. The open struggle was about to begin.

5

Open Struggle

His split with Vargas a matter of public record, Flôres accelerated state pacification. His goals were an alliance with the United Front and the reconstruction of the "fortress Rio Grande" of the 1929-32 era. To demonstrate his goodwill, Flôres refused to participate personally in the campaign for the November 1935 municipal elections. This probably made little electoral difference, as by now Flôres' PRL machine was functioning well enough to capture sixty of the eighty-four mayoralty contests.[1]

While Flôres enticed them locally, United Frontists received outside pressure from fellow members of the national Opposition Coalition, a loose alliance of antigovernment forces in the various states. Anxious to bring the powerful Flôres into the opposition camp, the Rio-based coalition heartily encouraged the potential PRL-FU agreement.[2]

The union finally came as an aftermath of a series of revolts by military units in late November 1935 in the cities of Recife, Natal, and Rio de Janeiro. Instigated by Brazilian Communists (working through a popular front, the National Liberation Alliance), the revolts failed to generate significant popular support. Faced with strong, rapid reactions by loyal police and military forces, the rebels capitulated within a week.[3]

Learning of the Rio revolt, Flôres immediately mobilized twenty thousand men and telegraphed Vargas, placing them at his disposal. But Vargas did not, as he had in the 1932 revolution, need Flôres' Gaúcho troops to quell the 1935 revolt. Federal troops had crushed the rebels in short order. However, the Gaúcho governor's spontaneous gesture had an unintended impact. This

68

rapid, extensive mobilization reinforced Vargas' awareness of Flôres' military potential as an obstacle to the reestablishment of his dictatorship.

Taking advantage of the 1935 revolt, Vargas took immediate steps to use public panic over Communism in order to reach his goal of centralism, if only on a temporary basis. He extracted from congress a series of extreme measures that drastically increased Vargas' presidential powers, established a state of siege, and authorized the president to declare an even more rigorous state of war, which he did. The congressional opposition minority, led by João Neves da Fontoura, vigorously but unsuccessfully opposed this legislation, which gave Vargas the instruments not only to rid Brazil of Communism but also to suppress any opposition. Shocked by this sudden jeopardy, the opposition turned for security to the nation's greatest source of nonfederal military strength, Flôres da Cunha.

Galvanized by the fear of Communism, Integralism, and central government power, Flôres and the United Front reopened negotiations focusing on the possible adoption in Rio Grande of a parliamentarist formula developed by Raul Pilla and Rio journalist José Maria dos Santos.[4] But despite the favorable climate and the urging of opposition leaders in Rio, the negotiators encountered serious obstacles.

Those Liberators and Republicans who preferred Vargas over Flôres objected to the pact. Many Liberators, having fought Flôres on the battlefield and in the political arena, could not forget time-hardened enmity toward the caudilho. Some Republicans criticized the Pilla formula as a rejection of historical Castilhism. Pilla countered by citing his plan's similarity to that prescribed by Borges de Medeiros in his *Poder Moderador*. In addition, a group of young Liberals, increasingly frustrated by Flôres' autocratic party control, felt the pact would sacrifice the youthful PRL in favor of an alliance of old cronies.[5]

Vargas, too, did his part to impede the accord. While publicly lauding the patriotic aims of such a pact, he privately urged his brother Benjamin (a Liberal state deputy) to oppose it from within the PRL.[6] He also continued hinting at possible federal posts for the FU if the Rio Grande pacification talks failed.

Several times it appeared as if negotiations would collapse, but an agreement finally was reached. It was a special victory for

Lindolfo Collor, who had guided negotiations through numerous crises and obtained the key compromises. Most of the irreconcilably anti-Flôres United Frontists surrendered to the will of the majority of the FU leaders. However, they extracted the compromise that a Gaúcho accord would not preclude negotiations for a national agreement with Vargas.[7]

On January 17, 1936, Flôres, Borges, and Pilla signed the Gaúcho modus vivendi. During the emotional public ceremony in the Rio Grande legislature, Flôres and Borges embraced tearfully after more than three years of broken personal relations. According to the modus vivendi, Flôres accepted the Pilla formula and a number of United Front demands, including the guarantee of freedom of press and assembly, the rehiring of state employees who had been removed for political reasons, and the establishment of an effective civil service system.[8] In exchange the FU agreed to political peace and participation in the Gaúcho secretariat. As FU representatives, Flôres selected Pilla as agriculture secretary and Collor as finance secretary.

With state peace came a Gaúcho economic upsurge. In 1936 Rio Grande enjoyed a 20 percent industrial growth, while the state's export-import balance nearly quadrupled. Flôres also accelerated his progressive governmental program. He built food-processing plants, schools, railroad lines, and paved highways. He purchased refrigerated railroad cars and five refrigerated ships, the beginning of the Riograndense Fleet. Making double use of his human resources, Flôres transformed a number of mobilized provisional corps into two-hundred-man armed road gangs, which divided their time between road construction and military training.[9]

Liberals and United Frontists publicly described the modus as an administrative agreement, not a political alliance, but most Gaúcho leaders were more concerned with the pact's political benefits. The modus had brought FU participation in government spoils and had increased the FU's power position within the national Opposition Coalition. At the same time Flôres had severely muted FU criticism and had made the opposition co-responsible for future state acts. Furthermore, he had forged a base for national political action and had strengthened his ties with the Opposition Coalition. It appeared as if a united Rio Grande, led by Flôres, might now make a determined effort to reestablish national political hegemony and possibly even anoint the next president. With the help of many FU leaders, Flôres resumed his campaign for Antônio Carlos.

Stunned by the modus vivendi reversal, Vargas began a subtle campaign to undermine the Rio Grande pact, using his loyal agents within each Gaúcho party. He encouraged the nascent secret Liberal Dissidency, a group of young PRL state deputies led by his brother Benjamin and a junior caudilho named José Loureiro da Silva. The Dissidents opposed the modus as an opportunistic entente among power-hungry Old Republic politicians of all three Gaúcho parties. They also quietly opposed Flôres' dictatorial party leadership. Finally they saw a brighter future in alliance with the president than with the governor. 10

Vargas also renewed his enticement of the FU, via Gaúcho state deputy Maurício Cardoso, an indomitable opponent of the modus. The president commissioned Cardoso to develop plans for national political pacification and a compromise ministry in which the FU would play a major role. Whiffing the intoxicating scent of federal power, the FU allowed Cardoso to draw it closer to the president and further from both Flôres and the anti-Vargas Opposition Coalition, of which the FU was the official leader.

Already frustrated by the FU's drift toward Vargas, Flôres received another severe blow—the destruction of the Antônio Carlos de Andrada presidential candidacy. As president of the federal chamber of deputies, the normally astute Mineiro had committed the fatal error of becoming too absorbed by his presidential quest. This permitted pro-Vargas Minas governor Benedito Valadares, working subtly and unobtrusively, to take control of the state's dominant Progressive Party.

In league with Vargas and the president's new political hatchetman, owl-eyed Labor Minister Agamemnon Magalhães of Pernambuco, Valadares prepared a coup. The climax to the intraparty struggle came in August 1936, when Valadares announced the formation of an alliance between the majority wing of the Progressive Party and majority bloc of the opposition Minas Republican Party. The secretly prepared alliance omitted both Antônio Carlos and the titular Republican chief, former president Arthur Bernardes. 11 By preempting his political base and making him a man without a state, Valadares destroyed Antônio Carlos' presidential hopes.

On the heels of the Minas coup occurred a startling newspaper interview, in which Firmino Paim Filho, a leading Gaúcho Republican, came out strongly in favor of the extension of Vargas' term in office.[12] For Flôres, this not only reconfirmed his conviction of Vargas' continuist aims but also added the new element of FU support for the president. Aware that he was a marked man because of his opposition to Vargas' plans, Flôres decided to strike before the president could act militarily or further undermine him politically in Rio Grande.

As early as April 1936, Flôres had uncovered an armed conspiracy against him and begun to make serious military preparations. He had expanded the Gaúcho military arsenal through contraband arms from Europe and clandestine local production and had organized, trained, and strategically placed his armed road gangs, some consisting of prisoners from the state penitentiary. He also had drawn up plans for the mobilization of fourteen thousand provisional soldiers, subverted army ranks throughout the state, including the regional commander, and created an alliance with generals throughout southern and south-central Brazil. Flôres had prepared both a defensive plan for resistance against a Vargas invasion and an offensive plan for a 1930-type march on Rio. Now, with the political tide against him and time short, he decided to take the offensive militarily and try to disrupt Vargas' scheme to implant a new dictatorship.[13]

Flôres instructed his caudilhos to mobilize Gaúcho provisional corps in preparation for the drive north. However, the key to Flôres' offensive thrust was the support of General João Guedes da Fontoura, army commander in Paraná, the strategic state between Santa Catarina and São Paulo. Flôres sent an emissary to inform Guedes that the time had come to march north together and overthrow Vargas. Although he had been conspiring with Flôres, the indecisive Guedes backed out at the moment of truth, rejecting the Gaúcho governor's plea. When the emissary returned with Guedes' reply, Flôres responded, "Then our cause is lost."[14] His offensive plans shattered by Guedes' defection, Flôres switched to a defensive stance, with continued military preparations and even such subsidiary action as printing emergency currency.

Simultaneously with his military mobilization, Flôres struggled to sustain his collapsing Gaúcho political house. Despite the continuous disintegration of the Flôres-FU political alliance, the modus vivendi remained intact as an administrative accord until October 1936. Then the second vice-president of the state assembly died. As usual Flôres selected the PRL candidate for the vacant office, publicly declaring the election of his candidate a question of party loyalty and governmental confidence. The Liberal Dissidents decided to take this opportunity to reveal their movement. Receiving Vargas' encouragement, Dissidents and United Frontists collaborated to nominate and elect their own candidate—a bitter defeat for Flôres.[15]

Spurred by their victory, the fractious Liberal Dissidents lashed out with a series of anti-Flôres interviews, the most virulent statements coming from Benjamin Vargas, who openly rejected Flôres' party leadership.[16] Getúlio moved in for the kill. He tried to convince the PRL central commission to vote official support for the Dissidents, a move which could force Flôres to resign as governor and party chief.[17] However, still dominated by Florists, the commission worked out a partial compromise between the governor and the Dissidents. Flôres had to eat crow by publicly accepting the Dissidents' de facto freedom of action in the assembly.[18]

In the case of the FU, compromise was almost impossible. Prior to the assembly vice-presidential election, FU state government secretaries Collor and Pilla had tried in vain to convince their FU comrades not to join the Dissidents in this electoral insult to Flôres. Rejecting their pro-modus pleas, the Cardoso-led FU assemblymen had voted with the Dissidents and helped defeat the governor, forcing Collor and Pilla to resign their government posts.[19] Despite attempts to reach a compromise and Flôres' appeals to Collor and Pilla to remain in his cabinet, the modus vivendi collapsed. Its relations with Vargas now firmly reestablished, the FU soon officially left the national Opposition Coalition, which had become closely allied with Flôres.

Fearing a violent reaction, Dissident and FU assemblymen now hesitated to attack Flôres vigorously, claiming that Getúlio had agreed to take the initiative, with them seconding his acts. Some even asked Vargas to replace Flôres with an interventor on the grounds that the governor was arming against the federal government.[20] Traditional love of Gaúcho autonomy had succumbed to the hunger for victory over Flôres.

To weaken the governor's power, Vargas had named a new Third Region commander, General Emílio Lúcio Esteves. Getúlio even considered transferring direction of the state of war in Rio Grande from Flôres to Esteves in order to give the opposition more security and freedom to act.[21] However, despite his intense desire to topple Flôres, Vargas hesitated to take the offensive openly.

Although the army held an advantage of fourteen thousand men—twenty thousand to his six thousand—over Flôres' military brigade within Rio Grande, Vargas felt unsure of his military control. Furthermore, he was loath to make a public assault on his own state's autonomy without sufficient justification. Seeking a better excuse, Vargas urged Dissident and FU state deputies to launch a muckraking campaign against Flôres but counseled Benjamin not to participate in order to avoid accusations that the president had instigated the movement.[22]

Holding an assembly majority, the United Frontists and Liberal Dissidents initiated investigations into unsavory aspects of Flôres' government and passed legislation contrary to the governor's wishes. Flôres responded with threats of a St. Bartholomew's Day massacre, ominously loading the assembly gallery and surrounding the building with his police and hired gunslingers.[23] With money from the government-favored commercial cartels and from his profitable state gambling tax, Flôres tried to bribe opposition deputies. Vargas countered with his own bribery offensive, using federal funds and patronage.

It was this strife-ridden climate that faced Oswaldo Aranha when, in late 1936, he returned to Brazil from political exile as ambassador to the United States. Officially he came for the Buenos Aires Inter-American Conference for the Maintenance of Peace, but politics ranked above peace on Aranha's agenda. His hunger for the presidency undiminished by more than two years in the United States, Aranha saw the trip as an opportunity to establish his candidacy for the January 1938 election.

Like Flôres, Aranha posed a threat to Vargas' continuist plans. Since Aranha's presidential hopes rested on a united Rio Grande as his power base, Vargas was determined to abort his potential candidacy by keeping Rio Grande divided.[24] In contrast, Flôres needed Aranha's friendship as a shield in his struggle for political survival. For both personal and political reasons, Aranha too wanted to strengthen his old friendship with Flôres, severely strained by the Minas succession crisis. He realized that he could not capture the presidency without the support of a unified Rio Grande.

Arriving in Rio Grande in late December following the Buenos Aires conference, the ambassador immediately began to hammer at a single theme—the need for national cooperation for a peaceful presidential succession. Arguing with the Liberal Dissidents that their anti-Flôres campaign could lead to Rio Grande's political suicide, he convinced them to accept a truce until April 1937. This permitted Aranha to make his presidential bid armed with the potentiality of a reunited Rio Grande.[25]

Aranha had extracted from Vargas the mission of conciliating the federal and Gaúcho governments, but the president soon revealed his hopes for Aranha's failure. He began to sabotage the ambassador, using Liberator Alberto Pasqualini. As soon as Aranha arrived in Rio in January 1937 to continue his peace negotiations with Rio-based Gaúchos, Pasqualini opened fire with a series of vitriolic anti-Flôres interviews calculated to increase Gaúcho turmoil.[26] When the government censor banned them as agitation under the state of war, Vargas himself removed the censorship. Ignoring their promise to Aranha, the Dissidents followed Pasqualini's cue with their own anti-Flôres interviews.

Although willing to accept the Aranha candidacy, some Dissidents favored Getúlio's plan to continue in office.[27] After the January interviews the Dissidents restrained their public criticism of Flôres in accordance with the Aranha truce, but they actively undermined the governor. Throughout the state they organized pro-Vargas clubs. They also converted military brigade officers, railroad employees, priests, labor officials, and business leaders to their cause, so that when the assembly reconvened in April they could effectively break with Flôres at the first excuse.[28]

Aware that this truce deadline might also be the deadline for his presidential ambitions, Aranha frantically sought support nationally. Flôres detached himself from previous commitments and dedicated himself to the Aranha campaign, considering the ambassador's candidacy the surest means to save his own political skin.

The national presidential picture remained unclear in early 1937 as leaders in the major states jockeyed for position. In São

Paulo, the Constitutionalist Party supported Armando de Salles Oliveira for president. The opposition Paulista Republican Party agreed to accept Aranha, but only if he were also the candidate of the other major political currents. Pernambuco's Carlos de Lima Cavalcanti and Bahia's Juracy Magalhães, governors of the two most populous northern states, rejected the idea of another Gaúcho president, instead demanding a northern candidate. Minas Gerais governor Benedito Valadares opposed Aranha on more personal grounds. He feared that if Aranha became president, the Virgílio de Melo Franco forces would triumph in Minas.

With time running out, Aranha concluded that only one thing could save his candidacy—the reuniting of Vargas and Flôres. Convincing the distrustful Gaúcho governor to come to Rio, Aranha dragged him to Vargas' summer palace in Petropolis for a "renewal of friendship" on April 3. Flôres knew better. According to one reporter, as Aranha and Flôres left Rio, the governor remarked, "Since you demand it, I am going to the Rio Negro Palace to sign my death warrant."[29] He was right. Even as Flôres was flying to Rio, the president had initiated the final coup to destory a Gaúcho peace and an Aranha presidency.

In an attempt to extend the Liberal truce, Aranha was trying to convince the Dissidents to vote for Flôres' state assembly officer candidates when the state assembly reconvened on April 12. Vargas countered by sending federal deputy Baptista Luzardo to Pôrto Alegre to make certain that the Dissident-FU majority coalition remained solid and defeated Flôres' candidates.[30] Arriving in the Gaúcho capital, Luzardo announced Vargas' support of the opposition alliance. José Loureiro da Silva, a strongly pro-Vargas Dissident state deputy, followed with a stinging attack on Flôres.

Stunned by these events, Aranha appealed to Vargas to work out a compromise on the assembly election. Naturally the president refused, instead telegraphing brother Benjamin not to yield.[31] As a last resort Aranha sent an emissary to Pôrto Alegre with a compromise formula that Flôres had accepted, but the Dissidents rejected it.

The Dissidents' decision came as no real surprise to Aranha, who had even given his emissary an acrimonious reply letter to be delivered to the Dissidents if they refused his formula. Chastising the Dissidents for rejecting the compromise, Aranha wrote, "The contrary action merely confirms the political incapacity of which we (Rio Grande) are accused. ... "[32] When published, the letter caused a sensation. Not released to the press was a subsequent secret letter from Aranha to the Dissidents, correctly accusing them of being the architects of Brazil's next dictatorship.[33] His presidential hopes shattered, the bitter Aranha left Rio on April 12 to return to his ambassadorial post. That same morning Flôres da Cunha returned to Pôrto Alegre to prepare for Vargas' impending onslaught.

While undermining Flôres politically, Vargas was also besieging him militarily with the aid of former war minister Góes Monteiro. Both committed centralists, Vargas and Góes viewed state autonomist Flôres as public enemy number one. Vargas saw Flôres as the major obstacle to the reestablishment of his dictatorship; Góes, who had a personal score to settle, considered Flôres the embodiment of state armed power and the prime impediment to a strong, unified, obedient, nationalistic military.

In August 1936, Vargas and Góes had concurred on the necessity of destroying Flôres' power and the desirability of dissolving congress. In exchange for Vargas' commitment to the construction of a national military juggernaut and the reduction of the strength of state forces, Góes had agreed to support Vargas' dictatorial aims.[34] Commissioned by Vargas to "get Flôres," Góes immediately ran afoul of War Minister João Gomes. The latter rejected Góes' request for carte blanche to act as he saw fit and ignored the Third Region commander's urgent appeals for increased arms, ammunition, and officers. To remove this obstacle, Vargas and Góes forced Gomes to resign as war minister in December 1936 and replaced him with the ideologically compatible General Eurico Gaspar Dutra.[35]

Vargas, Góes, Dutra, and Justice Minister Agamemnon Magalhães then launched a campaign throughout Brazil to reduce state power, particularly that of Flôres and his potential allies. Góes and Dutra federalized and collected "excess" state arms and recalled a number of army officers previously assigned as advisers to state militias. When they recalled three pro-Flôres army officers from the Gaúcho military brigade, Flôres and his congressional supporters protested furiously.

Vargas and Agamemnon Magalhães intervened in the Federal District and in Mato Grosso, toppling that state's pro-Flôres governor. Pernambucan Agamemnon eroded the political position of Pernambuco governor Lima Cavalcanti, his rival for state supremacy. He also provoked a split in Bahia governor Juracy Magalhães' party. Juracy, Lima Cavalcanti, and São Paulo's Armando de Salles Oliveira had joined Flôres on Vargas' list of marked men in late 1936 when they rejected the president's proposal to extend his presidential mandate.[36]

Trying to counter federal repression, Flôres, Juracy, and Salles signed a tristate, anti-intervention defense pact of Rio Grande do Sul, Bahia, and São Paulo. Lima Cavalcanti refused to bring Pernambuco into the alliance. However, the pact had little real strength, since the three leaders were suffering from debilitating political illnesses within their own states.

Flôres da Cunha, the military cornerstone of the anti-intervention pact, found his armed strength being sapped by the state political battle. Dissident state deputy José Loureiro da Silva, one of the most brilliant grass-roots organizers in Gaúcho history, had traversed the state during the assembly recess, recruiting and solidifying Dissident support. The Dissidents' final break with Flôres came with the assembly officer election, when the opposition alliance elected its slate of assembly officers, climaxing the crisis that had wrecked the Aranha candidacy.[37]

The Dissidency carried with it nine Liberal state deputies, five federal deputies, one senator, two mayors, and other major PRL figures. These included Treasury Minister Arthur da Souza Costa and Protásio Vargas, Getúlio's older brother and a powerful Gaúcho political boss in his own right. Flôres retained twelve state deputies, nine federal deputies, one senator, most of the Liberal mayors, and other powerful Liberal leaders, like Bank of Brazil rediscount office director Antunes Maciel, Flôres' Rio agent. The seven nominally Liberal class deputies also divided, five remaining with Flôres and two joining the opposition.

The Vargas-Flôres struggle split not only the PRL, but also the two FU parties. The destruction of the modus vivendi had been an intraparty victory of pro-Vargas Republican Maurício Cardoso over pro-Flôres Republican Lindolfo Collor. Because Borges de Medeiros was serving as federal deputy in Rio, Cardoso continued to direct the Republican Party in Pôrto Alegre as he had during the years following the 1932 revolution. Having antagonized the vindictive Cardoso, Collor faced an uninviting party future; moreover, an ideological chasm separated the socio-economic reformer from most other Republican leaders.

At first Collor continued his struggle within the PRR, attempting to break Cardoso's stranglehold on the PRR central commission. He also appealed for a party congress to modernize the conservative Republican program. Receiving little support from the inert, conservative Republican mass, Collor called a rump convention, which established the small reformist Castilhist Republican Party (PRC–Partido Republicano Castilhista). Its new socioeconomic dimension attracted a number of young, progressive Republicans.[38]

Dissension also struck the Liberator Party. A young Pelotas lawyer named Bruno de Medonça Lima had been crusading in vain to transform the PL into a social democratic party. Inspired by the Collor dissidency, Lima withdrew from the PL and formed a tiny national reform movement known as the National Democratic Union (UDN–União Democrática Nacional).[39] Other Liberators formed a second PL dissidency, Liberator Action (AL–Ação Libertadora). In contrast to the ideological impetus of the National Democratic Union, this second movement had its genesis in the presidential succession question.

The presidential contest had generated a new configuration of political forces. A curious alliance, born of desperation, had developed between Flôres da Cunha and former São Paulo governor Salles Oliveira. During the reign of Justice Minister Vicente Ráo, Flôres had opposed Salles' bid to become Vargas' successor. He even had announced privately that he considered a Paulista presidential candidate a casus belli and that, if Salles were the candidate, he would lead a Gaúcho separatist movement.[40]

But as political reversals had shaken Flôres' Gaúcho fortress and Vargas ultimately had refused to support the young Paulista, adversity impelled the two former antagonists into an increasingly close relationship. They even united with Juracy Magalhães in the scarecrow tristate anti-intervention defense pact. When the Aranha candidacy collapsed, Flôres committed his support to Salles for president in exchange for vital Paulista money and arms.

Flôres' Liberal Republican Party and Salles' Constitutionalist Party were the only two state government parties to back the Paulista. The rest of Salles' national organization, the Brazilian Democratic Union (UDB–União Democrática Brasileira), was composed of diverse state opposition parties and coalitions. Unable to wrest control in their own states, these opposition groups attached themselves to the Flôres-Salles coattails as an alternative path to power.

As the opposition clustered around Salles and Flôres, Vargas commissioned Minas governor Benedito Valadares to coordinate the majority forces in selecting a candidate. Valadares moved more rapidly than Vargas had expected—or hoped. He quickly invited each governor to send a representative to a national nominating convention. From Rio Grande Valadares also invited the PRR, PL, and Liberal Dissidency. Upset by the rapidity of Valadares' action, Vargas and Agamemnon Magalhães tried to sabotage his negotiations, but the Minas governor kept the convention on schedule. The irate president referred to Valadares' unexpectedly independent action in holding the convention and refusing an army request to place three Minas battalions under its control as a "goring by a tame bull."[41] When northern leaders demanded that the presidential candidate be a northerner, the convention nominated Vargas' former transportation minister, José Américo de Almeida of Paraíba.

Vargas reluctantly gave his placet to José Américo, whose support came from the opposition parties of Rio Grande and São Paulo and the government parties of the other states. The Liberal Dissidents, the PRR, and even Oswaldo Aranha immediately supported José Américo. A number of Liberators championed Salles, citing the PL's historical alliance with the extinct Paulista Democratic Party, the ancestor of Salles' Constitutionalist Party. However, despite this nostalgic inclination toward Salles, the PL succumbed to the realities of the state political struggle. Since Flôres supported Salles, the PL central directory endorsed José Américo. Pro-Salles Liberators defected, formed the dissident Liberator Action, and announced their support of the Paulista.[42]

A third candidate was yet to come—Plínio Salgado, the Brazilian Integralist Action führer. Borrowing both ideology and tactics from European fascist organizations, the green-shirted Integralists "campaigned" with parades, monster rallies, public spectacles, and street violence. They played Vargas' game by condemning liberal democracy, dramatizing the threat of extremism for a weary Brazil, and softening up the country for a possible "law-and-order" coup.

As the presidential campaign proceeded, Rio Grande's new political lines hardened. The Vargas-Flôres clash had terminated the PRL-FU confrontation, but two new political camps had rapidly formed around the two Gaúcho titans. With Flôres stood the regular PRL, Collor's Castilhist Republican Party, Liberator Action, and the small National Democratic Union. Vargas counted on the Liberal Dissidency, the PRR, and the PL. In the presidential contest, Vargas' men backed José Américo, while Flôres' forces supported Salles Oliveira.

While the growing furor of the presidential campaign captured public attention, less apparent events of even greater significance to the nation's future were taking place, with Rio Grande the key. Although he publicly supported José Américo, Vargas was more concerned with preventing the election from occurring. Aware that only Flôres' military strength, which was seriously declining, remained as a meaningful guarantee of the election, Vargas concentrated his political and military firepower on Rio Grande.

Politically his major weapons were the state assembly opposition deputies, who held a precarious twenty-to-nineteen majority. Vargas instructed them to provoke Flôres into extreme acts so that the president would have an excuse to react with force.[43] But despite the opposition's continuous harassment with defamatory speeches, assembly inquiries, and other irritating acts, the explosive Flôres surprisingly maintained his composure.

Frustrated by this failure, Getúlio and Benjamin developed an alternate plan. Armed with Getúlio's promise to act, Benjamin convinced the twenty opposition deputies to request that the president strip Flôres of his right to execute the special state of war powers in Rio Grande.[44] In response Vargas transferred these extraordinary powers to General Emílio Lúcio Esteves, the regional commander, in late April. This was intended to be the ultimate provocation, prompting Flôres to react and giving Vargas the excuse to crush his rival militarily. However, once again Flôres restrained himself. As Benjamin informed his brother, " the beast snorted loudly, but retracted his claws."[45]

General Esteves himself helped spoil Vargas' plan. A Gaúcho and a believer in state autonomy, he resisted attempts to involve the army in anti-Flôres political maneuvers. Convincing Flôres to accept the transfer order peacefully, Esteves became a buffer between the Gaúcho governor and the Vargas-Dutra-Góes triumvirate.[46]

The angry Gaúcho opposition deputies accused Esteves and his staff of negotiating a truce with Flôres, even suggesting there might be an alliance between Esteves' staff and the governor.[47] But although disappointed with Esteves' deportment, the Liberal Dissidents, United Frontists, and pro-Vargas politicians from other states intensified their campaign against Flôres in May. By charging Flôres with violence and aggressive intentions against the federal government, they provided propaganda cover for Vargas' military offensive.

Behind this verbal smoke screen Góes and Dutra acted. They removed pro-Flôres army officers from posts in Rio Grande, sent four navy ships to the port of Rio Grande, and ordered troops south toward the Gaúcho state. So that Góes could coordinate the anti-Flôres offensive, Dutra named him Inspector of the Second Group of Military Regions (which included Rio Grande) and dispatched him to Curitiba, Paraná.

The movement received a momentary setback from Minas governor Benedito Valadares, who in February had offered thirty thousand state troops to Dutra for the final showdown against Flôres.[48] Suddenly afraid for his own political skin in Vargas' centralizing drive, Valadares refused the request of Vargas and Dutra to place three battalions of the Minas public force under federal control for action in São Paulo and Rio Grande.[49] Undaunted by Valadares' unexpected defection, Góes informed Esteves that army reinforcements were on the way south and exhorted him to take the offensive against Flôres. Promising Esteves his full moral and material support, Góes wrote, "I repeat the advice which, on a certain occasion of national crisis, I sent to my friend, the then Major Esteves: impel the caravan forward into the desert, scorning the dogs who howl in the moonlight."[50]

Flôres' congressional supporters and his newspapers throughout Brazil did howl, defending the governor with nearly daily criticism of the federal government's aggression, but the noise did not deter Góes. He dispatched a large army detachment under General Manoel de Cerqueira Daltro Filho to the Santa Catarina-Rio Grande border, forming a "belt of steel" which ultimately grew to twelve thousand men.

Góes' invasion plan called for simultaneous parallel southward thrusts from Santa Catarina across the Gaúcho northeastern frontier. At the same time the navy would protect the coast, blockade Rio Grande's Lagoa dos Patos (Duck Lake), and occupy the southern Gaúcho cities of Rio Grande and Pelotas. All forces would then converge on Pôrto Alegre and crush Flôres.[51]

While the congressional and press howling did not stop Góes, more potent was the growing antagonism of a number of officers, upset by the perversion of the army into a tool for Vargas' continuism and Góes' vendetta. Among these were Third Region Commander Esteves and General João Guedes da Fontoura, army commander in Paraná, who refused to obey Dutra's orders to occupy the Gaúcho town of Marcelino Ramos on the Rio Grande-Santa Catarina border.[52] Fifteen generals sent a telegram of solidarity to Guedes, supporting his opposition to the proposed invasion of Rio Grande, and a manifesto to War Minister Dutra, demanding the return of the army to a nonpolitical role and opposing military intervention in Rio Grande.

Stunned by this internal dissidency, Dutra and Góes canceled the Gaúcho invasion and turned their attention to neutralizing these opposition generals. In cooperation with Vargas, they devised a plot which led to the arrest of two of the generals and transferred other potential or active opposition officers to less strategic positions. Most important, they removed Guedes and Esteves, the two most vital military buffers between Flôres da Cunha and the determined trio. To replace Esteves as Third Region commander, they selected General Daltro Filho, commander of the invasion troops in Góes' previous master plan.

The collapse of the May invasion of Rio Grande and the ensuing June termination of the state of war had forced the Rio triumvirate to alter its approach to Flôres. In his invasion plan Góes had envisioned a civil war of at least two months. However, fear had developed that an invasion might unite proud, autonomy-minded Rio Grande around its governor. Even Oswaldo Aranha in Washington vowed that if Vargas decreed intervention in Rio Grande, he would return immediately to command Gaúcho forces in defense of Flôres and state autonomy.[53]

As history had demonstrated in 1930 and was to show again in 1961, a united Rio Grande represented a formidable military

force. This was not only because of Riograndense fighting experience and enthusiasm but also because army units stationed in Rio
Grande, generally composed heavily of Gaúchos, often identified
with the state against the rest of Brazil. Rather than invade the
state and risk a military confrontation with unpredictable results,
Vargas, Góes, and Dutra opted for a politically prepared solution,
choosing to let the politicians further undermine Flôres' military
position by increasing Gaúcho divisions.

The Gaúcho assembly had turned into a veritable battlefield.
Deputies attended sessions armed, debating with guns strapped to
their hips; fist fights became a matter of course. Flôres planted his
hoodlums conspicuously in and around the assembly. The opposition countered with its own gunmen, led by Gregório Fortunato,
the feared personal bodyguard of the Vargas family.[54]

Flôres and Vargas used every means at their disposal in the
no-holds-barred contest. The governor persecuted opposition state
functionaries with transfers and removals, while the president and
his henchmen coerced federal employees in Rio Grande to join the
anti-Flôres ranks. The two contenders spread jobs, political
patronage, and bribes to recruit and maintain supporters. Both
concentrated on the battle-torn assembly, where Flôres attacked
and Vargas defended the opposition's one-vote majority.

Opposition deputies had taken three basic positions. Two
small groups viewed the Flôres problem as essentially a national
one. The first group of deputies, including Benjamin Vargas and
José Loureiro da Silva, had dedicated itself to the overthrow of
Flôres in order to further Getúlio's continuist plans. In contrast,
the second group, led by Raul Pilla, believed that the opposition
should criticize and defeat Flôres electorally, but should not try to
depose him. According to Pilla, Flôres was the last bulwark of
Brazilian democracy and the only assurance of the January 1938
election.[55]

But most opposition deputies did not view the Flôres question in these national terms. Reflecting traditional Gaúcho
provincialism, they considered Flôres to be a regional problem,
with national ramifications of secondary importance. Unconcerned that their actions might be helping Vargas to reestablish
his dictatorship, they worked for the overthrow of Flôres at all
costs and in doing so became instruments of the president.[56] As
Raul Pilla recalled, FU leader Maurício Cardoso insisted that rather

than having Flôres as governor, it would be preferable to have Getúlio as emperor and Benjamin as crown prince.[57]

Backed by Vargas, Cardoso led a movement to impeach Flôres. Confident they could bring Pilla and the more reluctant opposition deputies into line, Cardoso and his allies set a September 15 target date.[58] But Flôres struck first, coercing an opposition class deputy into resigning his assembly seat despite heavy pressure from Vargas. The substitute class deputy, who supported Flôres, shifted the one-vote majority to the governor. Vargas and the opposition retaliated with a combination of threats and huge bribe offers to pro-Flôres deputies, but their efforts failed.[59]

Flôres had ruined Cardoso's impeachment scheme, but his political position remained precarious. His agents sought in vain to entice the Liberal Dissidents to reunite with the PRL. The governor even sent an emissary to Vargas with a plan for Gaúcho reharmonization. But with victory in sight, Vargas naturally rejected Flôres' peace feeler and counseled the Gaúcho opposition to remain united and prepare the terrain for intervention.[60]

While the opposition set the stage politically, army regional commander Daltro Filho arranged to bring down the curtain militarily if necessary. A Bahian with no love for Gaúcho autonomy, Daltro had arrived in Pôrto Alegre in the middle of August. He received his first shock when he read Esteves' war plan for army reaction if the Gaúchos should revolt. Reeking of defeatism, it called for immediate abandonment of Pôrto Alegre, despite the army's advantage of twenty thousand men to the six thousand men of the Rio Grande military brigade and the presence of the twelve-thousand-man army detachment on the Gaúcho border in Santa Catarina.* Such a retreat probably would have resulted in heavy army casualties due to Pôrto Alegre's narrow streets and the concentration of army units in the congested downtown area. It also would have given Flôres a stunning initial victory with which to galvanize support in Rio Grande and throughout Brazil.

Daltro revised the plan and prepared to hold Pôrto Alegre at all costs. Taking advantage of the annual "Nation Week" military parade in early September, Daltro brought army units from all over the state to the Gaúcho capital, where they provided an

---

*The Brazilian army had about eighty thousand men in 1937.

imposing public display of army might. Following the parade the commander kept some of the troops in Pôrto Alegre and stationed others in nearby São Leopoldo, from which they could be rushed to the capital. Daltro had wiped out Flôres' initial superiority in Pôrto Alegre.[61]

Flôres responded with his own military buildup in the capital. Yet for all of the psychological impressiveness of Flôres' military machine, there was a tremendous gap between image and reality. For years Flôres had undermined the loyalty of army troops, but he failed to realize that since the collapse of the modus vivendi the Gaúcho opposition had critically subverted his state brigade. Anti-Flôres officers even had established a secret brigade rump headquarters.[62] One major consideration remained. Although these brigade officers would not support a Rio Grande offensive venture against the federal government, they remained loyal Gaúchos, prepared to follow Flôres in the defense of the state against invasion. Their solution was for Vargas to federalize the brigade, placing it under army command and thereby relieving it of its official duty to Flôres.[63] With Flôres' military base eroded and Daltro's Third Army units prepared to react against any armed movement, the Third Army commander informed Dutra that he was ready.

As the Vargas-Flôres struggle sped toward a climax, events throughout Brazil helped prepare the way for the concluding action. The presidential campaign, with its rising level of rhetoric, had polarized the electorate and added to the weary nation's sense of uncertainty and uneasiness. In the heated ambience of electoral conflict, military maneuvering, and public strife, congressional debates had become increasingly bitter and vehement. The often-violent clash of opposing radical movements—legal Integralism and illegal Communism—further magnified the nation's desire for order and stability.

Upon the psychologically battered nation Vargas broke the news that the army general staff had apprehended documents revealing a great Communist terrorist plot, the Cohen Plan. When released to the press, this piece of fiction predictably horrified Brazilians, who still recalled the November 1935 revolution. Armed with this document, Vargas obtained congressional approval in early October for a new ninety-day state of war, another major step toward centralization.[64] Although governors became executors of the state of war in most states, Vargas selected Daltro Filho to direct it in Rio Grande do Sul.

Flôres' Gaúcho fortress was about to collapse. The opposition politicians had destroyed state unity and effectively subverted the military brigade. Daltro Filho had deployed army troops in such a way as to stalemate Flôres' brigade, road gangs, and provisional corps. Finally, Vargas had regained his exceptional state-of-war powers and had placed Daltro Filho in charge of Rio Grande. Everything was ready for the final coup.

Vargas set that machinery in motion on October 14, when he signed a decree federalizing the Gaúcho military brigade and the São Paulo public force, placing them under the regional army commanders. The order was not delivered to Flôres until noon on October 16, giving Daltro time to mobilize his troops. Receiving the order, the governor responded that he would meet with his secretariat, submit the decree to the state legal counsel for his opinion, and answer within twenty-four hours.

It was a stalling action. Flôres knew that the surrender of the brigade would be the penultimate step in the drama that would inevitably end with his deposition and possible arrest. Meeting with the brigade commander and commanders of the Pôrto Alegre units to assess the possibility of resistance, Flôres received a shock: only one unit commander opposed the federal decree; the rest favored acceptance. When he then met with his political supporters in the turbulent governor's palace, Flôres learned that they too were split over the question of whether he should resign to spare Rio Grande a bloody civil war.

Unwilling to submit easily, Flôres prepared for the final showdown. He gathered three hundred of his most faithful supporters to defend the palace, a move reminiscent of the early days of the 1932 revolution. He mobilized his three platoons of port employees, who cut small pieces of barbed wire to be used to blow out the tires of trucks bringing the seventeen-hundred-man São Leopoldo army detachment to Pôrto Alegre. He moved the provisional corps which had been camped around Pôrto Alegre into the brigade barracks, elevating his capital forces to four thousand men, and also ordered his troops to concentrate for an attack on federal forces near army headquarters. Finally he tried to send a telegraphic appeal to São Paulo for joint resistance, but Vargas already had isolated Rio Grande by cutting all communications with the rest of Brazil.

Despite his officers' willingness to accept federalization, Flôres was confident they would follow his orders. He believed he could mobilize thirty thousand men to resist, but the opposition had done its job well. The brigade rump headquarters instructed collaborating officers to ignore Flôres' orders.

Receiving reports that two brigade units had defected and that he could not depend on individual elements in other units, the stunned Flôres called a meeting of his supporters at the palace. There he agreed to accept their decision—resist with them to the death or resign as governor. A few called for resistance, but the moderates prevailed. The following morning Flôres informed Daltro Filho that he was relinquishing command of the military brigade. Later he sent word that he was resigning.[65]

Early on the morning of October 18 Flôres quietly left his palace and flew by special plane to his frontier hometown of Sant'Anna do Livramento. Crossing into Rivera for a prolonged Uruguayan exile, Flôres signed off with a flourish of Gaúchesque oratory before his train left for Montevideo:

> If democracy does not prevail again in Brazil, my friends and I will be ready to reestablish its sway, since everyone will remain ready. Tyranny will not last in Brazil and, within a few days, I will return to Rio Grande to struggle against it.[66]

Although Flôres believed he was escaping from Brazil, in reality the army permitted every move. It had orders to let him escape, since a defeated Flôres in exile was less dangerous than a martyred one in prison.[67]

After years of bitter struggle, the centralist Gaúcho president had defeated the federalist Gaúcho governor. Vargas' victory over Flôres da Cunha signaled the destruction of state autonomy. It also assured the return of dictatorship to the tired nation.

6

The Estado Nôvo

The fall of Flôres da Cunha was the opening curtain to the last act of the collapse of the Second Republic. However, the conclusion for this historical drama had been drawn up long before by that expert political playwright, Getúlio Vargas.

By February 1937, at Vargas' request, Francisco Campos, the Mineiro former education minister, had written a constitution for a centralist, corporative dictatorship.[1] The decreeing of the new constitution awaited only Vargas' removal of the prodemocratic obstacles, primarily the Gaúcho governor. After Flôres' exile on October 18 had opened the way, Vargas needed less than a month to attain the holy grail of dictatorship.

First he had to clear up the confusion in Rio Grande do Sul. Vargas was prepared to appoint Daltro Filho as interventor if necessary.[2] However, to avoid the stigma of intervening in his native state and possibly alienating those Vargas supporters who might still cling to the increasingly fragile myth of Gaúcho autonomy, he preferred to let his forces elect the new governor.

But even in defeat Flôres frustrated his rival. Before leaving Pôrto Alegre, the caudilho convinced his twenty state deputies to sign an agreement that they would vote as a bloc for his comrade Antunes Maciel as his gubernatorial successor. In contrast, the opposition bloc, having triumphed over Flôres, divided over the gubernatorial succession question. The FU closed ranks behind Raul Pilla. Still harboring distrust of the FU as a remnant of Gaúcho "old politics," a few Liberal Dissidents and Florist Liberals initiated discussions about reuniting the PRL in support of the apolitical Antônio Saint Pastous (brother-in-law of Góes Monteiro) for governor and Oswaldo Aranha as new party chief.[3]

Learning of Flôres' parting coup, Benjamin Vargas appealed to his brother to intervene at once. He did. To avoid a possible electoral defeat, Vargas named Daltro Filho, the Bahian general, to the Gaúcho interventorship. Daltro immediately organized a secretariat of Republicans, Liberators, and Liberal Dissidents. Having lost all concern for state autonomy, the three parties readily accepted a non-Gaúcho interventor as a step toward reconquest of state political power.

Daltro and his associates began at once to dismantle Flôres' political-military machine. They removed Florists from key government positions, dissolved road gangs, and collected Flôres' war materiel.[4] This was the death knell for the presidential hopes of Armando de Salles Oliveira, who needed the votes and military support which Flôres could guarantee. For a moment the Rio Grande disaster even made the Brazilian Democratic Union consider withdrawing Salles' candidacy. However, the UDB central directory finally issued a note half-heartedly reiterating its support of the former Paulista governor.[5]

With Salles' victory chances seriously jeopardized by the fall of Flôres da Cunha, the "official" presidential candidate, José Américo de Almeida, would have been a shoo-in for the presidency under normal conditions. But conditions in Brazil had long ceased to be normal, what with increasing national turbulence and Vargas' dedication to extending his own stay in office. Moreover, José Américo himself unwittingly helped Vargas in his dictatorial quest.

Rather than campaigning with moderation and letting the state government machines carry him to victory, José Américo had launched a radical, populist crusade. By declaring war on special interests (keynoted by his cryptic public declaration, "I know where the money is"), he had alienated many of the conservative leaders who had nominated him. José Américo's unexpectedly radical campaign further disrupted a political climate already superheated by Plínio Salgado's Integralism, the Salles coalition's anti-Getulism, and the growing fear of Communism. Campaign vituperation, accompanied by congressional turbulence and Integralist-Communist street fighting, made many Brazilians long for order at any cost.

Delighted by the change in mood and with no more Flôres to interfere with his plans, Vargas made his climactic moves. Little more than one week after Flôres' fall, Francisco Negrão de Lima, a Mineiro confidant of Benedito Valadares, made a rapid tour of northern Brazil, obtaining the agreement of the governors for the reestablishment of the Vargas dictatorship. He avoided Bahia's Juracy Magalhães, who previously had rejected Vargas' coup proposal and signed the anti-intervention pact with Flôres and Salles, and Pernambuco's Lima Cavalcanti, who also had opposed Vargas' plans. However, even Paulista governor J. J. Cardoso de Melo Neto accepted the idea, although his Constitutionalist Party still officially supported Salles for president.[6]

Vargas, Dutra, Góes, and the other conspirators set the coup for November 15, but a democratic last gasp forced them to move the date forward. The diminutive Raul Pilla, one of the few United Frontists who had viewed Flôres' departure with alarm, sensed the cataclysmic event. He flew to Rio on November 7 to try to convince Salles and José Américo to withdraw in favor of a compromise presidential candidate, a move he hoped would calm the nation and remove any excuse for federal action.[7]

Salles issued a desperation manifesto, appealing to the military to guarantee elections and the legal regime.[8] PRL congressional delegation leader João Carlos Machado read it in the chamber of deputies on November 9, and the Salles forces distributed it in army barracks. Proelection deputies of both presidential coalitions planned a massive parade for November 15, anniversary of the proclamation of the First Republic, to demonstrate their support of democracy.

Suddenly fearful that this wave of prodemocratic activity might upset their plans for dictatorship, Vargas and his associates moved the coup up to November 10. On that day, with the military poised throughout the country, Vargas issued a decree dissolving all legislative chambers and promulgating Campos' Estado Nôvo (New State) constitution. He then arrested Salles on the charge of having incited rebellion and replaced Lima Cavalcanti and Juracy Magalhães with his own men. The rest of the governors and interventors, all but one minister, and eighty of the three hundred federal deputies immediately pledged their support to the new regime. Quietly, bloodlessly, the Second Republic came to an end in Brazil.[9]

In Pôrto Alegre, Daltro Filho informed his secretariat of Vargas' action. The Liberal Dissidents, who long had supported Vargas unconditionally, announced at once their solidarity with the new government. Even the regular PRL commission capitulated, informing Daltro that it was advising all Liberals to co-operate with him.[10] The tired, dismayed Borges de Medeiros recommended that Republicans remain in the Gaúcho government as long as they were working for state interests, but the younger, unquenchable Pilla called a meeting of the PL directory to decide on its course of action.

Back from his Rio failure, Pilla made a last stand against the establishment of the Estado Nôvo. Citing historical Liberator resistance to tyranny, Pilla appealed to the directory to reject collaboration with the new dictatorship. Against Pilla stood Baptista Luzardo, whom Vargas once again had sent to Rio Grande to hold the Liberators in line. In contrast to Luzardo's tempting promise of power and spoils, Pilla could only offer the opposition-weary Liberators an uncertain future of suffering, persecution, and governmental ostracism. By a vote of fourteen to three, the directory chose to collaborate with Vargas. Pilla resigned as party president and, with his two supporters, quit the directory.[11]

Aware that Vargas and his interventor had become the only route to political success, most Gaúcho leaders temporarily purged themselves of past loyalties, ideologies, or democratic beliefs and chose cooperation with the Estado Nôvo. Only the dwindling ranks of the diehard Florists and a few unreconstructed Liberator followers of Pilla rejected compromise. Vargas had brought a new revolution to Gaúcho politics. Within a month he had overthrown one party chief, Flôres da Cunha, and caused the resignation of another, Raul Pilla. Only Borges de Medeiros remained, but his formerly absolute party control had become more mythological and sentimental than real.

The sudden collapse of the chieftain structure created a state power vacuum. Vargas, the natural heir to state leadership, was more concerned with directing national affairs than with deeply involving himself in Rio Grande's provincial aggravations, but he still wanted to prevent the emergence of a new local chieftain. Following his classical politics of compromise and equilibrium,

Vargas opted for collective leadership for the mutual checking of individual power and ambition.

He commissioned Luzardo and brother Benjamin to institutionalize the PRR-PL-PRL Dissidency alliance as a new progovernment political machine. On November 19 the three party central commissions met jointly and elected a three-man interparty commission to resolve Gaúcho political questions, the first step toward what would become the Gaúcho Social Democratic Party more than seven years later.[12]

The interparty commission, which included Getúlio's older brother, Protásio, immediately went about its primary task of redistributing county governments. Within a week it gave Daltro a list of which mayors should remain, which should be removed because of incompetence or Florist ties, and who should be their replacements. Daltro resisted briefly in favor of pacification through absorption of former Florists into his government, but when the hungry parties demanded their spoils, Daltro submitted.[13] Yet the parties, as such, had little time in which to savor their political delicacies. They soon were swept away by Vargas' national drive for centralization.

The Estado Nôvo marked the apparently definitive triumph of the central government over the states, symbolized by the banning of state flags, coats of arms, and anthems by the the new constitution. To dramatize this triumph, Vargas staged a Flag Day ceremony in which the state flags were burned publicly. More important, he took steps to solidify the centralist victory.

Vargas fulfilled his agreement with Dutra and Góes to modernize, reequip, and expand the federal military while reducing the relative strength of the state militias.[14] The new constitution and Vargas' subsequent decrees increased federal strength by transferring numerous state and county powers to the central government. They also gave the federal government sweeping new socioeconomic responsibilities and redistributed tax authority for its benefit. The states and counties lost traditional sources of tax revenue and became more dependent on federal funds, permitting the president to exercise greater state-level influence through the Bank of Brazil.[15]

With new taxes and responsibilities came an alphabet soup of federal agencies and the parallel bloating of the already padded federal bureaucracy. This further centralized political power by expanding the scope of federal patronage, controls, projects, loans, jobs, and favors.[16] With such a mechanism at his expert control, Vargas reduced the power of state bosses and increased dependence on his personal favor, which became the necessary condition for a political career. To maintain this control Vargas spent hours each day personally distributing individual government jobs and conducting state and county business.[17]

Vargas further altered the power structure on December 3, 1937, when he dissolved all political parties and auxiliary organizations. This came as a particular shock to the older Republicans and Liberators, whose pride in their parties had a historical depth unmatched in most other states. In contrast, many younger Gaúcho politicians, such as those of the Liberal Dissidency, hailed the disappearance of parties, which one Dissident labeled the "rancid residue of the end of the eighteenth century."[18] But despite some controversy within Gaúcho ranks, all three Rio Grande ex-parties continued to support Vargas and Daltro Filho.

The official termination of parties did not, however, erase individual political ambitions. The death of Interventor Daltro Filho in January 1938 once again complicated the Gaúcho scene by raising the question of his successor. To topple Flôres da Cunha, the opposition had sacrificed state autonomy, accepting both federal intervention and the appointment of a "foreign" interventor. With the spectre of Flôres gone, pride in state autonomy returned. Rio Grande politicians demanded a native Gaúcho interventor, but mutually vetoed each other. This prompted Vargas to complain, "If a son of Rio Grande can govern Brazil, why can't a son of Brazil govern Rio Grande?"[19] Yet he realized that he must make this nativist concession.

Getúlio faced a dilemma. He knew that if he chose one of the leading political contenders, he would provoke the wrath of the others. So he stepped outside of the political arena and selected Colonel Oswaldo Cordeiro de Farias, Daltro's chief of staff and a native Gaúcho but not a part of political Rio Grande. Vargas simultaneously appealed to the disgruntled and disappointed politicians to remain at their posts under Cordeiro. After a brief display of properly hurt feelings, they accepted his request.[20]

Vargas faced two other major Gaúcho problems—Oswaldo

Aranha and Flôres da Cunha. Saddened by Vargas' intervention in Rio Grande, Aranha had written a melancholy letter to the president protesting against what he termed "that brutal act."[21] The Estado Nôvo decree further embittered Aranha, who angrily resigned as ambassador to the United States and labeled the constitution as "a revocation of Brazil, seeking to graft on the immensity of our territory and on the goodness of our people a regime incompatible with our traditions and with my sentiments."[22]

Returning to Brazil, Aranha became the democratic loyal opposition within the Estado Nôvo government. He accepted the post of foreign minister, justifying his action as service to his country in a nonpolitical post. Aranha brought not only a degree of ideological equilibrium to Vargas' cabinet but also an international balance. Countering the pro-Axis propensities of Dutra and Góes Monteiro, who both openly admired Adolf Hitler's German regime and Benito Mussolini's Italian dictatorship, Aranha worked to preserve and strengthen Brazilian-United States relations.

While Aranha led the loyal opposition within the Estado Nôvo, Flôres da Cunha became one of its major external opponents. Five years had brought a reversal in the Gaúcho caudilho's fortunes. In 1932 he had been Vargas' bulwark against the continuous threats of exile invasions; now, in 1937, an exiled Flôres in Montevideo conspired to overthrow the Brazilian dictator. Ironically, Vargas' major weapon against Flôres was Baptista Luzardo, who had been in exile from 1932 to 1934. An enemy of Flôres since the 1923 revolution, Luzardo became ambassador to Uruguay with instructions to neutralize the exiled chieftain.[23]

Vargas sharpened the ex-governor's antipathy with a series of vindictive acts. He endeavored to erase the memory of Flôres in Rio Grande do Sul with such steps as removing his name from the Flôres da Cunha Education Institute and changing Pôrto Alegre's Flôres da Cunha Avenue to Independence Avenue. He stripped Flôres of one of his greatest treasures, his honorary army generalship, awarded for valorous service during the revolutions of the 1920s. He also instigated a series of investigations and trials of the ex-governor, with charges including the murder of Waldemar Ripoll, misappropriation of state funds, wire-tapping, and arms contraband. Ultimately all were dropped except the arms-contraband charge, for which Flôres later served a seventeen-month prison sentence upon returning to Brazil.

The moment Flôres crossed the border into Uruguay he had begun conspiring. Eager to overthrow Vargas, the ex-governor drew no limits in accepting allies, plotting at times with Communists, Integralists, military men, Sallist exiles, and democrats in Brazil. As in the post-1932 era, these conspiracies generally ended at the verbal level.[24]

The major exception was the Integralist revolt of May 11, 1938. Plínio Salgado and his Integralist followers had become disenchanted with the Estado Nôvo. They had assumed that Vargas would make Integralist Action the official party of his dictatorship, but Getúlio instead had extinguished it along with the other parties in December 1937. Excluded from power, the Integralists began to plot against the government. Mesmerized by the desire to topple Vargas, a number of military men and anti-Vargas politicians, like Flôres, Collor, and Salles, united with these Brazilian fascists in preparing the coup. Partners in this crusade, they planned to share the government after Vargas' fall.

In the early moments of May 11, 1938, forty-five Integralists staged a pitiful, comic-opera assault on Rio's Guanabara Palace, where Vargas was working in his office. Although the palace was only lightly defended, the timid revolutionaries remained firing from a distance and waited for reinforcements. Vargas also waited. Despite his telephone appeals for help, not for several hours did army troops arrive to lift the siege. Shaken by this close call, the president had his brother, Benjamin, organize a personal presidential guard composed of loyal Gaúchos from their home county of São Borja.[25]

Flôres was despondent. He had helped finance the abortive attempt and even had furnished the Montevideo newspapers with a story of Vargas' fall.[26] Despite this disappointment, Flôres continued to conspire; however, Baptista Luzardo limited his activities by convincing the Uruguayan government to restrict the ex-governor to Montevideo.[27] This appalled Flôres, who had been wandering the Uruguay-Rio Grande frontier at will, meeting with emissaries and organizing potential invasion columns.

Flôres also set up a newspaper, *A Democracia,* in the Uruguayan frontier town of Rivera. It spewed ferocious attacks on Vargas, his supporters, and the Estado Nôvo, called on the army to revolt, and even appealed to Rio Grande to secede from Brazil. After it had been published sporadically for eleven months, Luzardo persuaded Uruguay to suspend it.[28] In July 1939, Flôres tried to provoke a conflict between Vargas and Dutra by distributing throughout Brazil five thousand copies of a letter to the war minister, offering his support if Dutra would overthrow "the homunculus who pretends to exercise the functions of chief of government."[29]

But the years of exile weighed heavily on Flôres. His health took a turn for the worse, necessitating a series of operations. His notorious weakness for gambling cost him dearly at the Montevideo roulette tables. Watching Flôres bet three thousand to four thousand pesos on a spin became one of the city's public attractions. Shortly after Pearl Harbor he issued a manifesto in favor of Brazil's aiding the United States in continental defense.[30] Seven months later the sick ex-governor returned to Brazil, where he served more than a year in prison.

During Flôres' absence a series of deep socioeconomic changes had begun in Brazil. After a brief period of uncertainty, Vargas had committed the government to a program of industrialization and economic nationalism, with the goal of reducing Brazil's dependence on imported manufactured goods. The program included both protection and stimulation of private industry and direct government investment in transportation, communications, utilities, and basic industries.[31]

World War II gave added impetus to industrialization. By limiting the flow of manufactured goods into Brazil, it created the need for import substitution and stimulated the development of national industry. The war also brought significant U.S. technical and financial aid in exchange for Brazil's joining the Allies and permitting U.S. air bases on its northeastern hump. With industrialization came rapid urbanization, severely altering the base of Brazilian politics.[32]

Rio Grande do Sul shared in the Estado Nôvo prosperity. Benefiting from the end of the depression and the inauguration of an extended political peace, Gaúcho agriculture prospered.[33] But the reality of Gaúcho prosperity gave birth to a myth of renewed state economic progress. Increased profits obscured Gaúcho deficiencies—an inadequate economic infrastructure, an archaic agricultural system, an insufficiently developing industrial plant, and a population exodus. Despite an accelerated program of public works by the Gaúcho government, the Estado Nôvo era actually weakened Rio Grande's position in the national economic structure.

Vargas himself struck a severe blow against the Gaúcho economy. He had the national fleet, Lloyd Brasileiro, purchase the five refrigerated ships being constructed in Holland for the nascent Riograndense Fleet, Flôres' project to free Rio Grande from the economic strangulation resulting from the inadequacy of the nation's maritime fleet and the high cost of shipping Gaúcho products to Rio and São Paulo.[34] Intent on restricting state power, Vargas would not permit even his native Rio Grande to possess such a source of independent economic and potential military strength. In losing its fleet, Rio Grande suffered a loss for which it never has been able to compensate.

The south-central São Paulo-Minas Gerais-Rio de Janeiro triangle became the great beneficiary of the Estado Nôvo industrial surge. As in 1934, Vargas once again courted São Paulo, which readily accepted positions in and benefits of the Estado Nôvo. As active collaborators, the Paulistas concentrated the government's industrialization efforts in the triangle, particularly in their own state.

Meanwhile, content to relax on its agricultural base, Rio Grande did not take full advantage of the war-given opportunity for rapid industrialization. With its small and middle-sized artisan industry, the state maintained its tenuous hold on third position in the nation's industrial complex, but expanded at a far slower rate than its major competitors. As a result, the industrialization gap between Rio Grande and the south-central triangle increased.[35]

Nor did Rio Grande modernize its archaic agricultural system. For example, a 1965 Rio Grande government study revealed that the state produced annually only eighteen kilograms of meat per head of cattle. This contrasted with seventy-three kilograms per head in the United States, forty-eight kilograms in Argentina, twenty-eight kilograms in Latin America in general, and twenty kilograms in Brazil as a whole. A major reason was the failure of Gaúcho ranchers to provide winter pasture for livestock; each winter took a stunning toll of the animals, while the emaciated survivors spent a significant part of the following spring and summer regaining the weight lost during the winter. It took four to five years of summer fattening and winter dieting to prepare Gaúcho cattle for market, a most inefficient use of both animals and land.[36]

Sated with easy profits, Gaúchos did not heed the fact that, alongside industry, a competitive agriculture was developing in the south center, lessening that region's dependence on Rio Grande. Moreover, since Rio Grande did not produce coffee, the rise in its price and volume correspondingly reduced the Gaúcho percentage of national agricultural production. A coffee boom in the state of Paraná soon vaulted that state into third position nationally behind São Paulo and Minas Gerais, with Gaúcho agriculture slipping to fourth.[37]

The state also failed to attack the companion problems of latifundia and minifundia. Owners of large farms and ranches relied on size to provide profits despite inefficient land use. Since ranching offered limited employment, the frontier zone consequently began to suffer a rural exodus. Displaced ranch workers flocked to the major Gaúcho cities, where they brought increased pressure on an industrial sector that was expanding too slowly to provide the necessary jobs. Futhermore, much of Gaúcho industry was seasonal, based on the processing of agricultural products. Thus, urban slums grew, padded by incoming frontier-zone marginals.[38]

In contrast to the frontier region's population stagnation, the strongly Catholic colonial zone of northeastern Rio Grande underwent a rapid growth. But even the colonial zone suffered an accelerating exodus, a result of the dual pressures of limited land and unlimited birthrate. As family farms became so small that fathers could no longer follow the traditional colonial-zone practice of dividing their land among their multitude of sons, ambitious young colonists pushed on. They either moved to the cities, like the frontier-region exiles, or headed north into the fertile, inexpensive, sparsely settled lands of Santa Catarina and Paraná. By 1950, 120,710 native-born Gaúchos were living in Santa Catarina and 35,701 in Paraná. In contrast, economically stagnating Rio Grande had little appeal for foreign immigrants or other Brazilians. By 1950 native-born Gaúchos formed 97 percent of Rio Grande's population, the highest percentage of native born in any Brazilian state.[39]

These demographic changes would severely affect the nature

of post-Estado Nôvo Gaúcho politics. They increased the electoral power of the major cities and the colonial zone at the expense of the frontier region. In addition, they expanded the ranks of both urban labor and the urban unemployed.

The Gaúcho political spectrum was also altered by another phenomenon—the Estado Nôvo Brazilianization campaign. For more than a century, waves of German and Italian immigrants (as well as smaller numbers of Polish, French, and other European immigrants) had formed and maintained colonies in Rio Grande do Sul and the two states immediately to its north—Santa Catarina and Paraná. In Rio Grande they focused on the state's mountainous, forested northeastern quadrant, where they established communities and settled on small, government-granted family-sized plots of land.

As of 1927 these *colonos* (colonists—those of non-Portuguese European extraction) composed about 32 percent of the Rio Grande population.[40] Permitted relative cultural autonomy, they had their own foreign-language schools, churches, newspapers, and radio stations. In 1927, 937 German-Brazilian private schools operated in Rio Grande, the largest network of German schools in the western hemisphere. By 1937 there were 320 German Associations in the three southern states, while the German-Brazilian press numbered ten daily newspapers and forty periodicals.[41]

The isolated colono ethnics contributed mightily to the Gaúcho economy. Most were small farmers, but others became prosperous in crafts, commerce, and industry. In addition, colonial-zone birth and literacy rates surpassed those of the rest of the state; yet this economic and demographic strength was not mirrored in the political arena.

Prior to the fall of the Old Republic in 1930, Gaúcho colonos had maintained a principally economic orientation. To insure being permitted to work in peace and to avoid government retribution—excessive taxation, denial of services, or coronel violence—colonos traditionally voted en masse for government candidates. The language barrier further restricted opposition attempts to mobilize colono voters. Finally, in establishing the state's five electoral districts, the government effectively gerrymandered the colonial zone so that Lusos (those of Portuguese descent) held a clear majority in each district.

Although the colonial zone provided about one-third of the

state's voters during the Old Republic, colonos had only token representation in the state legislature and even less in the Gaúcho congressional delegation. The government party also imposed non-colono mayors on the colonial-zone counties; Caxias do Sul, the largest Italian zone city in Rio Grande, did not have an Italian mayor until 1947. Most ethnics who obtained government positions did so by becoming "Lusofied," entering the Luso-Gaúcho mainstream, and serving as cogs in the Luso-dominated Republican machine. [42]

The 1930 revolution and the 1932 establishment of the secret ballot, which mitigated the power of the Luso electoral coroneis, inaugurated the transitional era in Gaúcho ethnic politics. By intensively registering voters in the fervently Catholic Italian zone, the Catholic Electoral League provided another impetus toward colono political independence. The 1934 election gave indications of this emerging power, as both the PRL and FU relied less on coroneis to deliver the ethnic vote and instead sprinkled their legislative slates with non-Luso candidates to appeal to colono voters. Although capturing only two of twenty seats in the Gaúcho congressional delegation, these candidates won ten of the thirty-two publicly elected state legislative seats. [43]

In the late 1930s the Vargas government became increasingly concerned over the perceived penetration of Nazism and, to a lesser extent, Italian Fascism into the ethnic colonies of southern Brazil. So in 1938 the president and his nationalist advisers instituted a Brazilianization campaign to integrate the colonos into the nation—dump them into the Luso-Brazilian melting pot.

The government closed or nationalized all foreign-language private schools, ordered an emphasis on the teaching of Brazilian history, and made Portuguese the instructional language in all schools. It became mandatory to conduct church services and deliver sermons in Portuguese; foreign-language magazines and newspapers could be published only if Portuguese translations were included. Foreign languages were forbidden in public offices and barracks and during military service, while German-language shop signs were banned. All German associations were nationalized, and local army commanders assigned them new presidents and new Portuguese names. When the government banned German inscriptions on tombstones, some overly zealous local authorities even decreed the removal of existent German inscriptions, although this ex post facto cemetery assault was soon abandoned.[44]

At times government officials and private individuals committed excesses under the cloak of Brazilianization, including official and unofficial extortion, graft, and physical violence. Much of this stemmed from Luso economic frustrations and jealousy provoked by colono prosperity. World War II provided the ultimate rationalization for attacks on ethnics. Most of Rio Grande was pro-Ally, but many German merchants exuberantly celebrated Axis victories. As German submarine warfare took an increasing toll of Brazilian merchant ships, tensions rose, and the announcement on August 18, 1942, that German submarines had sunk five Brazilian ships near the Brazilian coast led to riots in Pôrto Alegre and interior towns. These included mass demonstrations, the systematic smashing of stores of supposed Axis sympathizers, and the destruction of street and business signs with German and Italian names.

The Brazilianization campaign, with the concomitant World War II violence, climaxed the political liberation of the colono. The coming of the secret ballot had set the stage by freeing colonos from direct coronel electoral control. The 1933 and 1934 elections had given colonos experience in political mobilization, an introduction to the secret-ballot process, and an indication of their electoral potential. Once the Estado Nôvo's Brazilianization campaign had broken down their linguistic and cultural walls, they actively entered the state electoral arena with the return of electoral politics in 1945.*

---

*A comparison of the last pre-Estado Nôvo Rio Grande assembly and Gaúcho congressional delegation with those of the post-Estado Nôvo era reveals the impact of the Brazilianization campaign on Gaúcho politics. In 1937 only ten of the thirty-nine state deputies and two of the twenty Gaúcho federal deputies had non-Portuguese surnames. However, in post-Estado Nôvo Gaúcho elections, beginning in 1947, persons of non-Portuguese surnames always captured at least 42 percent of the state legislative seats and only once won less than 45 percent of the Gaúcho congressional seats (computed from electoral statistics at the Tribunal Regional Eleitoral, Pôrto Alegre). In addition, ethnics captured five of the seven Gaúcho senatorships in the 1950-66 elections, and from 1954 through 1970, persons of Italian descent held the governorship, despite the fact that ethnics comprised less than one-third of the state's population. According to French historian Jean Roche, this assertion of ethnic power resulted from the colonial zone's greater population density and a greater sense of cohesion and mutual identification among ethnics than among Luso-Riograndenses. See Jean Roche, *La Colonisation Allemande et le Rio Grande do Sul* (Paris: Institut des Hautes Études de L'Amérique Latine, 1959), pp. 574-75. Even

Although socioeconomic changes provided the essence of Gaúcho history during the Estado Nôvo, political events of a less public variety were also taking place. Nationally a clandestine resistance movement, with branches in every state, functioned throughout the Estado Nôvo era. Despite severe government pressure, resistance leaders issued prodemocratic bulletins, circulars, and manifestoes.[45]

World War II increased antidictatorial rumblings within Brazil. During the early war years, Brazil maintained a precarious neutrality. While Dutra and Góes Monteiro publicly expressed their admiration for the Hitler and Mussolini regimes, Oswaldo Aranha labored to cement Brazilian-United States relations. Vargas, as usual, followed a sphinxlike course of noncommitment.

Following the Japanese attack on Pearl Harbor and the signing of a series of beneficial economic agreements with the United States, Brazil severed relations with the Axis powers and formed a military cooperation pact with the United States permitting U.S. forces to use northeast Brazil as a way station for transporting troops and supplies to Africa. When Germany retaliated by torpedoing Brazilian merchant ships, Brazil declared war on Germany and Italy in August 1942. Brazilian war activities ultimately included sending a twenty-five-thousand-man Brazilian expeditionary force to fight in Italy.

Brazil's entry into World War II and participation in this so-called democratic crusade provided further impetus for prodemocratic propaganda and activities despite government restrictions, with Gaúcho veterans among those in the forefront of the resistance. Oswaldo Aranha became vice-president of the Society of the Friends of America, which used its pro-Allied activities as an avenue for espousing political democracy. When Vargas sanctioned the government dissolution of this organization, Aranha irately resigned as foreign minister and openly aligned himself with the anti-Estado Nôvo forces.[46]

Aranha's sometimes-ally, sometimes-rival, Flôres da Cunha, also became a focus of resistance expression. Following his release

accepting the superficiality and lack of statistical rigor of the surname index, this evidence clearly indicates greater post-Estado Nôvo ethnic political participation and success in Rio Grande. For a more complete discussion of Gaúcho ethnic politics see Carlos E. Cortés, "The Political Rise of the White Ethnics in Rio Grande do Sul, Brazil" (Paper delivered at the Pacific Coast Branch Conference of the American Historical Association, Sept. 28, 1971).

from prison in 1943 and accompanied as always by omnipresent police agents, Flôres visited Pôrto Alegre. His arrival ignited a series of pro-Flôres, prodemocratic demonstrations, climaxed by an emotional homecoming mass in his honor. Startled by the extent of these manifestations, Vargas canceled an eighteen-hundred-person banquet in Flôres' honor and forced the ex-governor to leave Pôrto Alegre ahead of schedule.

Another Gaúcho ex-chieftain, Raul Pilla, also provoked a prodemocratic controversy. To nourish the Liberator oppositionist flame thoughout the Estado Nôvo, Pilla held biweekly luncheon meetings of his loyal followers. He also wrote a popular Pôrto Alegre newspaper column entitled "Microscópio," which he used to criticize the government and champion the return to electoral democracy. When the government reacted negatively to Pilla's articles, angry anti-Getulist Pôrto Alegre university students turned the "Pilla Case" into a cause célèbre for mobilizing prodemocratic student sentiment.[47]

Vargas' political problems in Rio Grande were not restricted to the opposition. He also encountered trouble among his own supporters. Gaúcho politicians had bitterly swallowed Vargas' selection of Colonel Oswaldo Cordeiro de Farias as interventor in 1938. In 1943, when Cordeiro resigned to join the Italy-bound Brazilian Expeditionary Force, Vargas forced Gaúcho aspirants into a repeat pride-swallowing performance.

Once again the president avoided elevating a Rio Grande politician to this post, which might serve as the basis for establishing a chieftainship. Instead he selected his first cousin, the relatively unknown army lieutenant colonel Ernesto Dornelles. Gaúcho politicians did not hide their unhappiness, particularly since Vargas had not consulted them prior to his surprise announcement. However, like Cordeiro, Dornelles appeased them in the time-honored manner—by retaining most of them in their posts.[48]

In addition, Dornelles even created some goodwill among anti-Getulists by appointing an advocate of political democracy, ex-Liberator Alberto Pasqualini, as his interior secretary.[49] As a socioeconomic reformer Pasqualini had eulogized the 1937 constitution, but as a political liberal he had criticized its dictatorial political system. During his six months as interior secretary Pasqualini increased the state sales tax, with the money to be used solely for social welfare. He also ended press censorship, in glaring contrast to the rigorous national muzzling of information. When the mayor of Cachoeira do Sul resigned, Pasqualini announced that the influential elements of that county would hold a plebiscite to "elect" the new mayor, a radical departure from the existing appointive system. This proved too much for Dornelles. He publicly disavowed Pasqualini's announcement, forcing him to resign.[50]

These sporadic manifestations of opposition to and deviation from the Estado Nôvo provided continuity to Gaúcho politics, although parties did not exist. When electoral democracy returned in 1945, Flôres, Pilla, and Pasqualini would reemerge as major state political leaders.

World War II hastened the demise of the Estado Nôvo. Despite the pro-Axis sentiment of many government leaders, including Dutra, Góes Monteiro, and Vargas himself, Germany's sinking of Brazilian transport ships had forced the unwilling Brazilian leaders to declare war on the Axis. The paradox of waging a war against dictatorship while that same system continued in their own country became increasingly unacceptable to many Brazilians, including officers of the Brazilian Expeditionary Force in Italy. Many military leaders concluded that the time had come for a return to electoral democracy in Brazil.

The military's defection removed the effective base of Vargas' regime. When in early 1945 Dutra informed Vargas that he should reestablish democracy, Vargas had no choice but to comply.[51] On February 28, 1945, Vargas announced that there would be an election. Three months later he set December 2 for the presidential and congressional elections, with the gubernatorial and state assembly contests to follow.

With elections came the reappearance of political parties, although not in their pre-Estado Nôvo form. The opposition united as the National Democratic Union (UDN–União Democrática Nacional)—no relationship to the party of the same name formed in 1937 by ex-Liberator Bruno de Mendonça Lima. A basically middle-class coalition, the UDN supported traditional political liberalism, civil liberties, and morality in government; its members' common antipathy for Vargas and the Estado Nôvo provided the party's unifying and galvanizing force. As its presidential candidate the UDN selected a former tenente, Air

Brigadier Eduardo Gomes, last survivor of the "Eighteen of Copacabana" and a giant in the building of the Brazilian air force.

In battling the UDN, Vargas again displayed his political genius. Even as his governmental empire was collapsing, he could count on such motley supporters as interventors, patronage-seeking officeholders, industrialists, large landowners, and urban labor. Following his time-tested politics of equilibrium—never permitting a single group or party to become too strong or his sole source of support—Vargas founded two parties.

On the one hand he formed the Social Democratic Party (PSD–Partido Social Democrático). A conservative "politicians' party," the PSD was led by interventors, other Estado Nôvo politicians, and their favor-seeking followers, who basked in the patronage of "clientelist" politics.[52] The PSD's economic base consisted of large landowners who continued to dominate agricultural Brazil and large industrialists who had benefited from the Estado Nôvo. To undermine Eduardo Gomes' military support, Vargas selected War Minister Dutra as the PSD presidential candidate, purchasing a political insurance policy in doing so. Dutra's long involvement in the Estado Nôvo assured his postelection benevolence toward a dethroned Vargas and his past government activities, something which could not be expected if the revenge-happy UDN won the election.

Vargas also founded the Brazilian Labor Party (PTB–Partido Trabalhista Brasileiro). Since Labor Minister Lindolfo Collor's triumphal 1931 northern tour, Vargas had hungrily eyed urban labor as a potential political force. Estado Nôvo industrialization had rapidly enlarged urban labor, and Vargas worked to corral it and make it personally loyal to him. His instruments included Brazil's first minimum wage law, a flood of labor legislation, and a paternalistic social welfare system. Moreover, the government propaganda machine continuously extolled Vargas' virtues as the "Father of the Poor."

But the key lay with the labor ministry's domination of the union structure. All workers had to pay the government an annual union tax consisting of one day's wages. To share in the disbursement of these funds or to use the labor courts, unions had to be recognized as legal by the government.[53] With such leverage the ministry succeeded in installing its agents as union leaders, who acquired the colorful title of *pelegos*—sheep hides. Brazilian saddles often consist of a number of such hides used to cushion the cowboy's ride. In a political sense pelegos were labor agents who cushioned Vargas and the labor ministry officials in their relations with the urban worker, allowing government leaders to "ride" the workers more easily.

With the return of electoral democracy, Vargas commissioned Labor Minister Alexandre Marcondes Filho to use this government-controlled union structure as the basis for building the Brazilian Labor Party.[54] Most of the PTB organizers were union leaders with limited political skill or experience.

In Rio Grande do Sul the return of democracy brought a repetition of traditional Gaúcho political patterns—the redivision of the state into two political camps through the alliance of former antagonists against a common enemy. In 1889 Republicans and Conservatives had united against the forces of Gaspar da Silveira Martins. In 1923 Federalists and ex-Republicans had joined to oppose the reelection of Borges de Medeiros. In 1929 Republicans and Liberators had formed the tenuous United Front to support Vargas for the presidency against Júlio Prestes. In 1932 ancient enemies Raul Pilla and Borges de Medeiros and their disciples had united against the Vargas-Flôres-Aranha PRL triumvirate. In 1936 the Liberal Dissidency had allied with the FU to support Vargas in his struggle with Flôres da Cunha. Now, in 1945, Aranha and Flôres united with their former antagonists, Pilla and Borges, to support Eduardo Gomes and oppose the Vargas forces.

Aranha, Flôres, and Pilla signed the national manifesto launching the Gomes candidacy. Although the eighty-one-year-old Borges at first announced his intention to remain in political retirement, the opium of politics soon proved too strong for him. He joined the pro-Gomes movement, sending a statewide invitation to Republicans to follow him.

Aranha and Flôres helped found the UDN nationally. As he had since 1930, Aranha continued to devote himself to national politics; in the meantime Flôres organized the party in Rio Grande. As a result the Gaúcho UDN became essentially a party of Flôres and his followers, augmented by other anti-Vargas democrats, including members of the UDN's national Democratic Left coalition. Among the Democratic Left Gaúchos were José

Antônio Aranha, an ex-Liberal Dissident and youngest brother of Oswaldo, and Bruno de Mendonça Lima, former Liberator social reformer.[55]

Borges and Pilla found their organizational activities restricted by the new electoral law, which outlawed regional parties and limited registration to national parties—those with the signatures of ten thousand voters, including at least five hundred from each of five states. The law exploded Borges' dream of reincarnating the Riograndense Republican Party; so he joined the UDN, reestablishing his old friendship with Flôres. Hoping to rekindle loyalties of nostalgia, Borges sent a circular letter to old Republicans, appealing to them to follow him into the UDN. To his bitter disappointment, his letter brought a lukewarm response. Only a relatively small number of former Republicans joined the UDN.

For Borges and Flôres, both products of the old PRR, this renewed unity within the UDN was comfortable and natural, but Raul Pilla rejected integration into a party led by his former enemy Flôres. He also refused to admit that Vargas' electoral law could prevent the rebirth of his cherished Liberator Party. In a personal tour de force, Pilla organized a party state convention, established branches in other states, and obtained enough signatures to qualify the PL as a national party, but it remained essentially a Gaúcho phenomenon. In the 1945 congressional election Liberators received 51,324 votes in Rio Grande do Sul and only 6,017 in the rest of Brazil. In later years dissidents from parties in other states joined the PL, but not until 1950 did a non-Gaúcho become a member of the party's national directorate.

Unlike the old PL, which had left the parliamentarism-presidentialism question open, the new PL made parliamentarism its ideological base. Parallel to the UDN in its anti-Getulism and its appeals for government morality, the PL became the party of parliamentarists, personal followers of Pilla, and the more radical anti-Vargas oppositionists. Within Rio Grande the PL had one enormous advantage over the UDN in Gaúcho political recruitment. In contrast to the UDN, a new party with no tradition, the PL offered budding oppositionists a proud heritage of over fifty years of struggle dating back to the Federalist Party at the beginning of the Old Republic. Despite their separate organizations, the UDN and PL generally functioned during the next twenty years as a single, anti-Vargas political camp, reminiscent of the 1932-37 United Front.

Flôres, Pilla, and Borges failed to attract most of their former followers, particularly those who had collaborated with the Estado Nôvo. More than seven years of participation in government by Liberal Dissidents, Liberators, and Republicans had eroded previous party and personal loyalties. A community of interest had developed based on preservation of political power.

At the request of his brother, Protásio Vargas transformed the Rio Grande government organization into an electoral machine—the Gaúcho Social Democratic Party. Although new in name, the PSD embodied the historical governmentalist tradition developed by the Riograndense Republican Party during the forty years of the Old Republic and continued by the Liberal Republican Party from 1932 until the Estado Nôvo. Unwilling to sacrifice their governmentalist plenty for a future of prospective oppositionist famine, most of the veterans of the pre-Estado Nôvo parties rejected the appeals of their old chieftains. Instead they joined the PSD, the new government party, along with many ambitious young political hopefuls.

During the Estado Nôvo an alliance had developed among ex-Liberal Dissidents Protásio Vargas and Cylon Rosa and ex-Liberators Walter Jobim and Oscar Carneiro da Fontoura. They also held four of the six posts on the Gaúcho PSD provisional commission. By organizing PSD county committees throughout the state, they made sure that their supporters dominated the party's July 1945 state convention. There they secured the PSD gubernatorial nomination for Jobim, who had been Gaúcho public works secretary during much of the Estado Nôvo.[56]

This stacked convention angered José Diogo Brochado da Rocha, former director of the Rio Grande do Sul Railroad, who also had serious gubernatorial ambitions. He based his strength on youth and labor, which were given official, if patronizing, status as the PSD Labor Wing. José Diogo (as he is usually referred to in Brazil to avoid confusing him with his politician brothers, Francisco and Antônio) tried to organize enough labor-oriented county committees to block the pro-Jobim coalition, but his efforts failed. By his defeat José Diogo learned that his labor-oriented populism had little future in the PSD.[57]

As on the national level, Vargas did not put all of his political

eggs in one party's basket. Instead he also encouraged the formation of the Gaúcho branch of the Brazilian Labor Party. However,
as in the rest of Brazil, the Gaúcho PTB of 1945 had unknown
leaders of questionable political skill and organizational ability.

Not all Estado Nôvo politicians entered the PSD. The most
notable exception was Alberto Pasqualini, the controversial former
interior secretary. Rejecting both the hyperpolitical PSD and the
pelego-led PTB, Pasqualini formed his own socioeconomic reformist Brazilian Social Union (USB–União Social Brasileira),
which nominated Pasqualini for governor and chose congressional
candidates.[58] Although USB attracted a certain reformist elite, it
had little public impact and soon formed an alliance with the PTB
to run a joint slate of candidates in the 1945 election. This was the
preliminary step to what would ultimately become the PTB's absorption of USB.[59]

In addition to the state's pro- and anti-Vargas alliances,
parties appeared on the left and right flanks of the Rio Grande
political spectrum. On the left stood the Gaúcho branch of
Luis Carlos Prestes' Brazilian Communist Party (PCB–Partido
Comunista Brasileiro).* On the right stood the Gaúcho section of
Plínio Salgado's Popular Representation Party (PRP–Partido de
Representação Popular), a reincarnation of the old fascist Brazilian
Integralist Action. Since 55 percent of the Gaúcho Integralist
leaders had been of German extraction, the PRP had great strength
in the colonial zone, particularly in the German regions.[60]

As the presidential campaign progressed, Vargas tried to re-
enact his 1937 feat of preventing the elections, using similar con-
fusionist tactics. To divide the PSD and UDN forces, Vargas used
his old trick of suggesting compromise or substitute candidates.
On October 10 he decreed that state and county elections would
be held simultaneously with the national election, permitting
Vargas, as president, to influence the choice of officials at all
levels.

Vargas' greatest threat came in the form of *queremismo*
(from the Portuguese verb *querer*, to want), a movement launched

---

*Formed in 1922 as the Partido Comunista do Brasil (PC do B), the Communist Party
changed its name to Partido Comunista Brasileiro (PCB) in August 1961. See Vladimir
Reisky de Dubnic, *Political Trends in Brazil* (Washington, D.C.: Public Affairs Press, 1968),
p. 74. For purposes of clarity, PCB and Brazilian Communist Party will be used throughout
this book.

General José Antônio Flôres da Cunha (second from right) and his sons during the Revolution of 1930.

Getúlio Vargas and his staff leaving Pôrto Alegre for Rio de Janeiro during the Revolution of 1930.

Joaquim Francisco de Assis Brasil

Gaúchos preparing to leave Pôrte Alegre during the Revolution of 1930.

Oswaldo Aranha at a meeting of the Liberal Republican Party.

President Getúlio Vargas (left) and Governor José Antônio Flôres da Cunha during the Farroupilha Centennial of 1935.

Júlio de Castilhos

João Goulart

Raul Pilla

Getúlio Vargas on his ranch in São Borja.

Antônio Augusto Borges de Medeiros

Gaúcho leaders of the Brazilian Labor Party, including Getúlio Vargas (second from left), João Goulart (center), and Leonel Brizola (second from right).

Rioting in Pôrto Alegre following the suicide of President Getúlio Vargas in 1954.

Governor Leonel Brizola during the Legality Movement of 1961.

Fernando Ferrari, José Diogo Brochado da Rocha, and Leonel Brizola in the Rio Grande do Sul legislature.

by his PTB pelegos. Deriving their name from their chant, "We Want Getúlio," *queremistas* championed a principal demand—"A Constituent Assembly with Getúlio." They wanted the presidential election to be postponed until after congressional elections and completion of the constitutional convention à la 1933-34. This would have automatically extended Vargas' mandate, giving him more time to develop new political strategies, including a possible reelection bid. Released after nearly ten years in prison, Gaúcho Luis Carlos Prestes, with his Brazilian Communist Party, joined the queremista chorus. For fear of provoking military wrath Vargas did not openly endorse queremismo, but he made his support clear by appealing to workers to join the Labor Party.[61]

Concern grew within the Dutra and Gomes camps over events in neighboring Argentina, where in October labor demonstrations helped reinstall populist Juan Perón in power eight days after the military had imprisoned him. The final straw came when Vargas named his brother, Benjamin, to be the new Rio police chief, an act viewed by military leaders as an unmistakable sign that Vargas was preparing to cancel the election, possibly through a revolution of workers and slum dwellers led by Laborites and Communists.

The military reacted. With the support of Dutra and Gomes, War Minister Góes Monteiro, who had succeeded the campaigning Dutra in that post, mobilized his troops and issued a resignation ultimatum to Vargas. Having no means to resist, Vargas resigned and flew into "exile" on his São Borja ranch.[62] Vargas' fifteen-year reign had come to an end as bloodlessly as he had established the Estado Nôvo eight years earlier.

PART THREE

The Third Republic

7

Return of Vargas

With the departure of Vargas for São Borja, Supreme Court Chief Justice José Linhares assumed the interim presidency of the Third Republic. He postponed state and county elections, limiting the December 2 confrontation to the presidential and congressional contests. He also named new interventors, mainly selecting judges, such as Appellate Judge Samuel Figueiredo da Silva in Rio Grande do Sul.

Vargas' interventors had been instrumental in organizing the PSD and could have been counted upon to mobilize state government machinery behind Social Democratic candidates. Their replacement by nonpartisan interventors seriously jeopardized the PSD's electoral chances. In particular, without government support the PSD presidential candidate, the phlegmatic Eurico Gaspar Dutra, became critically vulnerable to the challenge of the UDN's Eduardo Gomes, a popular tenente hero.

The PSD realized that its hopes for electing Dutra now rested on obtaining Vargas' support in order to capture the labor vote. With Vargas neutral or against Dutra, the ex-war minister would have little chance against Gomes.[1] The discouraged Dutra even contemplated renouncing his candidacy to avoid suffering the expected crushing defeat.[2]

In early November Protásio Vargas and Gaúcho PSD gubernatorial candidate Walter Jobim visited Getúlio in São Borja. There the ex-president restated his support for Jobim's candidacy. As for the presidency, he suggested João Neves da Fontoura as a possible PTB civilian alternative to the two military candidates.[3]

115

Like Oswaldo Aranha, João Neves yearned for the presidency. However, he refused to accept the role of Vargas' last-minute vendetta candidate, as this would split the PSD vote and assure Gomes' victory. Declining the nomination, Neves reaffirmed his commitment to Dutra, although admitting he might reconsider if elections were postponed, giving his candidacy more time. Neves' refusal appeared to convince the ex-president to sit out the presidential election.[4]

Floundering without instructions from Vargas, the PTB national convention declined to endorse a presidential candidate, and the party began to splinter. The crucial labor vote was up for grabs. In a bid for this vote, the Communist Party selected a civilian non-Communist candidate, engineer Yedo Fiuza. As Fiuza was a close friend of Vargas, the Communists even entertained the outside hope of winning the ex-president's support. For the UDN Oswaldo Aranha swung a number of influential PTB leaders into the Gomes camp.[5] Dutra also sought PTB votes, agreeing to support its program, improve labor and social welfare laws, and select a labor minister in accord with the party.[6] A few PTB state directories backed the ex-war minister, but many queremistas planned to vote blank rather than for the man who had agreed to the overthrow of Vargas.[7] Urban labor had become the election's critical unknown, with Vargas the key to its action.

Panicked PSD and pro-Dutra PTB leaders poured into São Borja to try to convince Vargas to save the Dutra candidacy and keep the federal government out of UDN hands. Influential in the Linhares interim government, the UDN already was persecuting the PTB, unrestrainedly attacking Vargas, and even threatening to banish him from Brazil if the UDN captured government control.[8] But the sphinx of São Borja remained uncommitted.

One week before the election João Neves made a final appeal to Vargas. He informed Getúlio that he had obtained a written agreement of "reciprocal loyalty" from Dutra and urged Vargas to support Dutra as the only way to avoid a Gomes and UDN victory. Neves' words broke Vargas' resolve of neutrality.[9] On November 28 the ex-president issued a note to the press calling on the PTB and the workers to vote for Dutra.[10] Once again Vargas had worked his political magic. His note gave Dutra a smashing victory over his more popular UDN rival, 3,251,507 to 2,039,341 votes. Communist candidate Fiuza trailed badly with 569,818.[11]

Dutra won the presidency, but Vargas won the election. Although Getúlio had not campaigned, he had been nominated for congress in various states. In a tribute to Vargas' widespread popularity, São Paulo elected him senator as candidate of the PTB, while six states and the Federal District elected him federal deputy. Rio Grande do Sul elected him senator on the PSD ticket and federal deputy on the PTB ticket. All this was possible because of the bizarre electoral law which permitted a person to be a candidate in more than one state and for both houses of congress from the same state. Forced to choose among the various seats, Vargas selected the Gaúcho senatorship.

The election proved that, even out of power, Vargas was still Brazil's greatest political force. It also demonstrated that his conservative creation, the PSD, was the nation's strongest party. Even with judges running the state governments, the former interventors showed that they had made good use of the Estado Nôvo era to build powerful political machines. The PSD elected 26 of the 42 senators and 151 of the 286 federal deputies; the UDN trailed badly with 10 senators and 77 deputies. The poorly organized, weakly led PTB elected only 2 senators and 22 federal deputies, mainly from the heavily urban Federal District and São Paulo. The PCB established itself as the fourth-largest party with 511,302 federal deputy votes, 14 deputies, and a senator.

The PSD scored an impressive national victory. In Rio Grande its triumph reached landslide proportions. Riding the coat-tails of senatorial candidate Vargas, the PSD also elected its other senatorial candidate, former interventor Ernesto Dornelles, and seventeen of the state's twenty-two federal deputies. With Vargas' support, PSD presidential candidate Dutra crushed Gomes by 447,462 to 110,444.

The Gaúcho results demonstrated both Vargas' popularity and the effectiveness of the PSD state machine. They also reflected a Gaúcho protest against Vargas' removal and the UDN's national vilification campaign against him. Gaúchos took these acts personally as renewed expressions of the long history of national scorn and persecution of Rio Grande do Sul.

Despite the leadership of veteran party chieftains Flôres da Cunha, Borges de Medeiros, and Raul Pilla, as well as Oswaldo Aranha, the anti-Vargas movement elicited little response among Gaúchos. In the senatorial contest Vargas received 461,913 votes, slightly more than his cousin and running mate, Ernesto Dornelles. The two anti-Vargas senatorial candidates, including former justice minister Antunes Maciel, received little more than 95,000 votes each. The federal deputy balloting mirrored the senatorial results. The two Vargas parties, the PSD with 389,975 votes and the PTB with 40,146, nearly quadrupled the total of the two anti-Vargas parties, the UDN with 58,663 and the PL with 51,324. Of the two extremist organizations, the Communist Party received 38,759 votes and the ex-Integralist Popular Representation Party received 21,197, its highest state total in Brazil.

The 1945 election revealed two Gaúcho political verities. The Rio Grande electorate had sharply rejected the attempt of the old political chieftains to reestablish their state domination. More important, Rio Grande had declared itself Vargas country; his forces held undisputed state control. For the time being at least, anti-Getulism had little appeal to the Gaúcho voter.

Following the 1945 election Rio Grande do Sul began its first true, though short-lived, experiment with a multiparty system. Because this was a transitional period during which loyalties to the new parties had not yet solidified, there was considerable switching from party to party with the principal flow from the PSD to the PTB. The next five years brought the establishment of PTB state hegemony, the parallel atrophy of the PSD electoral machine, and feeble minor party efforts at anti-Vargas opposition. But the political spine of the period was Vargas' intelligent, persistent, and unwavering dedication to his basic goal—the return to the presidency.

To accomplish this Vargas decided that he needed something with which he had never bothered before—a unified personalist party inflexibly loyal to him. The PSD could never fill that role. Nationally it consisted of a motley assortment of rural oligarchs, industrial magnates, and professional politicians whose loyalty to him had become questionable now that he could no longer lavish government favors on them. In Rio Grande the PSD was led by politicians who had chosen the government party rather than follow former chiefs Borges, Pilla, and Flôres. Getúlio realized that most PSD politicians had supported him nominally in 1945 for their own electoral benefits and that their fidelity would diminish in proportion to his length of time out of power.

Vargas' problems were complicated further by growing alienation between himself and President Dutra, the highest-ranking politician in the politicians' party. Vargas never forgave Dutra for his complicity in the 1945 coup, and this antipathy grew when Dutra selected a moderately conservative compromise cabinet which included two members of the anti-Vargas UDN.

Getúlio was further angered by Dutra's abandonment of Vargas' policy of government direction of the economy and rapid government-galvanized industrialization. Instituting a policy of laissez-faire economic liberalism, Dutra removed government economic controls and opened the door for a flood of foreign-manufactured finished goods. By the middle of 1947 luxury consumer imports had eroded most of Brazil's wartime-built $708 million in foreign-exchange reserves.[12]

Dutra looked askance at Vargas' political activities. The president became particularly disturbed at Vargas' urging of Brazilian workers to join the PTB rather than the PSD, and he turned increasingly sensitive as Vargas and the PTB intensified their criticism of his policies.[13] It soon became clear that Dutra would never permit Vargas to become the PSD presidential candidate in 1950.

Facing the impossibility of capturing control over the PSD, Vargas turned his attention to harnessing the electoral potential of the growing urban laboring class. He decided to expand the weak PTB and lead the urban masses into an electoral corral, personally obedient to him.

The ex-president faced a fourfold problem in constructing a powerful PTB: he had to attract the uncommitted elements of the labor electorate, detach blocs of voters who had cast their ballots for other parties in 1945, provide an ideological framework for party legitimacy, and build a political machine capable of regimenting and giving expression to the heretofore voiceless urban masses. This final problem provided a special challenge, as, in contrast to the PSD, the PTB sorely lacked skilled political leaders. Its ranks abounded with union bosses, students, Pasqualini-style idealists, and minor politicians adept at little more than carrying out Vargas' orders.

As it had been in 1930, Rio Grande do Sul became the foundation for Vargas' new political revolution. Always the headquarters strategist, Vargas saw the need for a set of Gaúcho field commanders. To construct the Gaúcho PTB, the base for his national party, he selected three veterans of the 1930s, who also represented the three pre-Estado Nôvo political parties–Alberto Pasqualini of the Liberator Party, José Diogo Brochado da Rocha of the Riograndense Republican Party, and José Loureiro da Silva of the Liberal Republican Party. Their political careers reflected the deep changes in the Rio Grande political scene from 1930 to 1945.

Pasqualini, a former seminarian, had joined the youthful Liberator Party because of its opposition to government authoritarianism and defense of political liberalism. He soon became disenchanted with both Raul Pilla's rigid party control and the PL's refusal to expand its program to include socioeconomic reform. In 1933 Pasqualini tried to form an ideologically oriented reform movement, Riograndense Civic Action, but he had little success in a state divided over men, not ideas.[14] In 1936 he and Loureiro da Silva contemplated establishing a party committed to socioeconomic change.[15] Their plans never materialized, as they became two of Vargas' most outspoken supporters during his 1936-37 struggle with Flôres da Cunha. During the Estado Nôvo Pasqualini served for a brief, stormy period as interventor Dornelles' interior secretary. With redemocratization in 1945 he formed the Brazilian Social Union, but its failure to attract mass support led to its integration into the PTB following that year's election.

Pasqualini became the PTB ideological leader, providing Vargas the party philosopher necessary to give the PTB doctrinary legitimacy and differentiate it from the unabashedly political PSD.[16] However, it is doubtful that many Laborites, including Vargas, ever read Pasqualini's ethereal treatises. Party leaders certainly did not base their decisions on Pasqualinist doctrine. For the next nine years Getúlio milked maximum political advantage from the ex-seminarian without allowing him to obtain enough strength within the party to challenge Vargas' leadership.

José Diogo Brochado da Rocha, second of the triumvirate of new Gaúcho PTB leaders, contrasted sharply with Pasqualini. Lacking the latter's philosophical temperament, José Diogo contributed populist appeal, two decades of political experience, and a knack for grass-roots organizing. During the grim years after the

1932 revolution, this young Republican had received his higher education in party organization as secretary of the PRR central commission under Maurício Cardoso.

Becoming director of the Rio Grande do Sul Railroad during the Estado Nôvo, José Diogo applied this political experience. Refusing to adopt the office-bound administrative style of his predecessors, he roamed the state, made personal contacts, and solidified his relations with workers, political bosses, and economic leaders. In this way he used his post to create his own electoral machine based on the state's fourteen thousand railroad workers.[17]

With the resumption of party politics in 1945, José Diogo was instrumental in convincing former Republicans to join the PSD rather than follow Borges de Medeiros into the UDN. However, the 1945 PSD state convention rejected his bid for the party's gubernatorial nomination, most Social Democrats preferring the conservative Walter Jobim to the labor-oriented ex-railroad director.[18] Despite this failure José Diogo demonstrated his electoral strength by receiving 45,579 votes in the 1945 election, third-highest total among Gaúcho PSD federal deputy candidates. But once he went to Rio for the constitutional convention, he found himself a veritable pariah. The Social Democrats had no use for José Diogo's populism.

Noting José Diogo's increasing friction with the PSD and savoring the addition of his railroad workers to the PTB fold, Vargas invited the frustrated labor leader to switch parties. Realizing he had no future in the PSD, José Diogo decided that the PTB furnished a more natural outlet for his labor populism. He resigned his congressional seat and returned to Rio Grande to help prepare the PTB for the 1947 election.[19] The addition of this experienced organizer and dynamic campaigner to the Labor Party provided a sudden shift of votes from the PSD to the PTB.

Vargas' state commander-in-chief and the main organizer of the Gaúcho PTB was José Loureiro da Silva, a gun-toting lawyer-cowboy who fit the caudilhesque mold of Pinheiro Machado and Flôres da Cunha. Originally a Republican, then a Liberal, in the 1930s he had been a progressive mayor of the county of Gravataí and a fine state deputy. When the PRL became too small to hold both Flôres and Loureiro, the latter bolted and led the pro-Vargas Liberal Dissidency.

Loureiro naturally shared in the spoils of Vargas' triumph, becoming mayor of Pôrto Alegre. The most brilliant administrator in that city's history, he gave the Gaúcho capital a dramatic face-lifting, including the construction of a modern arterial system.[20] Following this stint he became director of industrial and agricultural credit for the Bank of Brazil, traveling extensively throughout the state in this role. Using his control over federal loans, he established a network of political ties throughout the interior to complement his Pôrto Alegre power base.[21]

Upon the resumption of party politics in 1945, Loureiro joined the PSD with most of the other pro-Vargas Gaúcho politicians. But, being a socioeconomic reformer like Pasqualini and José Diogo, he responded eagerly when Vargas asked him to carry out the grass-roots organization of the PTB.[22] Soon the PTB ranks began to expand with other PSD defectors, both sincere Getulists and ambitious politicians who considered Getúlio the key to their political futures.

Leaving Loureiro da Silva and José Diogo to organize the Gaúcho PTB and Pasqualini to write ideological prose poems, Vargas returned to Rio to claim his PSD senatorial seat. He arrived in June 1946, four months after the opening of the constitutional convention. When revenge-minded UDN congressmen opened fire on the ex-president's governmental record, the angry Vargas left the convention and returned to São Borja. He refused to sign the resulting 1946 constitution although it incorporated much of the Estado Nôvo's social and labor legislation and maintained some of Vargas' prize creations, particularly a robust executive and strong central government. The constitution also guaranteed civil liberties, free elections, and private property.

After the constitutional convention was transformed into the first congress of the Third Republic, Senator Vargas dropped in occasionally to defend his record and criticize the Dutra government. He labored at remolding his image from the inveterate dictator to a potential democratic candidate for president. But Vargas, like his political mentor Borges de Medeiros, had little use for talk-prone legislative bodies. These seemed worse than useless to the little Gaúcho, who had run the nation without congress for eleven of the fifteen years between 1930 and 1945.

More important to Getúlio was the upcoming election of January 1947 and the electoral debut of his reorganized PTB.

During the months prior to the election, Vargas campaigned throughout the country for PTB legislative candidates; however, the ex-president refused to stake his political future solely on PTB urban electoral strength. While focusing on the PTB, he also sought to retain the support of some of the PSD rural bosses, even endorsing select PSD gubernatorial candidates. [23]

The major PTB thrust came in Rio Grande, where Vargas had concentrated on creating a base for his national party. There the PTB faced an uphill battle. The PSD had captured nearly half the state's votes in 1945. Its gubernatorial candidate, the tall, brawny Walter Jobim, had been campaigning since the 1945 state convention, with the well-organized PSD machine conducting an intensive electoral drive. Finally, President Dutra had named Jobim's political ally, Cylon Rosa, as state interventor. [24]

Against such formidable opposition Vargas selected the ideological Pasqualini to head the PTB ticket as gubernatorial candidate. A third senatorial seat was to be filled in 1947 (two senators had been elected in 1945), but Vargas experienced considerable difficulty in finding a senatorial candidate willing to challenge the PSD machine. His first choice, the populist José Diogo, opted instead to run for the state assembly.* Next Vargas turned to Oswaldo Aranha, but the former ambassador declined the offer, realizing his long absence from Rio Grande would jeopardize his chances for victory and fearing a defeat might destroy his eternal presidential hopes. José Loureiro da Silva, who had eyes on the governor's palace, decided to remain in Rio Grande as party organizer. In semidesperation Vargas drafted former labor minister Joaquim Pedro Salgado Filho, a native Gaúcho who had long resided in balmier Rio de Janeiro. During Getúlio's hibernation Salgado Filho had directed the PTB nationally as Vargas' personal agent. [25]

A perplexing situation had developed in Rio Grande. The pro-Vargas PTB was challenging the PSD, but the Gaúcho PSD was by no means anti-Vargas. Getúlio had been elected senator on the Gaúcho PSD ticket in 1945, and many Gaúcho Social Democratic leaders maintained close relations with him. In particular, Walter

---

*In an interview in Pôrto Alegre on January 10, 1967, José Diogo explained to the author that he declined Vargas' invitation in order to avoid the charge that he had resigned his PSD federal deputy post out of political opportunism to obtain the PTB senatorial nomination.

Jobim avoided any trace of anti-Getulism in his campaign. He had been one of Vargas' most ardent supporters during the Estado Nôvo, had obtained Vargas' pledge of support for his candidacy in 1945, and was closely tied to Getúlio's brother, Protásio.[26]

As in 1945 the anti-Vargas role fell to the PL and UDN. Although they had suffered a crushing defeat in 1945, the two opposition parties took heart from the split in the Getulist forces and felt they might win by offering a clear anti-Vargas alternative. Together they nominated veteran Liberator Décio Martins Costa for governor and diehard UDN Florist João Carlos Machado for senator.

Getúlio had to walk a political tightrope. He wanted a PTB victory without alienating the PSD or permitting the individualistic, independent Pasqualini to threaten his own party hegemony. Therefore he campaigned vigorously for Salgado Filho and the PTB state assembly slate but virtually sat out the gubernatorial contest. At the PTB state convention Vargas extolled the virtues of both Jobim and Pasqualini, calling them "worthy of the mandate of the people, who certainly will choose the man best suited to defend the public interest."[27] At the urging of Laborites, Vargas later endorsed Pasqualini perfunctorily, but it was evident that he had no real preference.[28]

Despite such obstacles, Pasqualini's late-starting campaign gathered momentum, and it ultimately became clear that he was threatening PSD statehouse control. In a search for Catholic votes the formerly anti-clerical Jobim avidly defended a series of demands issued by the Catholic Electoral League. But even the success of the PSD Catholic leaders in convincing the politically active priests to support Jobim against what was labeled Pasqualini's "Communist" threat did not assure a Jobim victory.[29]

The win-at-all-costs PSD then entered into the first of a series of bizarre alliances which were to characterize the Gaúcho electoral cockpit during the Third Republic. This was a PSD alliance with the far left and the far right, the Brazilian Communist Party and the Popular Representation Party. Both threw their support to Jobim. Communist Party chief Luis Carlos Prestes even campaigned in Rio Grande for the conservative Social Democrat against the socialistic Labor idealist. Prestes feared Pasqualini might institute basic socioeconomic reforms, which would undermine the PCB appeal and deprive the Communists of a conservative governor to criticize. [30]

With this electoral alliance, the general support of priests, a much longer electoral campaign, a well-organized party machine, and PSD control of the state government, Jobim managed to edge Pasqualini by 20,000 votes, 229,129 to 209,164. In nearly every county Jobim's vote corresponded closely to the PSD-PRP-PCB state deputy totals. Décio Martins Costa, the anti-Vargas candidate, received only 105,164 votes. This shockingly low total shattered the UDN-PL dream of victory on the basis of the split of the Vargas forces and further underscored the strength of Getulism in Rio Grande. [31]

More important, Pasqualini led the PTB to unexpected victories in the senatorial and legislative assembly contests. In the senatorial race PTB candidate Salgado Filho received 195,658 votes, nearly 15,000 fewer than Pasqualini. Yet he easily defeated the weak PSD candidate, Oswaldo Vergara, running without the support of the PRP and PCB, who had their own candidates. The PTB also captured a razor-thin victory in the state legislative contest, defeating the PSD slate by 172,059 to 171,528. This marked a PSD decline of more than 200,000 votes and a PTB increase of more than 130,000 votes from the 1945 election. Despite this minimal, 531-vote victory, the PTB captured twenty-three seats in the state legislature to sixteen for the PSD.*

The PL, which replaced the UDN as Rio Grande's largest minor party, received only 54,972 votes, a 3,000-vote gain over 1945 but less than one-third the PTB and PSD totals. Both the

---

*The electoral code permitted each party to register as many candidates as there were assembly seats. Each voter would cast his ballot for one candidate; after the totaling of each candidate's votes, their individual totals were grouped by party for cumulative party totals. An electoral quotient was then determined by dividing the total number of valid and blank votes cast in the election by the number of seats at stake. In turn each party's vote total was divided by the electoral quotient to determine the number of seats captured. Of necessity such a distribution system left an unpredictable number of undistributed seats, which were awarded entirely to the party with the highest vote. The Gaúcho PTB earned only a seventeen-to-sixteen margin over the PSD in the state assembly on the basis of the electoral quotient; however, the winner-take-all system for undistributed seats enabled the PTB to capture six of these "bonus" seats by virtue of its 531-vote triumph over the PSD. Each party's candidates were then ranked within the party by their individual totals, and seats were awarded in descending order. The unsuccessful candidates became official substitutes according to their vote ranking. This every-man-for-himself, dog-eat-dog system forced each candidate to either build his own electoral machine or be at the mercy of the party bosses, who would instruct party members in the various counties or districts to vote for selected candidates.

UDN and PCB votes declined sharply, as anti-Getulists flowed into the historically appealing PL and urban workers switched to the PTB. In contrast, the PRP, which showed great strength in the colonial zone, more than doubled its 1945 total to 46,783, its highest vote in Brazil and less than 1,000 votes behind the UDN.

Nationally the PTB did not fare so well. Outside of Rio Grande the PTB vote dropped 4,000 from 1945, although this loss in absolute figures represented a percentage gain, as there was an 11 percent national decline in votes cast. Counting the Rio Grande election, the PTB total rose by more than 125,000 votes. In contrast, the PSD lost more than 865,000 and the UDN lost more than 335,000, although both parties maintained sizable margins over the PTB.

Vargas had triumphed again in the 1947 election. His party gained nationally while the PSD and UDN declined severely. In Rio Grande the PTB vaulted to the top of the political heap and captured the largest bloc of seats in the state assembly, giving Getúlio an operational base for the 1950 presidential election. Only the governorship had escaped the PTB, but, with the assistance of the PL, the Laborites soon engineered a cynical political coup which temporarily checked Governor Jobim.

The reborn Liberator Party had committed itself to the principle of parliamentarism under party chief Raul Pilla. The national apostle of that governmental philosophy, he viewed parliamentarism as the necessary, if not sufficient, condition for the solution of Brazil's problems. To Pilla, Brazil's greatest onus was excessive presidentialism, which led to the abuse of power and in turn generated revolutions as the only means to restrict this power.[32] Pilla had devoted his life to the pursuit of parliamentarism. In the 1930s he naïvely attempted to persuade Vargas to support his schemes for a parliamentarist federal government. In 1936 he accepted collaboration with his enemy, Flôres da Cunha, in order to install a modified parliamentary-style government in Rio Grande do Sul. Now, in 1947, with the PL a minor party, Pilla once again allied with an enemy in favor of his obsessive principle.

The Gaúcho constitutional assembly had been in session for two months when, on May 14, the twenty-three PTB and five PL deputies signed a pact establishing PTB-PL cooperation in drafting and approving the state constitution and selecting subsequent state secretariats. In exchange for Liberator votes in organizing a

PTB-dominated state secretariat, Laborites supported the PL-proposed constitutional amendments that instituted a parliamentarist Gaúcho state government. As the PTB-PL bloc held a twenty-eight-to-twenty-seven assembly majority, it had no trouble pushing through the necessary constitutional provisions.[33]

The pact came as a shock. A number of Laborites had vigorously criticized parliamentarism in past floor debates and eleven were declared presidentialists. But for the PTB this was a pact of impeccable political logic if not ideological consistency, as the constitution limited Governor Jobim's powers and increased those of the state assembly. Furthermore, the alliance assured Laborite domination over the assembly and state secretariat, which, according to the constitution, was to be chosen from the assembly.[34] In exchange Liberators fulfilled their impossible dream—a Gaúcho parliamentarist constitution—although to realize it the anti-Vargas PL had to deliver state control to the pro-Vargas PTB. This was neither the first nor last time Liberators would make a pact with the devil to secure their goals.

Victory, however, was short-lived. Five days prior to the signing of the 1947 state constitution, Governor Jobim brought action to have the parliamentarist articles declared unconstitutional because they diverged from the presidentialist pattern required by the 1946 federal constitution.[35] The Brazilian Supreme Court quickly ruled in accordance with the governor's wishes, ending the abortive experiment.[36] By overcoming this PTB-PL obstacle, Jobim regained his full governmental powers.

Rio Grande benefited from Jobim's victory. Although the droopy-eyed "sleeping giant" lacked Flôres' imagination and Vargas' political dexterity, Jobim proved himself a fine administrator. He also received significant federal help, as the fall of Vargas and the ascension of Dutra had brought an influx of Gaúchos to high governmental posts. João Neves da Fontoura, who had won the presidency for Dutra by convincing Vargas to support his candidacy, had received the post of foreign minister as his reward. Adroaldo Mesquita da Costa, the essence of Gaúcho political Catholicism, had become justice minister. Most important, Dutra had named Clovis Pestana, an able Gaúcho engineer, to be transportation minister.

There was a clear political rationale behind the apparent paradox of the increase of Gaúcho federal influence despite the removal of Vargas from power. As president, Vargas had worked to escape the taint of regionalism and expand his base nationally, particularly emphasizing his political and economic courtship with the large, powerful states of São Paulo and Minas Gerais. Unlike Vargas, who could count on considerable Rio Grande support, Dutra had to work to strengthen his Gaúcho political base. The president gave the task of economically solidifying his strength in Rio Grande to Transportation Minister Pestana. In cooperation with Governor Jobim, Pestana poured in federal funds for such items as major trunk roads and dams for electrification and irrigation. Under Dutra's presidency, the number of schools in Rio Grande rose 25 percent and the Gaúcho highway network nearly quadrupled in size.[37]

While the 1947-50 period meant good state-federal relations for Rio Grande do Sul, the era also witnessed a series of other important developments in Brazil. In the economic realm, the Dutra government reversed its laissez-faire policy, which had decimated Brazil's foreign-exchange reserves. Instituting a system of exchange controls, import licensing, easier credit, and maintenance of a high Brazilian currency valuation, the government stifled luxury imports and stimulated industrial development and economic growth.[38]

On the political scene, the era saw the legal disappearance of one political party and the emergence of another. In 1947 the Brazilian Supreme Court declared the Communist Party illegal on the basis of a constitutional provision prohibiting antidemocratic parties.[39] In that same year a populist Paulista ex-interventor named Adhemar de Barros captured the governorship of São Paulo as candidate of his fledgling Social Progressive Party (PSP–Partido Social Progressista). Once in office, Adhemar created an administration characterized by massive public works, free-flowing patronage, social welfarism, and government corruption. Adhemar's slogan, "Roubo mas faço" ("I steal but I get things done"), best reflected his distinctive style. By the eve of the 1950 election, Adhemar had transformed his state PSP into a political machine more powerful than either the Paulista PTB or PSD.[40]

The election of 1950 clearly reflected the growing socioeconomic divisions of Brazilian politics. On one side stood the forces of conservatism, centered in the PSD, the UDN, the Minas-based Republican Party (PR–Partido Republicano) of former

President Arthur Bernardes, and the Rio Grande-based PL of Raul Pilla. The PL and PR were the only legal pre-Estado Nôvo parties that survived in permanent form during the Third Republic by qualifying as national parties under the electoral law. On the other side stood the rising forces of populism, represented by Vargas' PTB and Adhemar de Barros' PSP.

The PSD, UDN, and PR had formed a congressional coalition to support the Dutra government. Conservative politicians now contemplated the selection of a unity presidential candidate for the 1950 election to stem the tide of populism, but agreement on a candidate proved extremely difficult. Being the nation's largest party the PSD insisted that the candidate come from its ranks. Further complicating matters was the fact that many leading Social Democrats were friends of Vargas. The PSD had named Vargas its first national party president in 1945; when he refused, the post remained vacant with Vargas as symbolic president until he left the party in 1948 to become PTB national president.

Despite his official defection from the PSD, Getúlio continued to cultivate his old Social Democratic allies, who in turn insisted upon trying to find a candidate whom the ex-president would support. As usual, time and patience proved to be Vargas' most effective weapons. To every proposed solution or list of suggested candidates, the sphinx of São Borja replied with temporizing comments, while he simultaneously prepared his own candidacy.[41]

From his old friend and intermittent ally, General Góes Monteiro, Vargas obtained the assurance that the military would not veto his candidacy. To solidify his military security, Vargas asked Góes to be his vice-presidential running mate on the PTB ticket, but Góes declined on the grounds of his commitment to Dutra and the PSD.[42]

Vargas also concluded an alliance with his populist rival, São Paulo governor Adhemar de Barros, whose PSP had supplanted the PTB in the hearts of the Paulista workers. Adhemar himself would have liked a crack at the presidency in 1950. However, with Vargas determined to run, Adhemar agreed to support him in exchange for a PSP vice-presidential running mate, PTB support of the PSP gubernatorial candidate in São Paulo, and some vague promises of Vargas' future political aid. Adhemar hoped that a grateful Vargas would support him for president in the 1955 election. Ironically, the PSP vice-presidential nominee was João Café Filho, never a Getulist and one of Vargas' harshest congressional critics in 1936-37.[43]

Vargas' success in uniting the populist forces was paralleled by the conservatives' failure to find a PSD-UDN-PR compromise candidate. Many of Vargas' PSD supporters were lukewarm about the idea and successfully undermined the negotiations. Finally losing patience with the PSD's indecision, the UDN renominated the old tenente Eduardo Gomes, who had lost in 1945.

The remaining PSD-PR coalition came up with a candidate of sorts, a run-of-the-mill Mineiro congressman named Cristiano Machado. Gaúcho chances for the PSD presidential nomination were destroyed by the conflict between the two major Rio Grande hopefuls, Governor Walter Jobim and Justice Minister Adroaldo Mesquita da Costa, who had received Dutra's blessing.[44] The collapse of the conservative coalition virtually assured Vargas' victory. A close friend of Gomes, Machado was certain to draw votes from the same middle-class, liberal constitutionalist electoral sectors as the UDN candidate.

The national political arrangements played havoc with Gaúcho party alignments. Senator Salgado Filho, the original 1950 PTB gubernatorial candidate, died in an airplane crash during the early stages of the campaign. So Vargas called on his cousin, PSD senator Ernesto Dornelles, to accept the PTB gubernatorial nomination, selecting Alberto Pasqualini as PTB senatorial candidate. The task of organizing the PTB nationally for the electoral campaign was given to another Gaúcho, new national party president Danton Coelho.

The Gaúcho PSD had been suffering from a severe case of political schizophrenia. The exodus of Social Democrats to the PTB had thinned the PSD ranks of many Vargas supporters and started a process of "de-Vargasization" of the party. The development of a strong anti-Vargas current within the PSD had pushed it closer to the PL-UDN opposition camp. Growing PSD-PTB friction in the state, heightened by the continuous confrontation between PSD governor Jobim and the PTB as the largest party in the state assembly, had deepened divisions between Rio Grande's two strongest parties. On the other hand, the influence of pro-Vargas national PSD leaders and rear-guard efforts of the declining pro-Vargas wing of the Gaúcho PSD had slowed the party's movement toward the PL-UDN bloc. Furthermore, Getúlio's brother, Protásio, remained PSD state president.

The perplexing situation reached its climax in the 1950 election, when the Gaúcho PSD found itself opposing Vargas as PTB presidential candidate and Dornelles as PTB gubernatorial candidate, although both had been elected PSD senators from Rio Grande in 1945. In an effort to defeat the PTB, the Gaúcho PSD joined another complex electoral alliance, this time involving the UDN and the PRP.

The national UDN, in its quest for presidential victory, obtained PRP backing for UDN candidate Eduardo Gomes by agreeing to support the senatorial candidacy of the PRP's Plínio Salgado, the former Integralist chief. Since the PRP was strongest in Rio Grande, Paulista Salgado decided to run in the Gaúcho state as the UDN-PRP candidate.[45] Many Gaúcho UDNists opposed this national party imposition, considering it another display of scorn for Rio Grande; however, in his zeal to defeat Vargas, Gaúcho UDN chief Flôres da Cunha forced his reluctant compatriots to accept the Paulista carpetbagger.[46] The Gaúcho PSD also agreed to support Salgado in exchange for UDN-PRP backing of Social Democrat Cylon Rosa for governor. Although favoring the UDN's Gomes for president, the PL refused to support either Cylon Rosa or Salgado and nominated its own gubernatorial and senatorial candidates.

The Gaúcho political maelstrom exemplified the chaos which the Vargas candidacy had brought to Brazil. The conservative forces were in disarray nationally. Vargas' message of *trabalhismo* (laborism)—a blend of social welfare paternalism, governmental centralism, economic nationalism, and expanded presidentialism—had galvanized voters, particularly the urban working class, whose real income had declined under Dutra.

In some states, particularly Minas Gerais and Rio Grande do Sul, a number of PSD leaders openly supported Vargas against their party's official candidate, Cristiano Machado. At Getúlio's request some pro-Vargas Gaúcho Social Democrats, led by João Neves da Fontoura and João Baptista Luzardo, formed the Autonomous PSD (PSDA—Partido Social Democrático Autônomo), which supported the PTB candidates and ran its own legislative slate on the PTB ticket. After the election most of the PSDA members joined the PTB.[47]

Out of this turmoil came a resounding victory for Vargas, with 3,849,040 votes to 2,342,384 for Eduardo Gomes and 1,697,193 for Cristiano Machado.[48] The extent of the pro-Vargas PSD defection can be seen by comparing Machado's votes to the 2,284,612 votes for the PSD and PR congressional candidates. In contrast, Vargas more than doubled the 1,820,792 congressional votes of his two supporting parties, the PTB and PSP. Even in Minas Gerais, where the PTB was a nonentity, Vargas defeated Machado. The PSD defection spawned a new verb in Brazilian political lexicography—*cristianizar*, to nominate one candidate but support and vote for the opposition.

In the vice-presidential contest (voting was separate for president and vice-president), Vargas narrowly carried his running mate, the PSP's João Café Filho, to victory. Clinging to Vargas' coattails, Café won despite fierce opposition by the Catholic Electoral League. For example, in Rio Grande do Sul, Café Filho ran only slightly behind Vargas in the frontier region, where the Catholic Church was relatively weak. However, in the devout colonial zone, where the priests exercised great political power, Café Filho suffered an immense vote erosion; in some colonial-zone counties he received only one-fifth to one-tenth of Vargas' votes.

Vargas' triumph also swelled the national vote total of PTB congressional and state legislative slates, reducing the margin separating the PTB from the UDN. In alliance with Vargas the PSP vaulted into fourth place nationally, both populist parties profiting from the disappearance of the Communist Party, which forced thousands of workers to find a new political home.

To nobody's surprise Vargas carried Rio Grande do Sul and led his party to victory. Now firmly established as the state's leading power, the Gaúcho PTB won the presidential and vice-presidential contests, elected Dornelles as governor and Pasqualini as senator, captured ten of the twenty-two Gaúcho congressional seats, and placed twenty-one deputies in the fifty-five-seat legislature. The election completed the exodus of most pro-Vargas elements from the PSD to the PTB, particularly via the PSDA. In the balloting for the state assembly, the PTB broke the 1947 popular vote deadlock with the PSD and leaped to a 250,316-to-209,518-vote margin over its closest competitor. The PL finished a distant third with 70,355 votes, while the PRP and UDN remained in a virtual deadlock for fourth place in the state.*

The 1950 election also brought the less-than-sensational electoral debut of the Brazilian Socialist Party (PSB—Partido Socialista Brasileiro). This elitist splinter movement of Socialist intellectuals and former Communists had emerged from the UDN's Democratic Left following the 1945 election. Led by Bruno de Mendonça Lima, a philosophical social reformer who had diverged from the PL in 1936, the Gaúcho PSB captured only 12,917 votes in the Rio Grande state assembly contest.

The remarkable rise of the Gaúcho PTB from a weak fourth in the state in 1945 to dominant state status and national preeminence among PTB state parties in 1950 resulted from five major factors. First, the Gaúcho economy had failed to develop at a rate sufficient to absorb the state's expanding labor force, stimulating a rural exodus and creating an increasing unemployment problem. An army of jobless marginals was growing in the slums of Rio Grande's major cities and the frontier region's urban centers, the two areas of greatest PTB electoral strength.[49]

Second, Rio Grande had a literacy rate of 66.23 percent, second only to that of the Federal District.[50] In electoral terms this meant that a relatively higher percentage of those in the Gaúcho lower class could qualify as voters than in the other states where illiteracy disenfranchised a greater percentage of potential PTB voters. Third, the termination of the Communist Party, the PTB's major competitor for the lower-class vote, had released thirty-two thousand Gaúcho voters.

Fourth, Vargas furnished the magnetic appeal to bring the urban workers and unemployed marginals into the PTB. The party became a sort of statewide *compadrio* (extended family) under the "Father of the Poor." Paradoxically, Vargas also attracted a large part of the Gaúcho ranching elite into the PTB.[51] These great landowners viewed Vargas as a brother rancher who might work for the urban laborer but would never create problems for them by extending these reforms to the rural worker. History supported

---

*The electoral law was changed prior to the 1950 election to provide for the proportional distribution of the excess seats not awarded according to the electoral quotient. Therefore, although the PTB state assembly slate received a higher percentage of the votes cast in 1950 than it had in 1947, it lost two assembly seats.

this logic. Although the 1930-45 Vargas era had brought dramatic progress for urban labor, these benefits had not reached the rural areas. As a result many ranchers joined the PTB out of a sense of community with Getúlio. This helps to explain why the PTB, a party based on urban labor, was stronger in Rio Grande than elsewhere although Rio Grande was only the fifth most urbanized state in 1950. [52]

Finally, as PTB organizers in Rio Grande, Vargas had such Gaúcho political veterans as José Loureiro da Silva and José Diogo Brochado da Rocha, experienced in the machine politics of the First and Second Republics. One of the major reasons for the PTB's rapid expansion in Rio Grande as contrasted with other states was this legacy of pre-Estado Nôvo leadership. Throughout Brazil the PSD and UDN were built around politicians with lengthy experience in political recruitment, party organization, and voter manipulation, while in most states political neophytes led the PTB. However, in Rio Grande do Sul political veterans directed the PTB, adapting their pre-Estado Nôvo experience and organizational abilities to the previously untapped urban lower-class electorate. They also indoctrinated their young lieutenants with their political savvy. These veterans were able to make maximum use of Vargas' charisma in building PTB votes, while in most other states the inexperienced PTB leaders could not rapidly transform Vargas' coattails into an avenue to state electoral hegemony.

The 1950 election terminated one era and inaugurated another for Getúlio Vargas and Rio Grande do Sul. It brought an end to Vargas' exile and initiated for him a new, if abortive, period as Brazilian chief of state. For Rio Grande do Sul it marked the end of multiparty experimentation and led to the reestablishment of traditional Gaúcho two-party polarity, with the state divided into pro-Vargas and anti-Vargas camps.

8

Fall of a Titan

Getúlio Vargas had won a great victory in the 1950 election, but the little Gaúcho quickly discovered that the political war was far from over. Even before he returned to the presidential palace, he found himself under serious opposition fire.

In October 1950, the UDN challenged the electoral results before the Supreme Electoral Tribunal. Citing the legal requirement that a majority of votes was necessary for electoral victory, the UDN claimed this meant "absolute majority" and asserted that since Vargas had received only 48.7 percent of the votes, he had not been elected. The court disagreed, declaring Vargas and Café Filho to be legally elected, but the episode reaffirmed the opposition's resoluteness.

Vargas also realized that he faced serious congressional problems, as his PTB held only 51 of the 304 chamber of deputies seats. A master at mending political fences, Getúlio once again bartered government positions and patronage in an attempt to secure the friendship of the large states and form an interparty coalition. As always, the PSD emerged triumphant with three ministries, including foreign affairs. This went to João Neves da Fontoura, leader of the Gaúcho PSDA and one of Vargas' campaign chiefs, who remained in the PSD following the 1950 election. Adhemar de Barros' PSP obtained one ministry, as did the anti-Vargas UDN (the Pernambuco UDN leader—repayment for having supported Vargas in the 1950 election while the Pernambuco PSD had remained loyal to Cristiano Machado).

Although it was Getúlio's party, the PTB did no better than the PSP or the opposition UDN, receiving only the labor ministry.

Even Vargas' choice for labor minister caused consternation and disappointment among many Laborites, particularly the idealists. They had hoped and even believed that Vargas would select party philosopher Alberto Pasqualini, the new Lindolfo Collor.[1] But Vargas, more concerned with political organization than with labor philosophy, chose PTB national president Danton Coelho, a vigorous Gaúcho who had been instrumental in restructuring the PTB nationally for the 1950 election. Coelho's task was clear—to maneuver the PTB into control of the government-sponsored labor unions.

Vargas was back at the game he knew best, the politics of compromise and manipulation. Yet the game did not go as well as it had from 1930 to 1945. Vargas' old techniques did not bring the glittering successes of the past. For one thing, nearly seventy, he had lost his fine touch. More important, the conditions of the game had changed. Vargas now faced a set of economic, social, and political problems which defied even his manipulative genius.

Brazil's economic ills were multitudinous: structural bottlenecks in such areas as transportation, hydroelectric power, and fuel sources; sectoral lags involving such industries as chemicals and metal-working; regional disequilibria between the industrializing south-central triangle and the agricultural remainder of Brazil; a sudden increase in the rate of inflation; an unpredictable balance of payments which restricted the nation's capacity to import; and excessive profit remittances from foreign companies in Brazil to their parent companies at home.[2] As always, Brazil's dependence on coffee exports lay at the heart of the economic crisis.

These economic woes exacerbated the nation's social problems, particularly the class question, which was shaking Brazilian politics as never before. Since the 1930 revolution Brazil's industrial complex, urban working class, and middle class had grown dramatically. In particular, the middle class felt the squeeze from the industrializing giants above, from increasingly militant labor below, and from the run-away inflation that threatened to erode the middle class' socioeconomic position.

Finally, Vargas faced an increasingly turbulent, unstable political situation. Support for the president was as undependable as opposition to him was implacable. Vargas' postelection maneuvers, including the spreading of ministries among the various major parties, proved only partially and transitorily successful. The PSD accepted its ministries in exchange for supporting Vargas, but this motley party was so factionalized that the president could not count on it as a bloc. The PSP at first continued to support Vargas, but as the president began to hedge on backing Adhemar de Barros for the presidency in 1955, the alliance disintegrated. Most intractable was the UDN, which maintained unrelenting pressure on its traditional enemy in the Catete Palace.

Congress provided the major battleground. Getúlio's Gaúcho training had predisposed him against having to cooperate with legislative bodies. He had held them off as long as he could from 1930 to 1934, lived unhappily with them from 1934 to 1937, and closed all legislative bodies in 1937 as one of the first acts of the Estado Nôvo. Even the 1934-37 congress had been better than the 1951 version, since the pro-Vargas majority generally had approved his legislative requests.

In contrast, Vargas' 1951 congressional majority was based on his unstable alliance with the PSD and PSP, and many of his favorite bills died a legislative death. Moreover, irregularities involving the Vargas government and the president's cohorts received ample publicity from both the UDN congressional delegation and the powerful UDN press. Unfortunately for Vargas, these irregularities occurred in abundance, including massive influence peddling and bribery of government officials.[3]

Vargas also had problems with the military, which had split into two polarized blocs and a centrist swing group. On one side stood the economic nationalists, who combined a developmentalist-nationalist view of economics with an aggressive anti-imperialism directed primarily at the United States. They received support from Brazilian leftists, including the Communists. On the other side stood the right-wing, anti-Communist Democratic Crusade bloc. Although many members of this bloc considered themselves nationalists, they believed that Brazil faced a Communist threat more dangerous than U.S. imperialism.[4]

Vargas placed his bet on the leftist military, selecting war and air ministers linked to this wing. Ensuing years brought numerous ministerial shake-ups and a series of military ministers representing various factions, but these original choices helped identify Vargas with the left. They also reinforced the natural ties between the right-wing, anti-Communist military men and the anti-Vargas politicians.

Getúlio leaned to the leftist nationalists because they supported his policy for correcting Brazil's economic ills. In attacking these problems, Vargas followed general developmentalist, nationalist, and anti-imperialist guidelines, his programs including the establishment of state petroleum and electrical corporations and the issuance of a profit remittance limitation decree.* But political and economic pressures mitigated against the maintenance of a consistent developmental nationalist policy.

The increasing tension of the international cold war (made hotter by the Korean War) had a polarizing effect on Brazil, including the military. As the Communist Party and army radical nationalists championed economic nationalism, proclaiming it an expression of anti-Americanism, pro-U.S. military men responded by opposing even moderate economic nationalism. Caught in the increasingly virulent verbal crossfire, nationalist war minister General Estillac Leal resigned in March 1952. When the radical nationalist slate suffered a stunning defeat in the May 1952 election for control of Rio's powerful Military Club, Vargas' position was further undermined.

Inflation and accompanying social tensions also eroded Vargas' political base. As the president retreated to a flexible, centrist course, he found himself being criticized by both the left and the right. His politics of compromise was collapsing. In mid-1953, out of desperation and nostalgia, Vargas tried to shore up his ministry with a pair of Gaúchos who reflected past and future Rio Grande—Oswaldo Aranha and João Goulart.

Getúlio had a peculiar ability to rekindle dormant personal loyalties in those he had alienated. Aranha was a case in point. He had served Vargas in many state and federal posts but had also received countless slights from Getúlio, particularly in the thwarting of his presidential ambitions. Breaking with Vargas during the Estado Nôvo, Aranha had helped found the UDN and had supported Eduardo Gomes in both 1945 and 1950. But when

---

*When projected from the state to the national level, the Rio Grande do Sul love of autonomy often emerged as a vigorous anti-imperialism, i.e., national autonomy. This was reinforced by the Gaúchos' conception of themselves as super Brazilians and by the state's historical tradition of defending Brazil against foreign aggressors. Even Borges de Medeiros reflected a sort of basic anti-imperialism in his treatment of foreign companies in Rio Grande do Sul.

Vargas appealed to him in 1953 to become treasury minister again, he accepted, out of both friendship for his old comrade and hope for Vargas' support of his long-frustrated presidential ambitions in 1955.[5]

The president could not have given Aranha a more difficult task—to bring stability to inflation-ridden Brazil and correct the deficit in Brazil's balance of payments. In response, the new treasury minister developed the Aranha Plan, an economic stabilization program based on new restrictions on credit and foreign-exchange transactions. The plan failed due to a combination of foreign pressures and severe domestic problems. Vargas himself must accept part of the blame; in fact, he may have doomed the Aranha Plan from birth when he named the other member of the Gaúcho ministerial rescue team, Labor Minister João Goulart, who had little interest in either stabilization or stability.

Goulart was one of the Gaúcho PTB new breed. Son of São Borja rancher Vicente Goulart, a political ally of the Vargas clan since the Old Republic, Jango (nickname of João Goulart) had become a wealthy rancher in his own right. During Vargas' political exile he provided constant companionship for the deposed president and learned the art of politics directly from the master.

Jango helped found the PSD in São Borja, but when PSD state president Protásio Vargas denied him a place on the party's state assembly ticket in 1947, he ran on the PTB slate with Getúlio's support and won after a lavish campaign.[6] Elected to congress during the PTB sweep of 1950, he remained in Rio Grande do Sul as interior secretary of the Dornelles state government. When Labor Minister Danton Coelho broke with Vargas, the latter selected Jango to be the new national PTB president. He took up residence at the Catete Palace with Vargas and began to encourage labor militancy, often working in direct opposition to new labor minister José Segadas Viana.

The appointment of Goulart as labor minister in June 1953 marked a political shift for Vargas. During the first two years of his presidency, in line with his politics of compromise, Vargas had given little support to the strengthening of the PTB or to the efforts of Labor Ministers Danton Coelho or José Segadas Viana to institute PTB control over the unions. But having failed to placate the opposition, Vargas turned to a policy of confrontation. With

Jango as labor minister, the president reemphasized his 1945-50 drive to mobilize working-class support.

From the point of view of personal fidelity, Goulart was an ideal choice. Unlike such relatively independent Laborites as Pasqualini, Coelho, and Segadas Viana, Jango was Vargas' political creation and his most trusted follower. Yet his selection reflected the decline of Getúlio's famed political sensitivity. The choice of Goulart alienated the centrist, uncommitted military and middle-class elements, who feared the consequences of Vargas' shift toward the proletariat.

Although no radical, Jango collaborated openly with radical, militant labor leaders, including Communists. As labor minister he dominated the union structure with the control of vast sums of union money. The opposition press accused him of stimulating labor agitation, deposing independent union leaders, and replacing them with his own party hacks. Even more frightening to conservative and moderate elements was the prevalent rumor that Goulart had been conspiring with Argentine dictator Juan Perón to establish a Peronist-type syndicalist labor dictatorship in Brazil under Vargas.[7]

The Goulart crisis came to a head over the issue of the minimum-wage increase. Fearing that Jango was planning to double the minimum wage, eighty-one colonels and lieutenant colonels issued a lengthy memorandum on February 8, 1954, protesting that the wage increase would severely reduce the salary differential between the working man and the lower army officer.[8] In the face of this military challenge, Goulart resigned as labor minister. However, before leaving his post he recommended the feared 100 percent minimum-wage increase, which, of course, applied mainly to urban labor, not to workers on the ranches of the PTB cowboys.

The political arena had turned into a nightmare for Vargas, and Rio Grande do Sul was no exception. Even Getúlio's home state afforded no relief for the beleaguered president or his party. Unlike his cousin in Rio, PTB governor Ernesto Dornelles (referred to by his opponents as "the stopped watch") had not tried to play the politics of compromise. Rejecting the idea of a multiparty state secretariat, he named Laborites to all cabinet posts and made it clear that he would govern with the PTB and nobody else.

The PTB's main rival, the PSD, was in disarray. Between

1945 and 1950 the Gaúcho PSD had committed the serious tactical blunder of seeking a middle ground, neither fervently pro-Vargas nor openly anti-Vargas. Until the very eve of the 1950 election, PSD leaders had sought an electoral compromise with the PTB, even contemplating the sacrifice of the Cylon Rosa gubernatorial candidacy.[9]

These years of indecision and centrism had proved fatal to the PSD. The party suffered a continuous decline in its appeal to the Gaúcho electorate, accustomed to viewing politics as a war without compromise, a struggle between clear, distinct alternatives. Moreover, pro-Vargas elements had been abandoning the party since 1946, a process nearly completed via the PSDA in the 1950 election. The time had come for the PSD to take a stand or sink slowly into oblivion.

At this moment of maximum PSD despair a new leader stepped forward to pick up the party reins, so badly mishandled by the former leadership cadre. This was Walter Peracchi Barcellos, head of the PSD state assembly delegation. Peracchi epitomized the old-style Gaúcho—rugged, pugnacious, resolute in the face of adversity. A retired colonel and former commander of the state military brigade, he had fought Flôres da Cunha from 1932 to 1937 and also had been a major executor of the purge of the Gaúcho German colony during the Estado Nôvo. Peracchi drove the party into a critical policy decision: from this point forward the Gaúcho PSD would adamantly oppose both the PTB and Getúlio Vargas. This position contrasted sharply with that of the party's national leaders, who maintained their mutually profitable alliance with Vargas. By their decision the Gaúchos took the first step in what would become an open rebellion against the national PSD.

The 1950 election had proved to the PSD and the minor parties that only a united opposition could hope to stand its ground against the increasingly powerful PTB. To oppose the Laborites, the PSD, UDN, and PL formed an anti-PTB alliance known as the Democratic Front (FD—Frente Democrática).[10]

After five years of multiparty experimentation, Rio Grande had returned to its two-camp tradition. Minor parties continued to function outside of the two principal camps, but they had no chance for victory. Their only feasible route to a share of governmental power and its resulting spoils was through electoral

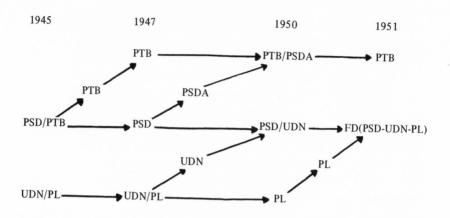

alliances with one of the two major camps. The essence of Gaúcho political history since 1951 has been this two-camp struggle, with third parties and independents furnishing the swing votes which decided the elections between the evenly matched pro-Vargas and anti-Vargas political armies.

The Democratic Front's electoral debut came in the county elections of November 1951, with the focus on Pôrto Alegre. The new alliance faced an uphill battle in the Gaúcho capital's first mayoralty contest of the Third Republic. The PTB ticket had obtained the highest vote during the 1947 county council election, receiving nearly one quarter of the vote,[11] and its power had grown in Pôrto Alegre since then. It had momentum from the 1950 election and support from both the federal and state governments. Also, it offered a popular, attractive candidate, a fiery young engineer named Leonel Brizola, whose 16,691 votes were more than double the vote of any other state deputy candidate in the 1950 elections.

To meet this challenge the Democratic Front nominated Ildo Meneghetti. The squat, rotund, personable Meneghetti had won a seat on the county council in 1947, mainly on the strength of his reputation as president of the International Sport Club, one of Pôrto Alegre's two major professional soccer clubs.* A year later

---

*The importance of professional soccer clubs in Brazilian politics cannot be ignored. Unlike U.S. professional teams, Brazilian teams are fielded by private clubs with large, fanatical, dues-paying memberships, which in turn periodically elect club presidents and boards of directors. Many a politician has begun his career as a club president. If the club's team has a good season, club members and fans often demonstrate their appreciation for the president at the ballot box.

Governor Jobim appointed him mayor of Pôrto Alegre. Although Meneghetti was a Social Democrat, his campaign in the 1951 clash was managed by a National Democratic Unionist, José Antônio Aranha, with Liberators also playing an important role in the contest.[12] Following a tense, vituperative campaign, Meneghetti defeated his Labor rival by a razor-thin 41,939-to-40,877 margin, although the PTB received more than one-third of the council vote and captured nine of its twenty-one seats.[13]

Victory in this vital mayoralty contest was to prove of utmost importance to the Democratic Front in counterbalancing PTB statehouse control in the next electoral confrontation in 1954, when the governorship, two senatorial seats, the chamber of deputies delegation, and control of the state legislature were to be at stake. The three years following the 1951 elections exacerbated PTB-FD antagonisms and hardened battle lines. In 1954 the FD repeated the successful 1951 formula—the three anti-Vargas parties in alliance behind Meneghetti, this time for the governorship. Because the FD gubernatorial candidacy went to a Social Democrat, the UDN and PL received the two FD senatorial nominations.

Eager for victory after the repeated defeats of its venerable veterans since 1945, the parliamentarist PL nominated Armando Câmara, who was neither a Liberator nor a parliamentarist. However, he was one of the state's leading intellectual lights and a leader of the Catholic Electoral League. Since Câmara was sure to draw support from the new Gaúcho Christian Democratic Party (PDC—Partido Democrata Cristão) and some Catholic Laborites, his election was considered a certainty. Considered just as certain was the defeat of the UDN senatorial candidate, former state deputy Daniel Krieger, one of the last remaining members of the anachronistic Flôres da Cunha cult.[14] An explosive orator in the tradition of his political chief, Krieger had failed in his congressional bid in the 1950 election.

While the Democratic Front swaggered with unity and vitality, the PTB shuddered with internal dissension and the burden of an unpopular state government. Too many Laborites wanted to be governor—José Diogo Brochado da Rocha, PTB congressional leader; José Loureiro da Silva, engineer of the PTB state machine; Alberto Pasqualini, senator and party philosopher; and João Goulart, PTB national president and ex-labor minister. It was an

encore to the 1938 competition for interventor after the death of
Daltro Filho, except that this time Getúlio could not personally
"elect" the governor. He could only choose the candidate to head
the PTB ticket against the FD challenge.

After months of infighting among the four potential candidates, Vargas selected the ailing Pasqualini. Jango received a
senatorial nomination as consolation prize, since Vargas wanted to
keep his neighbor in Rio to continue his politicizing of the unions.
The oft-disappointed Loureiro da Silva once again came away
empty handed and looked pessimistically toward 1958. But for
José Diogo, having been passed over by the PSD in 1945 and by
Vargas in 1950, this was the last straw. He bitterly rejected Vargas'
offer of the other senatorial candidacy.

José Diogo's frustrations caught the eye of Adhemar de
Barros, the Paulista presidential hopeful whose honeymoon with
Getúlio had long since ended. Adhemar planned to run for the
presidency in 1955, and he needed to establish bases of strength in
the other major states. A prime target was Rio Grande do Sul,
where his PSP federal deputy ticket had received only 11,329
votes in 1950. Moreover, he sought strong political allies who
could conduct an Adhemar-style populist campaign. José Diogo
filled the bill perfectly. With guarantees of support from Adhemar
and his Paulista money machine, José Diogo agreed to run as the
PSP gubernatorial candidate, hoping to win on the basis of his
personal following throughout the state.[15]

To complicate matters further the ex-Integralist PRP, which
had made an art of selling its votes to the highest bidder, decided
to experiment with its own gubernatorial and senatorial
candidates. The PRP hoped to build up party strength and loyalty
by running alone without the divisive effects of an electoral
alliance. Offering a choice, not an echo, the PRP fully expected a
statewide ground swell of right-wing voters.[16]

As Rio Grande primed for the 1954 electoral showdown,
Vargas found his national problems mounting. Jango had gone,
but his legacy lingered on. The accusations of Peronist ties, which
had been heaped on Goulart, now fell on Vargas. These attacks
increased following the publication of a purported secret speech
by Argentine president Perón incriminating the Brazilian president
as part of a pact with Argentina and Chile to establish domination
over all of South America.[17] The irate João Neves da Fontoura,

who again had broken with Vargas and resigned as foreign minister, added to the furor. Neves announced that without his knowledge Goulart and Baptista Luzardo, Brazilian ambassador to Argentina, had been negotiating for an ABC pact among Vargas, Perón, and Chilean president Carlos Ibáñez del Campo.[18]

The ghost of Jango also hung over Getúlio in the matter of the minimum wage. In his final act as labor minister, Goulart had recommended a 100 percent increase. Vargas could not disappoint his urban labor following and, after two months' hesitation, approved Goulart's proposal. Furthermore, in a populistic May Day speech, Getúlio vibrantly praised Goulart and called on Brazilian workers to unite as a class to make their will felt.[19]

The UDN congressional delegation initiated impeachment proceedings against the president for mishandling public funds, but the evidence was flimsy. Although Getúlio always followed an "anything goes" philosophy in his quest for political power, he apparently did not use this power for great personal economic gain. Such could not be said for many of his friends, relatives, and associates, who engaged in widespread fraud, peculation, embezzlement, corruption, and influence peddling, of which Getúlio was generally unaware.[20] Predictably, the UDN's impeachment attempt failed. Vargas could still count on the PTB delegation, while most of the PSD preferred to keep Getúlio in office rather than remove him and possibly be drowned in a UDN deluge.

The anti-Vargas military refused to accept this legal setback and began to plot to overthrow the president.[21] While the military conspired, the opposition press increased the tempo and virulence of its attacks on Vargas. This press campaign was spearheaded by a brilliant, vitriolic, Communist-turned-UDNist named Carlos Lacerda, whose daily diatribes angered Getúlio's friends, particularly his personal bodyguard, Gregório Fortunato.

Gregório had a profound emotional attachment to Getúlio. For more than three decades he had served the Vargas family. During the struggle against Flôres da Cunha in the 1930s, the husky gunman had been Benjamin Vargas' constant companion and had led the opposition "militia" which appeared daily at the turbulent state assembly sessions. He even had been imprisoned after a gun battle with Gaúcho police in downtown Pôrto Alegre. Now he protected Getúlio, directing the presidential palace guard, accompanying Vargas everywhere he went, and sleeping outside of his bedroom.

A specialist at resolving political problems with violence, Gregório decided that this was the fitting solution for Lacerda. Without informing Vargas, Gregório hired a gunman, who attacked Lacerda outside of his Rio apartment building just after midnight on August 5, 1954. Although he only succeeded in wounding Lacerda in the foot, he killed the journalist's companion, Air Force Major Rubens Florentino Vaz. [22]

From his hospital bed, Lacerda lashed out with an editorial accusing Vargas of having instigated the attack, leading to anti-Vargas demonstrations in Rio. The military captured the killer and the member of the palace guard who had contracted the assassin for Gregório. When the guard incriminated Gregório, the military investigators confiscated the latter's personal file, in which they found documentary evidence of so much corruption that Vargas stated, "I feel I am standing in a sea of mud." [23]

Demands for Getúlio's resignation exploded throughout the country, led by the raging Lacerda in daily newspaper and radio editorials. Former presidents Arthur Bernardes and Eurico Gaspar Dutra called on Vargas to resign for the good of the country. Air force officers and army generals issued ultimatums that Getúlio relinquish his office. Vice-President Café Filho suggested to Vargas that they both resign so congress could elect an interim successor to serve until the 1955 election, but Vargas responded, "Under no circumstances will I resign. If they try to take the Catete, they will have to pass over my corpse." [24]

As so often in the past, the military became the final arbiter. In a cabinet meeting in the early hours of August 24, the military ministers informed Vargas that bloodshed was likely if he sought to remain in office. Vargas agreed to take a leave of absence. A few hours later War Minister General Euclides Zenóbio da Costa sent word that the leave of absence would have to be permanent. [25]

Getúlio refused. To return to São Borja would inevitably be followed by a flood of investigations which would destroy his honor and possibly terminate with his imprisonment. Instead he entered his bedroom shortly after 8 A.M. on August 24 and put a bullet through his heart. On the table beside his bed lay a two-page typewritten suicide note, a manifesto to the Brazilian people, in which Getúlio accused international and national forces and interests of exploiting the people and trying to silence him because he opposed their spoliation. Offering his life to the cause, Vargas pledged, "My sacrifice will keep you united and my name will be your battle standard. My blood will be an eternal flame in your conscience to maintain the sacred spirit of resistance."[26]

By this act of violent self-martyrdom Getúlio underwent instant metamorphosis from devil to demigod. His death plunged most of the country, particularly lower-class and Laborite Brazil, into a state of mourning. In some places mourning turned into rioting.

Hardest hit was Pôrto Alegre. As soon as news of Vargas' suicide reached the Gaúcho capital, people poured into the downtown area, where a pro-Getúlio rally developed. This soon turned into an eight-hour riot spurred by lust for both revenge and pillage. Rioters sacked the Gaúcho PSD, PL, and UDN headquarters, opposition newspapers and radio stations, the United States Consulate, the First National City Bank of New York, firms with U.S. names, and many stores with U.S. merchandise.

But even as they smashed and burned, the rioters displayed a trace of Gaúcho quixotic romanticism. In UDN headquarters they destroyed everything but the huge protrait of long-time Gaúcho hero and UDN state president Flôres da Cunha. This they removed and displayed as they marched down the street, while the emotional Flôres stood sobbing on a hotel balcony above them. It was a spontaneous mob tribute to the aging Flôres, who recently had resumed personal relations with Vargas through the efforts of Oswaldo Aranha.[27]

Rioting began at 9 A.M., but despite appeals from newspapers and radio stations, Governor Ernesto Dornelles refused to dispatch military brigade troops or ask for army help until the afternoon. By the time control was established at 5 P.M., three people had been killed and thirty injured and forty buildings damaged or destroyed.[28]

Getúlio's suicide struck Brazil electorally amidships, with Rio Grande feeling a special impact. Riograndenses viewed Vargas' suicide as the murder of a Gaúcho by the military and the national opposition—another in the more than two centuries of federal crimes against Rio Grande. Representatives of all parties, including veteran anti-Getulists, protested against this new blot on the

Gaúcho name, as Vargas' death brought a momentary political truce to Rio Grande.[29] For a moment it appeared as if 1954 would bring a repetition of the 1945 phenomenon, when Rio Grande had united in electoral protest against the deposition of Vargas. In all likelihood, had the election occurred immediately after Getúlio's suicide, the emotional impact would have carried the PTB to victory. But six weeks separated his death on August 24 and the election of October 3.

With traditional Gaúcho bravado and lack of subtlety the PTB overplayed its hand, turning the campaign into a metaphysical crusade for revenge. It soon became clear that a PTB state-level victory would go well beyond expressing Gaúcho resentment against Brazil as during the Farroupilha War and the 1930 revolution. It would also lead to Gaúcho PTB revenge against Vargas' local enemies, principally the Democratic Front. The PTB campaign became characterized by inflammatory speeches and threats of violence, led by senatorial candidate Ruy Ramos and congressional candidate Leonel Brizola. Moderates, independents, and state autonomists, who might have voted in protest for the PTB, instead were frightened into the FD camp.[30]

The centrist backlash was accentuated further by the presence in the campaign of FD senatorial candidate Armando Câmara. His impact on the Catholic electorate became even stronger because of Labor senatorial candidate Ruy Ramos, a Protestant radical whom the PTB priests would not support. The PTB ticket was further undermined by the debilitating illness of gubernatorial candidate Alberto Pasqualini. The declining party philosopher, campaigning under the banner of "Social Justice," sometimes nearly fainted at rallies and usually needed days of rest between public appearances.[31]

Attempting to maintain a reformist position, the newly formed Gaúcho Christian Democratic Party refused to join the conservative FD, but it did endorse Câmara and Meneghetti.[32] The PSP nominated only a single senatorial candidate and supported the UDN's Daniel Krieger for the other senatorial seat. Its aim was to defeat João Goulart, Adhemar de Barros' major competitor for national populist leadership.

Party divisions, momentarily weakened by Getúlio's death, had become even further solidified by the emotion of the ensuing electoral struggle. Party-line voting returned as the norm, reflecting the historical-psychological Gaúcho predisposition to vote a straight ticket. This predisposition was reinforced by the mechanical inconvenience of split-ticket voting, since each party distributed its own ballots. For this reason a powerful vote-getter to lead the ticket was of paramount importance.

Vargas had filled this role in 1945 and 1950, when he led his followers to victory. In 1954 it fell to the popular Armando Câmara. Receiving 402,438 votes, Câmara helped the other FD senatorial candidate, Daniel Krieger, with 383, 010, and gubernatorial candidate Meneghetti, who defeated the ailing Pasqualini 386,821 to 356,183. Saddled with a radical Protestant senatorial running mate, João Goulart received only 346,198 votes, not enough to defeat Krieger.[33]

Getúlio's death did not bring Gaúcho PTB gubernatorial and senatorial victories. On the other hand it did destroy the gubernatorial chances of a former Laborite, PSP candidate José Diogo Brochado da Rocha. José Diogo's electoral calculations were based on the hard core of 44,812 voters who had supported him for congress in 1950 and on his ability to attract reformist Laborites. He appealed to petulant party members to follow him in his rebellion against the rigidity, corruption, and clan control of the PTB.

However, Vargas' suicide made a vote for the PTB a vote of revenge for Getúlio and defense of Gaúcho honor and made it a sin for Laborites to vote against their party's candidates. Realizing this, José Diogo asked Adhemar de Barros to let him withdraw from the race and support the PTB for populist unity. More concerned with strengthening his 1955 presidential chances than with the personal fate of José Diogo, Adhemar held him to his candidacy commitment.[34] José Diogo was right; in his electoral denouement he received a disappointing 7,396 votes.

Although losing the gubernatorial and senatorial contests, the Gaúcho PTB nonetheless increased its popular vote lead over the PSD as well as its proportion of seats captured in the congressional and state legislative races. The Gaúcho PRP gubernatorial and senatorial candidates did not run as strongly as their supporters had hoped, but the party moved solidly ahead of the declining UDN as the state's fourth-largest party behind the PTB, PSD, and PL. The Social Progressive Party and Brazilian Socialist Party captured their first seats in the Gaúcho legislature.

Nationally the PTB also slightly increased its congressional delegation (from fifty-one to fifty-six seats), as did the PSD, PSP, PR, PL, PRP, and a number of other minor parties, aided by a twenty-two-seat growth in the size of the chamber of deputies. The UDN delegation suffered the major loss, from eighty-one to seventy-four seats.

The 1954 election also brought the debut of the Gaúcho Christian Democratic Party, which had been founded the year before (the national PDC had been founded in 1945). The PDC hoped to galvanize clerical support and form a great party based on Catholicism. However, the political priests already firmly committed to the PSD, PRP, and PTB did not move in mass to the new, weak party.[35] The PDC state legislative slate received only 11,370 votes and the congressional slate obtained only 4,518.

Despite the existence of the PDC and other weak minor parties, the essence of the Gaúcho political struggle had become the clash between the PTB and the Democratic Front, the anti-PTB alliance. The PSD, PL, and UDN did continue to run separate chamber of deputies and state legislative slates of candidates. However, in senatorial and gubernatorial electoral confrontations with the PTB, as well as generally in clashes within the Gaúcho legislature, the three FD parties functioned essentially as a single force.

As party roots deepened and the two political camps solidified, voter loyalties had calcified. This in turn precluded victory by third electoral forces, exemplified by the mere 70,000 votes for the PRP gubernatorial and senatorial candidates. Moreover, it limited the impact of charisma, demonstrated by José Diogo's failure to lead his personal following out of the PTB.

At the same time a delicate electoral balance had developed between the PTB and the anti-PTB alliance. The frontier region, with its pro-Vargas ranchers, large urban pockets, and city-girdling slums, and the major cities had crystallized as the centers of PTB power. This was offset by the small businessmen and small farmers of the rapidly growing north, who found the Democratic Front their stronghold against Getulism and Laborism.

From 1954 on, slight shifts in electoral behavior by uncommitted voters or the addition of another party to one of the two major camps would decide state elections. Governors could not depend on a solid majority in the evenly divided state legislature. Control of the governorship from 1947 on alternated between the two major forces. Neither could sustain itself in power for more than one term because of the electoral balance and the inevitability that the incumbent governor would alienate enough swing voters to insure his party's defeat in the next election. Administratively it meant the impossibility of long-range government programs. Instead state governments emphasized short-range, voter-oriented activities to repay political debts and prepare for the next election.

In the less than ten years since the fall of the Estado Nôvo, Rio Grande had become emotionally polarized and equally divided, primarily on the issue of Getulism. This politics of equilibrium was to have consistently noxious effects for the state and its people.

9

Triumph of the Vargas Heirs

The year 1954 marked the Gaúcho PTB changing of the guard, with ramifications for the national Labor Party because of the Gaúcho stranglehold on national party machinery. It brought the death of Getúlio Vargas, founder and chief of the Labor Party. It ended the era of the three original state commanders who had built the Gaúcho PTB—the dying Pasqualini, the defeated José Diogo, and the frustrated Loureiro da Silva. Finally, it signaled the ascension to power of a new young trio of PTB leaders, the Vargas heirs—Leonel Brizola, Fernando Ferrari, and João Goulart—who took charge of the party upon their benefactor's death.

The fiery Leonel Brizola, one of the founders of the Gaúcho PTB and a leader of its youth wing, had been elected state deputy in 1947 and 1950. Defeated by Ildo Meneghetti in his 1951 Pôrto Alegre mayoralty bid, the young engineer had served as Governor Ernesto Dornelles' public works secretary from 1952 to 1954. In the 1954 election he demonstrated his electoral charisma and the strength of his personal organization by obtaining 103,003 votes, the most of any candidate for federal deputy in Brazil. His vote exceeded that of each Gaúcho party slate except those of the PTB and PSD.

The career of Fernando Ferrari paralleled that of Brizola. Ferrari had helped found the Gaúcho PTB and had risen from state to federal deputy with Brizola. Both men had been legislative protégés of José Diogo; both had tirelessly and skillfully built personal political machines. But in contrast to the inflammatory

152

populism of Brizola, Ferrari nurtured the mystical mantle of Pasqualinist idealism.

Foremost of the trio was João Goulart. Jango's rapid political rise had suffered two major 1954 setbacks—his forced resignation as labor minister and his senatorial election defeat. But even before his electoral loss, Jango had begun his comeback, launched by the arrival of Vargas' body for burial in São Borja. Brazilian politicians, some out of sincere grief, others for political capital, descended on the reddish, dusty town by the Uruguay River. Vargas' grave became the platform for vibrant funeral orations, climaxed by the tearful speech of Oswaldo Aranha. Led by Aranha and Jango, still PTB national president, the funeral turned into a summit conference of preparations for the 1955 presidential election.[1]

Vargas' death created dual crossroads for the PTB and for Jango. The PTB could follow the 1950 model of running its own presidential candidate, or it could accept second position on a ticket with another party's presidential candidate. Jango also faced the dilemma of his own political future. Vargas had left him in firm control of the PTB national presidium, bolstered by fellow Gaúchos Brizola and Ferrari. He probably could have claimed the PTB presidential nomination, but such a move would have had serious drawbacks. Although as labor minister he had made his "down-payment with the masses," Jango at this point merely reflected Vargas' prestige.[2] Lacking credentials of his own, Goulart faced severe competition for the Vargas vote.

Two other potential presidential candidates—Minas governor Juscelino Kubitschek of the PSD and former São Paulo governor Adhemar de Barros of the PSP—also claimed the Vargas mantle. Moreover, on the basis of the 1954 election, the PTB electorate only equaled that of the UDN and was merely two-thirds of that of the PSD. Finally, in the unlikely event of a Goulart presidential triumph, the question of whether the military leaders who had forced him into resignation and Vargas into suicide would permit Jango to bring Getulism and PTBism back to the Catete Palace would be problematical.

A Goulart presidential candidacy obviously was ill advised. If the PTB wished to present its own candidate, the logical choice would be Oswaldo Aranha, whose presidential ambitions stretched back to the early 1930s. Since his appointment as finance minister in June 1953, Aranha had been viewed as Vargas' choice as his presidential successor.[3] He combined the dual legitimizing credentials of his UDN background and his friendship with Getúlio.

But what might have been a logical candidacy for the PTB seemed far less so to Goulart, who realized an Aranha victory would jeopardize his personal domination of the PTB. Rather than take such a risk, Goulart opted for a more secure route—a renewal of the traditional electoral accord between the two Vargas-created parties. This alliance between the urban-based PTB and the rural-based PSD had operated openly for Dutra in 1945 and surreptitiously for Vargas in 1950. In the 1955 election, Goulart provided PTB support for Mineiro Juscelino Kubitschek's presidential candidacy in exchange for PSD backing of his own vice-presidential candidacy. Kubitschek also promised Jango that he could fill all federal posts in Rio Grande do Sul and control the labor ministry, including the enormous resources of the ministry's social security institutes.[4]

It was an ideal electoral compact. While Kubitschek courted the upper and middle classes by championing rapid industrialization and heavy public investment, Goulart organized and placated labor sectors. By this action Goulart rejected any true PTB shift to the left. According to Thomas P. Skidmore:

> The effect was to preclude any remaining chance, however slight, that the PTB might develop into an independent leftist party. Instead, it became increasingly the manipulable collection of "ins" among the organized working class and their government-appointed leaders.[5]

In short, Jango chose to further PSDize the PTB.

The Kubitschek-Goulart alliance came as a blow to the Gaúcho PSD, which since 1951 had been at open war with the Vargas forces. When new president Café Filho had appealed for an interparty unity presidential candidate capable of preventing the Getulists' return to power, Gaúcho Social Democrats had voiced their support. At the party's national convention, Gaúchos attempted to block Kubitschek's nomination and a PSD-PTB coalition. Gaúcho PSD president Walter Peracchi Barcellos presented a choice of four moderate Social Democrats who were acceptable as presidential candidates to the UDN, PL, and PDC. When the party rejected this Gaúcho formula and later formed an alliance with the PTB, the Gaúchos, along with the PSD branches in Pernambuco and Santa Catarina, refused to endorse their party's candidates. Utlimately they supported the UDN ticket of former tenente Juarez Távora and Mineiro Milton Campos.

The PSD-PTB alliance also disappointed presidential hopeful Adhemar de Barros, the PSP populist. Defeated in his 1954 attempt to recapture the Paulista governorship, he had attempted unsuccessfully to attract Jango as his running mate in a populist united front. When Jango rejected his offer, Adhemar turned to another Gaúcho Laborite, former PTB national president and labor minister Danton Coelho. Like José Diogo Brochado da Rocha before him, Coelho had defected from the PTB rather than accept subservience to Goulart and the Gaúcho Young Turks. Adhemar hoped Coelho would bring with him many other Laborites who could not accept Goulart's party domination.

Adhemar's candidacy posed a threat to the Kubitschek-Goulart ticket by splitting the populist forces. Fearing this division might permit the victory of the UDN's Juarez Távora, the only anti-Vargas candidate in the field, Kubitschek engineered a deft coup. He convinced PRP president Plínio Salgado to run for the presidency to erode Távora's support on the right.

Salgado's well-recompensed candidacy guaranteed Kubitschek's victory. The Mineiro defeated Távora by less than 470,000 votes, 3,077,711 to 2,610,462, while Salgado received 714,379.[6] However, with 2,222,725 votes, Adhemar hurt Kubitschek more than Salgado hurt Távora. The 5,300,136 total for the two claimants to the Vargas mantle reflected the tremendous electoral legacy left by the deceased president and the weakness of the stale UDN appeal to moralism and anti-Getulism.

The power of the urban labor vote became even clearer in the vice-presidential contest. Goulart received 3,591,409 votes—500,000 more than Kubitschek—even though 500,000 fewer votes were cast for vice-president than for president. Jango was helped by the thousands of Adhemar's labor supporters who split their tickets and voted for Goulart rather than for Adhemar's running mate, Danton Coelho. The latter's 1,140,261 votes were merely half of the PSP presidential candidate's total. But despite Jango's impressive showing, he defeated the UDN's Milton Campos by only 200,000 votes. In obtaining 3,384,739 votes, Campos benefited from the absence of a PRP vice-presidential candidate (Plínio Salgado ran alone for president) and the split-ticket voting for fellow Mineiros Kubitschek and Campos.

In the Rio Grande do Sul voting, Goulart gained revenge for 1954. He defeated the Democratic Front's candidate, Milton Campos, by 423,484 to 382,105 and crushed his former PTB rival, Gaúcho Danton Coelho, who received only 27,376 votes in his home state. Goulart also helped Kubitschek to a 329,562-to-302,595-vote victory over Távora, even though the Gaúcho PSD had rejected its national party candidate and had supported Távora. Adhemar trailed with 175,185 votes, including thousands of Laborites who voted an Adhemar-Jango split ticket. Plínio Salgado received 66,109 hard-line PRP votes.

Like his brother-in-law, Jango, Leonel Brizola also avenged himself electorally in 1955. In his second try he won the race for mayor of Pôrto Alegre, crushing Democratic Front candidate Euclides Triches 67,077 to 37,158, while the PTB took eight of the twenty-one county council seats in the Gaúcho capital.[7] With labor support secure, Brizola had also appealed to business interests by campaigning with the theme that, if elected mayor, he had Kubitschek's guarantee of federal financial support for Pôrto Alegre. Furthermore, Brizola had warned businessmen that after the election Rio Grande would have two state governments. All successful requests for federal funds would have to come through him, not Meneghetti, since the Gaúcho PSD was supporting Távora.[8]

The 1955 election provided a great victory for the Vargas heirs. It also brought the critical decision of the Gaúcho PSD to elevate the state political struggle above loyalty to the national party. By rejecting the PSD presidential candidate in favor of maintaining Democratic Front unity behind the UDN candidates, the Gaúchos had staged their first open rebellion against the national party. This assertion of state party autonomy would continue as long as there was a PSD. From 1955 until the extinction of the political parties in 1966, the national-Rio Grande do Sul party relationship functioned in the following manner:

National	PTB	PSD	UDN	
Rio Grande do Sul	PTB		PSD	PL	UDN

The powerful Gaúcho PTB incorporated both the national PTB role of manipulator of urban labor and the unemployed and a large part of the national PSD role of party of the professional politicians and large landowners. With its "natural" PSD role in Rio Grande greatly preempted by the state PTB, the Gaúcho PSD split. A small group of Gaúcho Social Democrats maintained firm relations with the national PSD, but the vast majority wing moved closer to the national UDN. Just as the Gaúcho PTB was going through the continuous process of PSDization, the Gaúcho PSD was being constantly UDNized.

As a result, the small Gaúcho UDN never gained major party status. Its traditional UDN anti-Getulist position was preempted both by the majority of the larger Gaúcho PSD and by the Liberator Party, whose vivid combative past appealed more to the historically minded Gaúcho than did the young, Flôres da Cunha-dominated Gaúcho UDN. In short, the Gaúcho Democratic Front became the functional equivalent of the national UDN, while the Gaúcho PTB became the functional equivalent of the national PTB-PSD alliance.

The 1955 election further solidified the state's two-camp division and projected a Gaúcho, João Goulart, into the vice-presidency, but, as in 1950, the anti-Vargas opposition decided to try to amend the election results. The UDN half-heartedly repeated its 1950 tactics of claiming that an absolute majority was needed for victory. Once again the Supreme Electoral Tribunal rejected the argument, but the more radical UDNists, like journalist Carlos Lacerda, and a number of army officers began to discuss the possibility of a coup to annul the election and block the inauguration of Kubitschek and Goulart.

The struggle on both political and military levels was complex and tortuous.[9] At first the tide seemed to be running in favor of the anti-inauguration plotters. On November 1 anti-Kubitschek army colonel Jurandir Mamede gave a rousing public oration in favor of military intervention. War Minister General Henrique Teixeira Lott, who had openly guaranteed Kubitschek's inauguration, asked President Café Filho to discipline Colonel Mamede (who at that time was directly under the president). Before he could decide how to respond, Café Filho suffered a heart attack, entered the hospital, and was replaced temporarily by Carlos Luz, president of the chamber of deputies. When Luz, who reportedly favored a coup, refused to discipline Mamede, Lott resigned in protest.

But resignation did not mean inactivity. On November 11, the day after his resignation, Lott mobilized Rio army units, which occupied the major newspapers, radio stations, and government buildings in a preventive countercoup. Acting President Luz fled, accompanied by a number of plotters.

On the civilian side, Lott received support from the old Gaúcho caudilho Flôres da Cunha, then acting president of the chamber of deputies. To legitimize the dumping of Carlos Luz, Flôres convoked the chamber and supported a rapid vote approving the installation of senate speaker Nereu Ramos as interim Brazilian president. It was ironic that Flôres da Cunha, who had fought Vargas for twenty years, would give vital support to a military movement assuring the inauguration of five more years of Getulism. Yet, as in 1937, Flôres stood as the defender of the constitution, even though it meant supporting the forces of Getulism he had long fought against and opposing the majority of his party, the UDN. It was as if fate had given Flôres a final opportunity to strike a blow for Gaúcho autonomy by aiding the inauguration of Riograndense João Goulart against the plot of non-Gaúchos to prevent it.

With Lott in control of the military situation, Kubitschek and Goulart took office in January 1956. Turning his administration into a quest for "Fifty Years of Progress in Five," Kubitschek launched an all-out drive to expand industry, energy, and transportation through heavy public investment, increased foreign aid, and new incentives for domestic and foreign private investors. In addition, he dedicated his administration to the construction of a new federal capital—Brasília—in the interior state of Goiás.[10] For Brazil it meant the most dramatic five-year economic surge in the nation's history. For Rio Grande do Sul it meant an accelerated economic decline in comparison to the booming south-central triangle.

Rio Grande had traditionally been one of Brazil's economically strongest states. Its diversified agriculture and prosperous artisan industry contrasted sharply with the depressed economies of Brazil's poverty-stricken north and northeast. Yet Rio Grande found itself in an increasingly disadvantageous economic position in relation to the rapidly developing Brazilian south-center.

Years of neglect of agricultural modernization, industrial expansion, and infrastructural development had finally caught up with Rio Grande. While the south-central triangle had industrialized and also expanded its agriculture, Rio Grande had remained dependent on an increasingly archaic agricultural system. Gaúcho agriculture directly provided more than 40 percent of the state's income and more than 50 percent of its employment. Agriculture also indirectly generated additional employment and income through such related fields as the food-processing industry and commerce based on the distribution of agricultural products. In contrast, industry provided only 17 percent of the state's income and 13 percent of its jobs. Moreover, this industry depended perilously on Gaúcho agriculture, with 60 percent of industrial production resulting from the processing of Rio Grande's agricultural products.[11]

Year by year Rio Grande became increasingly dependent on south-central industry, while that region became less dependent on Gaúcho primary products. Rio Grande agriculture remained burdened by inefficient techniques, an inadequate state transportation network, and the lack of sufficient storage and warehousing. The various Rio Grande governments made sporadic attempts to correct selected infrastructural deficiencies. However, even the best of these programs fell short of satisfying the state's impressive needs. Furthermore, the consistent failure of administrations to continue programs begun by their predecessors led to lack of continuity and waste of the state's financial resources.

Location also restricted the state's ability to compete with developing south-central agriculture. Far from the focal Rio-São Paulo market, Rio Grande was limited commercially by the tenuous transportation links between itself and the south-center. Only a single highway connected Rio Grande to São Paulo and Rio, an unreliable thread that could be snapped easily, as it was by a 1965 flood which destroyed the single highway bridge connecting Rio Grande to Santa Catarina. For months Rio Grande was like an island, isolated from the rest of Brazil except by air and sea.[12] Riograndenses found no compensation in the inadequate, undependable, expensive national maritime fleet. While goods rotted in ports for lack of storage and shipping, Gaúchos mused about what might have been had Vargas not destroyed Flôres da Cunha's dream of a Riograndense Fleet to serve state producers.

Rio Grande had been living on borrowed time economically since the beginning of the Estado Nôvo. In 1954 the string ran out and economic atrophy set in, with agricultural stagnation. This was followed inevitably by the decline of Gaúcho industry, inextricably bound to the state's agriculture. By 1956 Rio Grande's gross income had ceased to rise. By 1957 the state showed a negative rate of per capita economic growth, just at the time that Brazil was making worldwide headlines with the glamour of Kubitschek's swashbuckling development program. [13]

The ascension of Kubitschek to the presidency actually aggravated the Gaúcho economic decline. His Target Program concentrated on the heavy industry and energy-transportation infrastructure of the south-central triangle. Rio Grande received only 2 percent of the program's financial benefits although it made the third-highest contribution of federal taxes. [14]

Furthermore, the Kubitschek government strictly oriented new foreign investment in Brazil under the Superintendency of Money and Credit's Instruction 113 of 1955. The latter gave the federal government the power to regulate the importation of capital machinery for industry based on the government's evaluation of the industry's contribution to Brazilian development. Under Instruction 113 the Kubitschek government favored the heavy industry of the south-central triangle at the expense of the medium and light artisan industry characteristic of Rio Grande do Sul. From 1955 to 1960 over 90 percent of the massive foreign investment flowed into the south-central region. Rio Grande received less than 2 percent. [15]

Despite being a minor partner in the Target Program and foreign investment boom, Rio Grande continued to bear a heavy federal tax burden. It ranked third behind São Paulo and the Federal District both in the percentage of its state income taken for federal taxes and in per capita federal taxes. These three states also made more than 50 percent of the federal social security contributions. Yet Rio Grande received compensation neither from a flood of foreign investment, as did São Paulo, nor from an equivalent expenditure of federal funds, as did the Federal District. Only São Paulo and Rio de Janeiro State received a smaller percentage of their federal tax payments back in the form of federal expenditures. [16]

The Target Program, the federal tax system, and the flow of foreign investments into the south-central triangle further accentuated the regional disequilibrium between the south-center and Rio Grande. In the words of one Brazilian author, the Gaúcho state was becoming "a New Northeast."*

In addition to the unfortunate confluence of state economic stagnation and Kubitschek's centrally oriented development program, Rio Grande also suffered the political consequences of the 1955 election. The new president had a score to settle with the rebel Gaúcho PSD, which had refused to support him in 1955. His vengeance fell on the state government, headed by the PSD's Ildo Meneghetti and run by the anti-Kubitschek Democratic Front.

Kubitschek's revenge took many forms. Rio Grande was denied the benefits of the Target Program and the surge of foreign investment. When the Meneghetti government began its own state-financed road-building program, the federal government denied permission to import the necessary machinery. When a 1957 drought decimated Gaúcho herds and Rio Grande tried to recuperate by buying fifty thousand calves from Argentina and five hundred thousand sheep from Uruguay, the government refused to issue an import license. The federal government also barred Gaúcho wool exportation, thereby forcing the state to sell its wool to Brazilian wool manufacturers centered in São Paulo. This made the Rio Grande rancher a virtual slave of the Paulista wool industry. [17]

All of this occurred although a Gaúcho, João Goulart, held the second post in the Kubitschek government. Like his mentor Vargas, Jango was more concerned with solidifying his national power than with helping Rio Grande. Furthermore, he had his own personal vendetta with the Gaúcho governor and the Democratic Front, which had defeated him in 1954 and opposed him in 1955.

Letting the Meneghetti government suffer for lack of federal support in order to weaken the FD for the 1958 election, Jango simultaneously helped Pôrto Alegre mayor Leonel Brizola, an

---

*Franklin de Oliveira, *Rio Grande do Sul: Um Nôvo Nordeste. O Desenvolvimento Econômico e as Disparidades Regionais,* 2d ed. rev. (Rio de Janeiro: Editôra Civilização Brasileira, 1961). Northeastern Brazil is the country's classic symbol of poverty, misery, and backwardness in contrast to the south and south-center, which are traditionally described as progressive and relatively prosperous.

eager claimant to the governorship. As in the case of the death of Júlio de Castilhos in 1903, when Pinheiro Machado had taken over the national leadership and Borges de Medeiros had run the state, Jango and Brizola had divided Vargas' political empire. Jango dominated the PTB nationally and ruled the national labor system as vice-president while Brizola directed the PTB state machine.

For three years Rio Grande languished under a de facto dual state government, as Brizola had warned. While Meneghetti governed officially, Brizola became the prime recipient of whatever federal money, benefits, and patronage came to the state.[18] Industrialists, merchants, and landowners in need of Bank of Brazil loans and federal favors were forced to plead their cases before the fiery Pôrto Alegre mayor, who also happily accepted their donations to his gubernatorial campaign fund. Brizola took full advantage of his powerful position to strengthen his political machine and prepare for the 1958 contest.

Brizola's gubernatorial candidacy was a foregone conclusion. But in a quixotic gesture, José Loureiro da Silva challenged the rising Pôrto Alegre mayor for the PTB nomination. Loureiro had suffered twenty years of gubernatorial frustration under Vargas' autocratic domination of Gaúcho politics, beginning with Getúlio's selection of Cordeiro de Farias as interventor in 1938. Now, with Vargas gone, Loureiro took his case to the PTB state convention. In complete control of party machinery, Brizola stacked the convention and crushed the aging veteran. It appeared to be the final victory of the Vargas heirs over the PTB old guard.

Leonel Brizola was a singular phenomenon in Gaúcho history, blending PTB populism and PSD political craft. A perceptive student of themes and techniques for arousing and mobilizing the masses, he excelled both in spellbinding oratory and Republican-style, grass-roots organizing. Since 1956 Brizola had expanded his following through a popular Friday night radio program in which he raged against the powerful interests and pledged himself to defend the downtrodden.[19]

In addition to his large personal following, his use of the Getulist mystique, and the support of the state's largest party, Brizola had a number of other advantages in the 1958 election. He warned voters that an FD victory would mean the continuation of federal disfavor toward Rio Grande. Citing his own good relations with the Kubitschek government, Brizola proclaimed that his election would assure federal aid for economically aching Rio Grande. This appeal had a powerful impact because the 1947 constitution gave the federal government control over most major sources of tax revenue. By severely restricting the tax resources available to state and county governments, the constitution made them dependent on federal assistance.[20]

Many businessmen, in quest of Bank of Brazil loans and federal favors, supported Brizola as the shortest route to federal largesse. Brizola also made full use of the enormous resources of the labor ministry, such as money, automobiles, and offices, which Jango contributed to his brother-in-law's campaign. Finally, Brizola was favored by the Gaúcho tradition of gubernatorial alternation, which had operated since 1947.

With all of these advantages, Brizola took one final step to insure victory—the formation of an ideologically bizarre electoral alliance reminiscent of the 1947 Jobim accord. For the 1958 election he united the PTB with Adhemar de Barros' populist PSP and Plínio Salgado's PRP, Rio Grande do Sul's most reactionary party. The PRP furnished support in the colonial zone, where the PTB was weakest. In return Brizola promised state government positions and PTB support for the PRP senatorial candidate, a little-known colonial-zone landscape painter named Guido Mondim.

The Democratic Front countered with Walter Peracchi Barcellos. Like Loureiro da Silva, Peracchi had long craved the governorship. As PSD state president and leader of the FD since its inception in 1951, he had been a key figure in Meneghetti's 1954 victory. In the 1958 electoral contest Peracchi and the FD senatorial candidate, the PL's oratorically volcanic Carlos de Britto Velho, conducted an intensive, five-month campaign. But they could not compete with Brizola's populism, Friday night radio program, and promises of federal aid.

Furthermore, Peracchi became the object of pent-up colonial-zone antagonism dating back to the Estado Nôvo. As chief of Interventor Cordeiro de Farias' personal military staff, Peracchi had been active in the local implementation of the Estado Nôvo's Brazilianization campaign, in which excesses had occurred against Germans and Italians. In 1958 he received his political compensation. Finally, while Brizola created a three-party alliance, Peracchi failed to attract the Christian Democratic Party. The PDC had supported Meneghetti in 1954, but it chose in 1958 to maintain its distance from the conservative coalition in an attempt to foster a reformist image.[21]

Brizola won by a landslide, receiving 670,003 votes to 500,944 for Peracchi Barcellos, and carried Guido Mondim to victory over the popular Britto Velho in the senatorial race, 617,385 to 494,316. The PTB scored advances in the congressional and state legislative contests. Its vote continued to grow at a faster rate than the state electorate, as it had since 1945. With 602,925 votes the Labor congressional slate topped the 544,942 votes for all of the other parties combined. Nearly one-fourth of the PTB total went to Fernando Ferrari; with 147,996 votes he repeated Brizola's 1954 feat of being the highest-voted federal deputy candidate in Brazil.[22]

Flôres da Cunha, the aging caudilho, furnished a sad footnote to the election. The national UDN directory had censured Flôres because of his collaboration with War Minister Lott in the November 11, 1955, countercoup, forcing the proud Gaúcho to leave the party. Because of gratitude for his 1955 stand and hope that he would attract votes to its slate, the Gaúcho PTB invited the dying Flôres to run for the chamber of deputies as a Labor candidate. But even Flôres' charisma could not overcome the Gaúcho predisposition against party-switchers. Although he received 10,777 sentimental votes, he fell more than 5,000 votes short of election. This was to be Flôres' last electoral battle. During the four years of the Brizola governorship, death came to three Gaúchos who had epitomized Rio Grande politics—Borges de Medeiros, Flôres da Cunha, and Oswaldo Aranha.

With the 1958 election Gaúcho Laborites controlled the Brazilian vice-presidency, Rio Grande do Sul governorship, Pôrto Alegre city hall, national PTB machinery, and, through Fernando Ferrari, leadership of the PTB congressional delegation. The Vargas heirs were triumphant, but the seeds of Labor disunity were present, seeds left by Vargas himself.

The basic problem was the type of national party Vargas had built. The PSD and UDN were based on interstate agreements in the Old Republic tradition of pluralistic party control and collegial decision-making. In contrast, the PTB had developed in the classic Gaúcho military mold, with an autocratic chieftain, his personally selected field commanders, and a disciplined rank and file. Although there was an unwieldy one-hundred-man PTB national directorate, real authority rested in a thirteen-man national executive committee, which Vargas had ruled absolutely.[23] This system had functioned successfully while Vargas was alive, as explained by Fernando Ferrari:

> Vargas, with his enormous prestige and charismatic personality, a lover of personal power, was the absolute chief of the PTB and the maximum inspirer of its policies. Although uninterested in giving organization to his party, apparently neglectful of its destiny and, therefore, of its internal dissensions, he always made the decisions. Nobody dared to oppose him. He was the lord of judgments, the master of decisions.
>
> Renovating groups, like those of Alberto Pasqualini, Lúcio Bittencourt, and others who advocated party restructuring on democratic bases, with a program and ideology based on the philosophy of native laborism, found their efforts trammeled by the heliocentrism of the President. Vargas clutched the chieftainship, which nobody disputed, in an endogenous manner. The circle of iron which he created in an enigmatic and crafty manner always prevented the individual initiative which a collegial administration brings to the party. From time to time the boldest PTB congressional representatives would attempt an assault. Finally they became convinced that it was not worth the trouble since Getúlio was the great obstacle which, curiously, nobody, not even the most reformist, wanted to remove, since they recognized that he was the great agglutinant of the electorate. "Let the President go," they said. "Afterwards, if possible, we will build a party."[24]

Vargas' death led to neither democratic restructuring nor ideological reformation of the PTB. Goulart, with Brizola's support, assumed dictatorial party control. Under his direction the PTB continued to follow opportunistic and clientelistic rather than ideological guidelines.

Becoming leader of the national PTB congressional delegation, Ferrari launched a congress-based reform movement. He called for structural reformation of the PTB organization along democratic lines and ideological reformation of the party program along lines proposed by the late party philosopher, Gaúcho Alberto Pasqualini. Whether Ferrari was a sincere disciple of Pasqualini's labor philosophy or primarily an opportunist seeking to further his own ambitions by destroying Goulart-Brizola party control is debatable. In either case, from the moment Ferrari began his campaign, his relations with Goulart and Brizola became increasingly strained.

By 1959 the reform movement had developed into an open PTB dissidency known as the "Clean Hands Campaign." It supported Ferrari for the Brazilian vice-presidency–a direct challenge to incumbent Goulart. When Jango and Brizola engineered his removal from his post as PTB congressional leader, to which he had been elected by his fellow Labor deputies, Ferrari established a Clean Hands office in Rio and launched a national campaign to "clean up" the PTB. Harassed increasingly by party leaders, Ferrari broke completely with the PTB and formed his own Labor Renovation Movement (MTR–Movimento Trabalhista Renovador).[25]

Parallel with Ferrari's national challenge, the PTB was undergoing a Rio Grande-centered challenge from yet another Gaúcho Laborite, José Loureiro da Silva. Following his annihilation at the hands of Brizola at the 1958 PTB state convention, Loureiro had been given up for politically dead by Brizola and his followers. But these were desperate times for the opposition.

The 1958 electoral defeat had severely jolted the Democratic Front statewide and had shattered it in Pôrto Alegre. The PSD insisted that, as in 1951 and 1955, the FD candidate for the 1959 Pôrto Alegre mayoralty election be a Social Democrat. The UDN concurred unenthusiastically, but the PL refused and instead allied with the young PDC. Together, Liberators and Christian Democrats convinced Loureiro to be their candidate.

Considering the Gaúcho tradition of party loyalty and the disastrous electoral records of the two previous major PTB dissidents–José Diogo Brochado da Rocha and Danton Coelho–the challenge of this human anachronism appeared doomed to failure. Moreover, in the 1955 Pôrto Alegre election the PL and PDC had received a combined total of less than 19,000 votes. This contrasted with the PTB's 36,774 votes and the more than 27,000 votes of the PSD-UDN combination.

But despite the odds, Loureiro da Silva accepted the invitation to battle. Twenty years earlier he had led the successful Liberal Dissidency against the dictatorial party control of Governor Flôres da Cunha. He could not resist this new opportunity to strike out against the authoritarianism of another governor, Leonel Brizola.

Loureiro's campaign began quietly, almost surreptitiously, with house-to-house visits in the forty-odd workers' villas, most of them on the outskirts of the capital. Campaigning tirelessly, accompanied by his team of mainly youthful Liberators and Christian Democrats, Loureiro visited 150 factories, gave more than six hundred speeches, and attended countless open forums with workers, students, and public functionaries. His basic message was laborism—true laborism as contrasted with the autocratic, opportunistic, self-aggrandizing practices of Goulart and Brizola.[26]

As his three-month campaign gained momentum, Loureiro became the target of pressure by the PTB-controlled state and county governments.[27] During the 1954 election PTB excesses had helped the FD expand and solidify its ranks. Once again, in 1959, these PTB attacks helped the opposition, making it clear to the anti-PTB and independent voters that Loureiro da Silva, not PSD state deputy Ary da Silva Delgado, was the significant candidate of the anti-Brizola camp. Even the PSD and UDN "cristianized" Delgado, campaigning openly in favor of Loureiro.[28] A few weeks before the election, Loureiro's candidacy received the added support of Fernando Ferrari and the newly formed MTR.[29]

Rallying the opposition from its 1958 depths, Loureiro won the intense struggle. He received 95,539 votes to 79,398 for the PTB's Wilson Vargas da Silveira (no relation to Getúlio Vargas), a federal deputy and Brizola's former secretary of energy and communications. Delgado was cristianized so badly that he received only 7,754 votes, contrasted to the more than 27,000 council votes of the PSD and UDN, his official supporting parties. But despite the glamour of Loureiro's victory, the PTB council candidates obtained nearly three times the vote of the runner-up PSD.[30] Labor power continued to grow in the cities.

The 1959 election dramatized the growing political division within Gaúcho labor ranks. José Loureiro da Silva's successful electoral bid and Fernando Ferrari's growing Clean Hands movement presented a direct challenge to the João Goulart-Leonel

Brizola brother-in-law tandem. The 1960 presidential election was to provide the next arena for the deepening labor political conflict. Having failed in his internal struggle to overthrow the Goulart-Brizola party dictatorship, Ferrari decided to take the issue to the voter. His battleground—an electoral confrontation with Jango for the Brazilian vice-presidency.

Goulart and Ferrari, however, played second fiddle to the major figure in the 1960 election—reformist UDN presidential candidate Jânio Quadros. A charismatic, nonparty politician, Quadros combined a colorful populist style with UDN-type appeal for governmental honesty and administrative efficiency. He had risen like a rocket, being elected mayor of São Paulo in 1953, governor of São Paulo in 1954, and federal deputy in 1958. Both as administrator and as vote-getter, the unpredictable Quadros had carved an excellent record.

In 1960 the independent Paulista accepted the presidential nominations of both the PDC and the victory-starved UDN, which selected him despite his refusal to commit himself to the party. Symbolic of his political autonomy, Quadros also accepted each party's vice-presidential candidate as his running mate. For vice-president the UDN renominated its losing 1955 candidate, Milton Campos of Minas Gerais. The Christian Democratic Party chose Fernando Ferrari, eager to take on his Gaúcho rival, Goulart.

As in 1955 the PSD and PTB united. Having nobody capable of stemming the Quadros tidal wave, the PSD-PTB coalition unenthusiastically selected War Minister Henrique Teixeira Lott, leader of the 1955 countercoup, as its electoral sacrificial lamb to oppose Quadros. The two parties also renominated João Goulart for vice-president. But rather than let Lott drag him down to defeat, the vice-president clutched at Quadros' already crowded coattails. Although he publicly backed Lott, Jango clandestinely fostered the formation of "Jan-Jan" committees, which appealed to voters to support Jânio and Jango.

Goulart had extended his national political power since 1955, particularly by manipulating the extensive funds and jobs under his control. Using the labor ministry's social security institutes and labor courts, Jango had solidified his hold on urban labor. He also had effected a working arrangement with the illegal Communist Party, which ran candidates on PTB tickets in return for helping Jango organize labor.[31]

Challenging Goulart with his messianic Clean Hands vice-presidential campaign, Fernando Ferrari lashed out at what he termed Jango's perversion of labor and the PTB for his own political and economic gain. Traveling throughout Brazil, Ferrari called for a more effective program for the urban worker, the extension of the Collor-Vargas reforms to the rural worker, and the moralization of governmental and political customs.[32] His campaign meshed smoothly with that of Quadros, who stressed the eradication of the corruption, inflation, and governmental inefficiency of the Kubitschek-Goulart administration.

The election results demonstrated that the three vice-presidential contenders had been correct in climbing on the Quadros bandwagon. With 5,636,623 votes, Quadros crushed PSD-PTB candidate Lott with 3,846,825 and the old war-horse, PSP chief Adhemar de Barros, with 2,195,709. As in 1955, the Gaúcho PSD had rejected its party's nominee in favor of the UDN candidate. Supported by the FD, the PDC, and Ferrari's MTR, Quadros won handily in Rio Grande do Sul, receiving 541,031 votes to 431,497 for Lott and 214,963 for Adhemar.[33]

In the national vice-presidential race Goulart once again edged Minas Gerais' Milton Campos, the UDN candidate, 4,547,010 votes to 4,237,719. Ferrari trailed badly with 2,137,382 votes. But in the home-state showdown between the two labor antagonists, he defeated Jango by 557,425 to 472,902. Campos received only 143,509.

The national effect of the Ferrari candidacy on the Goulart-Campos contest is still debated, but its impact in Rio Grande is uncontestable. In the 1955 vice-presidential race Goulart had defeated Campos by 41,379 votes in Rio Grande. In the 1960 contest, while Goulart's total rose 50,000 votes, Campos' vote fell 240,000, although the Gaúcho electorate increased 360,000 votes. The major variable was the presence of the messianic Ferrari in 1960.

As in every election since 1951, the Gaúcho electorate was divided into PTB and anti-PTB camps. Given the choice between a charismatic Gaúcho and a cerebral Mineiro, the anti-PTB Rio-grandense naturally opted for Ferrari. Ferrari restricted the increase of Goulart's vote by siphoning off some of his labor support. On the other hand, the MTR candidate received the bulk of the anti-PTB vote and virtually destroyed the Gaúcho electorate of

Campos, who ran 400,000 votes behind running-mate Quadros. In his quest for personal revenge Ferrari may have cost Campos the election, although a state-by-state analysis of the sources of Ferrari's vote would be necessary to ascertain which opponent he hurt most nationally.

The Rio Grande defeat of Lott and Goulart reflected increasing Gaúcho economic frustrations and a rejection of the Kubitschek government. During his campaign trips through Rio Grande, Lott had encountered penetrating silence whenever he mentioned the president's name. His vain attempts to defend Kubitschek's program had not endeared him to Gaúchos, now frantic because of their state's economic stagnation.[34]

Things had gone from bad to worse for Rio Grande during the Kubitschek administration. The flow of federal and foreign money into the south-central triangle and the Kubitschek-provoked inflation, the worst in Brazil's history, had further increased the disequilibrium between Rio Grande and the south-center.

Prices of manufactured goods rose on the free market while price ceilings prohibited a concomitant rise of agricultural products. Between 1954 and 1958 the cost of manufactured goods increased 34 percent more rapidly than that of primary goods.[35] This was a brutal blow to Gaúcho farmers, who had to purchase increasingly expensive farm equipment.*

Even in terms of comparative agriculture Rio Grande had slipped vis-a-vis the rest of Brazil. Plagued by the twin curses of inefficient latifundia and uneconomic minifundia, Rio Grande found itself running out of room. Agricultural properties covered 80 percent of the state. While the rest of Brazil could increase its production by developing new lands, Rio Grande was faced with the necessity of more intensive exploitation of existing agricultural land, much of it devastated by years of misuse.[36]

The Gaúcho cattle herd fell from third to fourth in size

---

*Franklin de Oliveira cites the following comparisons. A fertilizing machine, which in 1949 had cost the same as 120 sacks of wheat, rose by 1959 to a price equal to 227 sacks. Between 1955 and 1959 an automotive harvester rose in cost from 900 to 2,140 sacks of wheat. From 1955 to 1959 the cost of a tractor rose from 1,222 to 1,500 sacks of soybeans, while from 1949 to 1959 it rose from 945 to 1,250 sacks of rice. Other vital items such as petroleum and modern plows also rose in terms of agricultural products. F. Oliveira, *Rio Grande do Sul*, pp. 94-95.

behind Minas Gerais, São Paulo, and now Mato Grosso. From 1953 to 1958 Rio Grande's herd increased by only 1.2 percent annually, contrasted to the 4.8 percent national average, even though during the same period the slaughtering of Gaúcho cattle fell 7 percent. With the growth of the central and northeastern herds, the Gaúcho dried-beef industry began to lose its traditional hegemony to the more centrally situated producers.[37]

The growth of the Paulista sheep herd, challenging Rio Grande for national leadership, was even more ominous, since São Paulo was the greatest market for Gaúcho wool. In its increasingly dependent colonial relationship with São Paulo, Rio Grande imported more than 80 percent of the Paulista finished products made from Gaúcho wool—a depressing comment on the inadequacy of Rio Grande industry.[38]

Rio Grande's comparative industrial decline had been equally severe. Starved for credit, unable to obtain modern equipment, and faced with the growing giant of Paulista industry, small Gaúcho factories began to close. During the Kubitschek administration Rio Grande showed a 1.7 percent annual industrial growth contrasted to 12.7 percent for Brazil as a whole. At the same time Rio Grande's percentage of the national income fell from 10.3 to 9.3 percent.[39]

Quite naturally, economic stagnation brought unemployment. A Rio Grande do Sul government study revealed that fifty thousand new jobs were necessary each year to meet the demand of the growing state work force. The Gaúcho economy not only failed to meet this demand, but in some years the number of available jobs actually decreased. Between 1950 and 1960 Rio Grande's industrial work force increased by little more than 5 percent to only 105,134 employees. In 1963 the state government estimated a 10 percent state unemployment rate, with 300,000 Gaúchos out of work. Additional thousands worked only during harvest periods or in seasonal food-transformation industries.[40]

Part of the pressure on the inadequate Rio Grande job market was relieved by the continuing exodus of thousands of Gaúchos. Further "relief" was provided by the Rio Grande government, whose payroll became bloated with some 110,000 public functionaries. In turn, the state payroll became a raison d'être for political parties, who contributed mightily to the state's economic decline.

Since 1945 incessant party warfare had battered the state and impeded effective government programs. When governments presented beneficial programs to the evenly divided assembly, they were usually destroyed, delayed, or emasculated by the uncompromising opposition, which gave highest priority to the defeat of government proposals and the discrediting of the government. Individual politicians used public office to enrich themselves and build personal political machines for future elections. Moreover, a primary goal of the various state governments was to solidify their power and pad the employment list with legally irremovable party loyalists. As Gaúcho journalist-politician Plínio Cabral described the system:

> The problem is simple. But it is a true infernal machine. The leaders of the new government arrive with their entourages. And they find the entire personnel structure loyal to or at least organized by their adversaries. So they feel they must appoint "their people," people of their personal confidence. But it so happens that their predecessors left "their people" in a secure situation, protected by special laws. Nobody can be dismissed. So the new government leaders have no other alternative: they appoint their people, who are added to those already with jobs. And this is repeated every four years. The result—nearly 110,000 public functionaries in a state like Rio Grande do Sul. Public functionaries? No, strictly speaking. Merely people who were given jobs to fulfill political agreements or so that the new government could have "their people." When the government's term ends, naturally all will be protected by special laws. And the succeeding government will have to swallow them and, in its turn, name "its people"— and so on every four years. It is a true infernal machine. It is a process of self-consumption. The state devours itself, solemnly, constantly.[41]

Gaúcho businessmen and agriculturalists were little better than the politicians. They generally refused to reinvest their profits in the expansion and modernization of their enterprises or in new productive ventures. Instead they poured their savings into automobiles, imported from overseas or São Paulo, or into non-dynamic real-estate investments.[42]

Generally ignoring or downplaying their own part in the state's economic stagnation, Gaúchos accused the central government of relegating Rio Grande to its traditional role as victim of south-central discrimination and depredation. By voting against Lott in 1960 (even though Quadros and Adhemar were Paulistas), the Gaúchos vented their antagonism toward the federal government and south-central Brazil, symbolized by Kubitschek. Less than a year later they would give a far more dramatic demonstration of Rio Grande frustrations.

The key to this new Gaúcho outburst was President Jânio Quadros. Although elected as a UDN-PDC candidate, the eccentric Quadros quickly showed that he belonged to no party. The major split between Quadros and the UDN came on the issue of foreign policy, where the president charted an independent middle course for Brazil between the Communist and anti-Communist cold-war camps. He contemplated the resumption of relations with Russia, supported floor debate over the seating of mainland China in the United Nations, and awarded Brazil's Southern Cross to Cuba's Ernesto "Che" Guevara. These acts provoked criticism from the more radically anti-Communist military and UDNists, led as usual by Carlos Lacerda. Furthermore, Quadros' frustration grew as his programs were blocked by congress, where the opposition PSD-PTB coalition held more than half the seats.[43]

Finally, under heavy pressure from the Lacerda camp and in a rage against the obdurate congress, Quadros resigned unexpectedly on August 25, 1961. He had deluded himself into believing that his electoral popularity and the congressional-military dread of Vice-President Goulart's becoming president would force congress to beg him to return with expanded executive powers. Quadros was wrong. With little hesitation congress accepted his letter of resignation and let him sail into exile. Since Jango was then in mainland China on a special economic mission, chamber of deputies president Ranieri Mazzilli became provisional president.

Congress' action was logical. The PSD-PTB majority bloc had wearied of the reform-minded Quadros, who had been determined to clean out the PSD-PTB-dominated federal bureaucracy. On the other hand, Goulart represented the traditional PSD-PTB alliance. Social Democrats preferred Jango, who had cooperated thoroughly with the PSD in the political patronage game.

The anti-Jango military was another matter. It had won the first round against Goulart by forcing his resignation in 1954. It had lost the second when Lott's 1955 preventive coup secured Goulart's vice-presidential inauguration. Now the bell had rung for round three, and the anti-Jango military decided that Goulart would not become president. Although Provisional President Mazzilli officially governed Brazil, de facto power lay with the three military ministers, who made it clear that they opposed Goulart's assuming the presidency. On August 28 they informed Mazzilli that Goulart could not return to Brazil.

Congress refused to declare Jango ineligible for the presidency. Instead it discussed the possibility of resolving the crisis through a constitutional amendment changing the governmental system from presidentialist to parliamentarist and reducing presidential powers. Thwarted, the military ministers issued an August 30 manifesto vetoing Jango as a threat to national security. They cited his syndicalist labor ideas and his ties to agents of international Communism, underscored by his laudatory comments about the Russian and Chinese Communist regimes during his current official trip there.[44]

To unhappy, angry Rio Grande do Sul, the movement to block Goulart was one more flagrant example of the rest of Brazil's scorn for Rio Grande and assault on Gaúcho rights. The party struggle was forgotten. Coming on the heels of Rio Grande's frustrating years under the Kubitschek government, the federal challenge united Rio Grande as it had not been united since the 1930 revolution.

Informed by his agents in Brasília (Brazil's new capital) of the military ministers' intentions, Governor Brizola began preparations the day after Quadros' resignation for a Gaúcho "Legality" movement in support of his brother-in-law.[45] He closed all schools and banks, occupied the telephone company, and requisitioned Radio Station Guaíba in Pôrto Alegre. The station became the center of the National Legality Network, which soon included 104 stations in Rio Grande, Santa Catarina, and Paraná, with all broadcasts originating in the pressroom of Rio Grande do Sul's Piratini Palace. Throughout the dramatic days to come, the station functioned continuously, transmitting news of the crisis that was developing throughout Brazil.

Aware of the need to back up his words with force, Brizola

mobilized the eleven-thousand-man Gaúcho military brigade and the various police forces throughout the state. He turned the governor's palace into a citadel, filled and surrounded with sandbags. By August 27 the brigade was ready and the palace defenses were prepared, with 330 heavily armed soldiers and hundreds of armed civilians.

Although the Third Army had not yet stated its position, Brizola went on the air at 3:00 that morning and threw down the gauntlet to the military ministers. He issued his first in a series of manifestoes to Rio Grande and the nation. Stating he would support any movement to guarantee Goulart's inauguration, he announced, "I am here as the legitimate governor of Rio Grande do Sul and will not permit the honor of our state nor the Constitution of the Republic to be insulted in any manner. If it becomes necessary, I will react with bullets."[46] In a broadcast later that day, he pledged that "Rio Grande do Sul will resist even if it means being crushed."[47] Not since the days of Flôres da Cunha had a state so seriously challenged the federal government. What some of Flôres' supporters had wanted, Brizola prepared to do—turn the Piratini Palace into the last bastion of Brazilian constitutional legality.

For a few moments the following day it appeared as if this would be the fate of the palace and its defenders. Army tanks began to roll through the streets of Pôrto Alegre, and rumors spread that the Third Army had orders to crush the palace stronghold. Expecting an attack, Brizola broadcast his determination to resist. Volunteers flooded into the palace square to aid in the defense.

But the army did not attack. Instead the Third Army commander, General José Machado Lopes, arrived and announced that he would not comply with the war minister's orders. He added that he would defend legality even if it meant establishing a provisional national government under Jango in Rio Grande. Since the Third Army encompassed Rio Grande do Sul, Santa Catarina, and Paraná, Machado Lopes' declaration split the nation geographically over the succession question. The Legality movement received a further boost when Lieutenant Colonel Alfeu de Alcântara Monteiro, air force commander in southern Brazil, pronounced in favor of Jango.

Having made his decision, General Machado Lopes, the "Iron

General," wired the commanders of the First Army in Rio, the Second Army in São Paulo, and the Fourth Army in Recife, clearly stating his position. War Minister Denys tried to replace him with the virulently anti-Jango General Oswaldo Cordeiro de Farias, one of the architects of the 1937 overthrow of Flôres da Cunha. Notified of his removal, Machado Lopes replied tersely, "I will arrest my replacement."[48]

Federal forces were in readiness, and three marine regiments moved south. Legality troops took up strategic positions along the Paraná-São Paulo border. An aircraft carrier, the *Minas Gerais*, headed south toward Pôrto Alegre, but Brizola countered with Oswaldo Aranha's 1930 tactic of sinking two barges in the Rio Grande channel, the entrance to the state's Lagoa dos Patos. Within the state, troops were massed in the north and on the coast to resist a possible invasion. Army antiaircraft units were concentrated in Pôrto Alegre in preparation for expected bombing raids.

An avalanche of telegrams of support from unions, commercial, industrial, and rural associations, student organizations, and other groups poured into the governor's palace. The Gaúcho legislature transcended its traditional divisions and, by unanimous vote, sent a message to Provisional President Mazzilli demanding immediate removal of the military ministers. Pôrto Alegre artists and intellectuals formed their own committee to spread pro-Legality propaganda throughout the interior. Even Pôrto Alegre archbishop Vicente Scherer announced his support for the movement.

Pro-Legality committees emerged throughout the state. Although Goulart-Brizola-patronized labor leaders and the PTB machine galvanized much of this movement, support came from all political parties and all levels of Gaúcho society. In the interior pro-Legality volunteer battalions were formed, while the Central Committee of Democratic Resistance recruited actively in the state capital. In a preposterously anachronistic touch, the Pôrto Alegre Maragatos, the last remnants of the thirty-three-year-old Federalist Party corpse, established street stations, with recruiters clad in traditional red neckerchiefs, cowboy hats, and Gaúcho riding britches. Even the state's forty-four hundred Gypsies pledged their solidarity. As in 1930, Rio Grande do Sul was "on its feet for Brazil."

Brizola's defiance and Machado Lopes' decision had steeled

the rest of Brazil, including congress, which wired its solidarity. The governors of Paraná and Goiás announced their support. Thirty-seven Rio de Janeiro unions issued a pro-Jango manifesto, the partially muffled press began to speak out, and strikes and demonstrations racked Rio.

But for nearly a week the Legality movement was a revolution without its leader. Despite Brizola's appeal to Jango to return immediately to Brazil, not until September 1 did the vice-president complete his phlegmatic trip back from China. Finally arriving in Pôrto Alegre, he encountered a reception of some seventy thousand people.

Seeking to avoid the impending civil war, congress found a solution. On September 2 it approved a modified parliamentarist constitutional amendment presented several weeks before Quadros' resignation by Raul Pilla, the tireless Gaúcho who had battled for such a system for more than forty years.* With Jango's powers severely reduced, the military ministers accepted the compromise.[49] Less pleased was Brizola, whose resistance committees had already enlisted an estimated two hundred thousand Gaúcho volunteers and who felt strong enough to contest the reduction of his brother-in-law's power.

More compromising than Brizola, Jango accepted his modified position. The presidency came first; presidentialism could come later. As Jango flew to Brasília on September 5 for his inauguration, Brizola somewhat despondently dismantled his Legality network and disbanded the Gaúcho forces. Rio Grande do Sul had gained a partial victory in its struggle with the armed forces. The final triumph, with the destruction of the ad hoc parliamentary system, would have to wait. Once again Brizola would lead Jango's army.

---

*Raul Pilla later stated that he did not favor the establishment under emergency conditions of a parliamentarist government because such a system must be instituted carefully, properly, sincerely, and under the right conditions. According to Pilla, the system as established in 1961 was doomed to failure because Goulart never wanted it to work. Author's interview with Raul Pilla, Pôrto Alegre, June 29, 1967.

10

The Goulart - Brizola Era

The Legality movement was a great moment for João
Goulart, for Leonel Brizola, and for Rio Grande do Sul. It brought
Jango to the Brazilian presidency, even though he had to settle for
reduced powers under the new parliamentary system. It transformed Brizola from a successful regional politician into a national
leader and hero of the Brazilian left. For Rio Grande it meant the
first successful state military challenge to the federal government
since the Gaúcho triumph of 1930.

Although the Legality crisis was the most dramatic incident
of Brizola's administration, his entire four years as governor
proved a traumatic experience for him. According to one of his
loyal supporters, three major factors converted Brizola from
political opportunist into radical idealist by the end of his administration.[1] Some might take exception to such a eulogistic view of
the post-1962 Brizola, but the impact of the transformative
factors cannot be denied.

First, Brizola received an education in the fragility of the
Gaúcho economy, increasingly colonial and subservient to both
the federal government and the south-central triangle. In
particular, Brizola became dismayed over the economic domination of the industrial triangle, primarily São Paulo, over the rest of
Brazil, including agricultural Rio Grande. From 1950 to 1964 São
Paulo's percentage of Brazilian industry rose from 44.5 to 54.9,
while Rio Grande's portion fell from 7.4 percent to 6.1 percent.[2]
However, lacking the compelling poverty of the northeast, Rio
Grande failed to obtain a significant share of federal government
regional development programs.

Second, like his benefactor Getúlio Vargas, the Gaúcho governor became involved in the struggle against international capitalism. Convinced that Brazil could not progress until it rid itself of the economic suction of foreign enterprise, Governor Brizola turned his beliefs into action three times: he expropriated a Swift and Company packing plant, an American and Foreign Power Company subsidiary, and an International Telephone and Telegraph Company subsidiary despite U.S. government protests and pressure.

Finally, the Legality experience demonstrated to Brizola the anti-Vargas forces' determination to continue the struggle against the Vargas heirs. The 1961 crisis also dramatized Brizola's ability to galvanize the masses. Unfortunately for Brizola, this modified victory gave him a false sense of confidence that he could mobilize sufficient force to oppose the military. Elated by his post-Legality sense of power, the Gaúcho governor dedicated himself to solidifying his claim to the leadership of the Brazilian radical left. He helped form the leftist National Liberation Front and turned the last year of his state administration into a showpiece of extremist agitation and mass-oriented reforms. These activities made him a hero to the national left, but at the same time they increased political polarization within Rio Grande.

Brizola accelerated his primary education and literacy crash program, his goals being mass literacy and maximum popular impact. Choosing quantity over quality, he erected hundreds of inexpensive primary schools and hired thousands of minimally trained teachers to spread the rudiments of reading and writing, orchestrating his drive with an extensive publicity campaign.[3] Because illiterates could not vote in Brazil, the acquisition of basic reading and writing skills transformed nonvoters into voters. Since these new literates came from the lower echelons of society, they could be expected to vote heavily for the Labor Party. Therefore, Brizola's literacy campaign doubled as a PTB electoral registration drive. However, while concentrating on primary education, Brizola neglected the glaring, long-standing problem of the paucity of secondary schools.*

---

*This inadequacy, a widespread one in Brazil, causes tremendous frustrations for thousands of students who complete primary school only to find their education terminated by the absence of secondary-school openings. T. Lynn Smith, *Brazil: People and Institutions* (Baton Rouge: Louisiana State University Press, 1963), pp. 499-506.

The governor's weekly radio programs became more vibrant. Repeated strikes shook the state. Brizola's ad hoc agrarian reform program, in which he expropriated private land and distributed it to the Gaúcho landless, created an atmosphere of tension and impelled many frightened landowners to try to make an agreement with him. Opining that "it is better to give up your rings than to lose your fingers," they offered 10 percent of their land in exchange for the governor's promise to leave them in peace.[4]

Brizola fought one element after another, including the archbishop of Pôrto Alegre and the various rural, commercial, and industrial associations, many of which had supported the governor in the 1955 and 1958 elections. He alienated the PRP and PSP, his 1958 allies, and even to Goulart proved a mixed blessing. He embarrassed Jango by expropriating the National Telephone Company in Pôrto Alegre (a subsidiary of the International Telephone and Telegraph Company) just as the president was seeking massive U.S. aid for development projects and the foreign debt. On the other hand, Brizola continued to use Rio Grande as a military threat to exert pressure on the federal government in favor of his brother-in-law.

While Brizola expanded his influence, Jango launched a two-pronged offensive to regain full presidential powers. He tried to convince the United States, the International Monetary Fund, and Brazilian moderates that he was no devil incarnate, presenting himself instead as a responsible democrat who would fight Brazil's runaway inflation and could be trusted as a fully empowered president.

At the same time Jango conspired to discredit the parliamentary system with which congress had shackled him. The act establishing the parliamentary government also provided for a national plebiscite on the system in 1965, near the end of Jango's administration. The impatient president decided to alter the timetable by creating enough chaos to show that Brazil could not function without a strong president. He condoned strikes, turned his ministry into a game of musical chairs, and provoked legislative confusion. The PSD-PTB congressional majority, which had not wanted parliamentarism in the first place but merely had yielded under duress, let the system flounder. To provide military cover for his maneuvers, Jango placed friendly generals in vital positions.

By the time Jango nominated his third prime minister,

Gaúcho Francisco Brochado da Rocha (Brizola's former state interior secretary and José Diogo's brother), the president had softened up the country. Most of the Brazilian left and center wanted to terminate the parliamentarist experiment, and Brochado da Rocha submitted a bill to congress to move the plebiscite from early 1965 to December 1962. When the three military ministers issued a proplebiscite manifesto, congress set an April 1963 deadline, but even this displeased Goulart and Brizola.

Once again Brizola flexed his muscles, prompting General Dantas Ribeiro, the Third Army commander, to issue an ultimatum hinting at a possible "people's revolt" if congress did not move up the plebiscite date even further.[5] Brizola wanted the plebiscite to be held simultaneously with the October 1962 election, but, as during the Legality crisis, congress compromised in the face of Gaúcho pressure and scheduled it for January 6, 1963.[6]

Such tactics increased Brizola's national stature with the radical left. They also destroyed the state unity of August 1961, creating an even more extreme polarity than had existed prior to the Legality movement. Brizola was unconcerned, since his ambitions now reached far beyond the Rio Grande border and he planned to run for congress from the state of Guanabara.* But his activities created enormous problems for the Gaúcho PTB as the 1962 election approached. It soon became evident that the central electoral issue would be Brizola, a radical corollary to the state's traditional issue, Getúlio Vargas. Aware that the Gaúcho voter longed for tranquility after years of increasing agitation, both political camps selected gubernatorial candidates of order, who could attract the crucial centrist independents.[7]

The PTB chose Egydio Michaelsen, a wealthy banker and disciple of Alberto Pasqualini. One of the founders of the Brazilian Social Union in 1945, Michaelsen had served as state deputy and as interior secretary under Governor Ernesto Dornelles. A symbol of moderation, Michaelsen contrasted sharply with Brizola, who dedicated himself to courting the laboring and unemployed people of Guanabara in his bid to become a federal deputy. Michaelsen's senatorial running mates—José Mariano de Freitas Beck, Brizola's

---

*Guanabara, composed principally of the city of Rio de Janeiro, was created to replace the old Federal District when the new Brazilian capital, Brasília, was inaugurated in 1960.

education secretary, and Antônio Brochado da Rocha, another brother of José Diogo—provided a more populist image.

The PTB used the same campaign theme that had been successful in 1958. Labor leaders proclaimed that the election of Michaelsen would guarantee good relations between the Rio Grande and federal governments.[8] However, in the wake of Brizola's populist agitation, this theme lacked its 1958 appeal to Gaúcho businessmen and centrist independents.

The euphoria of the August 1961 defense of Gaúcho honor had worn off. Brizola's campaign for radical changes in the state's socioeconomic structure had so thoroughly frightened Gaúcho moderates and conservatives that the three Democratic Front parties now found themselves with new allies. These were the PDC, which had run independently in previous Gaúcho elections, and the PRP, which consistently had pandered its votes to the highest bidder. The PDC and PRP united with the FD in 1962 to form the Popular Democratic Action (ADP—Ação Democrática Popular) in an attempt to defeat the PTB and stem the tide of Brizolism.

The ADP immediately faced a major problem—the selection of a gubernatorial candidate acceptable to all five parties. Historical precedents and personal ambitions further exacerbated this dilemma. The 1954 and 1958 elections had established the tradition that the mayor of Pôrto Alegre ultimately would move up to the governor's palace. According to a second tradition, the PSD, as the alliance's largest party, should furnish the gubernatorial candidate as it had in 1954 and 1958. Added to this were the long-term gubernatorial ambitions of the two leading ADP possibilities, Pôrto Alegre mayor José Loureiro da Silva of the PDC and Federal Deputy Tarso de Moraes Dutra of the PSD. The latter, an old-style politician in the Republican Party mold, had worked doggedly toward the governorship. For years he had built a thorough, county-level machine based on his skill at providing personal favors.

The ADP split on the two candidates. The PRP joined the PSD in support of Dutra, a down payment for Dutra's future support for the 1966 campaign for reelection of PRP senator Guido Mondim. The PL and PDC, who originally had backed Loureiro in the 1959 Pôrto Alegre campaign, again supported the old caudilho. The fifth party, the UDN, divided into conservative, pro-Dutra and liberal, pro-Loureiro wings. Locked in a stalemate, the ADP seemed on the verge of disintegration, which would have meant dual candidates and a certain PTB victory.

But the fear of Brizolism prevented this division and provided the basis for a compromise candidate, former governor Ildo Meneghetti of the PSD. Although not one to attract emotional adherents in the manner of Brizola or Loureiro, neither was Meneghetti one to create enemies. The candidacy of the non-committal, likable industrialist held the ADP together and even attracted the support of Adhemar de Barros' PSP.[9] To balance the ticket, the ADP nominated two incumbent senators for reelection —the UDN's Daniel Krieger and the PL's Mem de Sá.*

Both Meneghetti and Michaelsen epitomized the moderate image necessary to attract the centrist swing votes. Both also were dreary public speakers and lacked charisma, contrasting sharply with the third gubernatorial candidate, the MTR's Fernando Ferrari. The messianic labor reformer contemplated his resounding triumph in the state's 1960 vice-presidential confrontation, decided that the same votes would carry him to victory in 1962, and entered the gubernatorial contest with the support of only his fledgling MTR.

But the 1962 election proved Ferrari's vote miscalculation and his misinterpretation of the Gaúcho political process. Meneghetti won his second gubernatorial term with a 502,356-to-480,131 victory over Michaelsen. The crusading Ferrari received a disappointing 290,384 votes, although his Renovation network provided statewide radio coverage of his rallies and newspapers gave him far more space than they gave his colorless opponents.[10] It was like Hamlet running third in Denmark to Rosencrantz and Guildenstern.

The election reaffirmed the futility of third party movements in Gaúcho state elections and the inability of popular leaders to challenge the two Gaúcho political camps. The PTB voter could be counted on to vote for the PTB candidate; the anti-PTB voter could be relied on to cast his ballot for the main anti-PTB candidate. In 1959 Loureiro da Silva became identified as the

---

*In 1954 Daniel Krieger had been elected senator and Mem de Sá had been elected senatorial substitute for Armando Câmara, since according to the electoral law senatorial substitutes were elected simultaneously with senators. Câmara soon found senatorial life depressing and resigned in favor of Mem.

prime anti-PTB candidate, so Ary Delgado, the official PSD-UDN candidate, became cristianized. In 1960 the anti-PTB camp myopically ignored the national impact of its votes, treated the vice-presidential election from a traditionally provincial perspective as a classic showdown between two Gaúchos, and voted for Ferrari rather than for the "foreigner," Milton Campos. Ferrari failed to comprehend that his heavy 1960 vote was primarily anti-Jango and anti-PTB, not pro-Ferrari.

In 1962 the situation was drastically different from 1960. Battle lines were drawn clearly between the PTB and the ADP, the primary anti-PTB camp. Furthermore, the ADP candidate was a personable Gaúcho, Meneghetti, not a reserved Mineiro like Campos. Both camps realized that an erosion of their vote in favor of Ferrari might mean victory for the opposition, so their machines rigidly enforced party discipline. The dynamic Ferrari, supported only by his personal machine and the makeshift MTR, could not detach enough votes to threaten his pedestrian opponents.

Although he failed to win, Ferrari's 290,384 votes had a significant impact on the gubernatorial race, but it is not clear whether he took more Labor votes from Michaelsen or more moderate and independent votes from Meneghetti. In the senatorial race the two ADP candidates received almost identical vote totals of 572,334 and 567,882 to defeat the two PTB candidates, whose votes of 539,665 and 513,601 were somewhat more divergent. These results reflected rigid Gaúcho party-line voting. Since there were no MTR candidates in this contest, it can be hypothesized that even without Ferrari in the race Meneghetti would have defeated Michaelsen. However, thousands of MTR former Laborites voted blank or for the FD senatorial candidates in reaction to the PTB's vindictive anti-Ferrari campaign. Had there been no MTR or Ferrari candidacy, the results of the PTB-ADP confrontation might well have favored the PTB.

The 1962 election reinforced certain basic constants of the Gaúcho political process. It continued the tradition of alternation in state gubernatorial and senatorial elections. It reaffirmed the hegemony of party loyalty over the attraction of independent or third party candidates. It reflected the continued balance between the PTB and anti-PTB camps. Finally, it demonstrated that, despite the controversy over Brizola and the exodus of some

Laborites to Ferrari's MTR, the PTB still remained the leading Gaúcho party. It captured fourteen of the state's twenty-nine congressional seats and twenty-three posts in the fifty-five-seat Rio Grande legislature.

Despite Ferrari's great personal popularity, his MTR elected only one federal and four state deputies. Whether he could have transformed this nascent labor reform movement into a significant political force soon became a hypothetical question. On May 25, 1963, he died in an airplane crash during a party-organizing trip in Rio Grande. At that time he was considering a try for mayor of Pôrto Alegre.[11]

The Gaúcho PTB lost the governorship in the 1962 election, but Brizola scored a stunning triumph in the Guanabara congressional contest. He captured 269,000 votes, the most ever obtained by a Brazilian federal deputy candidate, despite his being a Gaúcho in a foreign land. With this demonstration of power Brizola solidified his claim to the leadership of the radical left.

Three months later Brizola won another victory. Having helped push congress into rescheduling the plebiscite on parliamentarism for January 6, 1963, Brizola led the national campaign for the reestablishment of presidentialism under his brother-in-law. The plebiscite was strictly no-contest. Tired of the confusion of the parliamentary system, Brazil buried it by a five-to-one majority. Even in Rio Grande do Sul, home of parliamentarist spirit, the Liberator Party, and anti-Jangism, more than two-thirds of the voters favored presidentialism.[12]

Brizola's rapid rise to national prominence destroyed the well-functioning Borges de Medeiros-Pinheiro Machado working relationship that he and Jango had maintained since 1955. With no worlds left to conquer in Rio Grande, Brizola challenged his brother-in-law for national leadership of labor and the PTB while maintaining his stranglehold on the Gaúcho PTB. As in the 1930-37 era of Vargas, Aranha, and Flôres da Cunha, the struggle between Gaúchos became a national phenomenon.[13]

While Brizola moved further to the left, Goulart took the moderate route, relying as always on the Vargas-style politics of compromise. Unfortunately, although Jango had inherited some of Getúlio's political skills, he lacked the old master's sense of timing and uncanny ability to manipulate antagonistic elements.

During the first five months of his full-powered presidency, Jango tried to cope with Brazil's tremendous problems by means of a hybrid stabilization-development-reform program. This included such structural reforms as revisions in the tax system, a tepid assault on latifundia, restriction of foreign firms' remittances of profits, the purchase of foreign-owned utilities, and a mass literacy campaign. Like Brizola's literacy crash program in Rio Grande do Sul, this national literacy campaign doubled as a PTB electoral registration drive.

It was a modest reform program, as could have been expected from a rancher with conservative predispositions like João Goulart. But any governmental decision necessarily treaded heavily on some elements of the society. With his tendency to compromise and vacillate, Jango shifted from one economic policy to another under the influence of a myriad of advisers and pressure groups. By the end of 1963 Goulart's unpredictable, contradictory decisions had antagonized almost every economic interest, social group, political power center, and element of society.

To make matters worse, a growing minority of civilians and military men had concluded that the Third Republic had failed and they would have to resort to antidemocratic action to save the country. These included forces on the extreme right and the extreme left, both of which considered the Goulart government an unpalatable halfway house.

The extreme right consisted of those elements dedicated to bringing down the final curtain on the Vargas era. Their confidence in doing so by electoral means had declined after failing to defeat Vargas in 1950 and Goulart in 1955 and 1960. Twice they had ousted Vargas from the presidency; once they had pushed Goulart out of the ministry; twice they had failed to block Goulart's inauguration. They had just seen the voters restore to Jango the presidential powers which they had taken away. Although moderate anti-Getulists were willing to persevere with Jango until the 1965 presidential election, years of frustration had convinced those on the extreme right that only the surgery of force could remove the Vargas cancer which they felt had been poisoning Brazil for more than thirty years.

No less dedicated than the extreme right, the radical left was considerably less cohesive. The Communists were split between the more moderate, Moscow-oriented Brazilian Communist Party led by aging tenente Luis Carlos Prestes and the revolutionary, Peking-oriented Communist Party of Brazil. Both labor and students were splintered into various organizations, which jealously maintained their autonomy and cooperated only sporadically. These included the General Labor Command, labor's Unity and Action Pact, the National Union of Students, and Popular Action, the Catholic radical student movement. In the northeast the revolutionary Francisco Julião had formed the potentially powerful Peasant Leagues, which demanded an immediate redistribution of land.[14] Most important was Leonel Brizola, the self-proclaimed leader of the radical left. But while vying with Jango for national PTB leadership, Brizola had to face a new challenge to his authority in Rio Grande do Sul, this time from State Deputy Wilson Vargas.

Like José Diogo, Danton Coelho, Loureiro da Silva, and Fernando Ferrari before him, Wilson Vargas was rebelling against the authoritarian PTB chieftain structure. Vargas had been one of Brizola's former confidants and his state energy and communications secretary, in which role he had specialized in expropriations. He also had been Brizola's hand-picked candidate in a losing cause against Loureiro da Silva in the 1959 Pôrto Alegre mayoralty contest. But Vargas' immense popularity within the Gaúcho PTB had made him a threat to Brizola's autocratic state control.

The climax came when Vargas decided to make a second bid to become mayor of Pôrto Alegre in 1963. In a bitter struggle for the PTB nomination, Brizola succeeded in imposing State Deputy Sereno Chaise. One of Brizola's best friends and his former roommate, Chaise was a weak populist imitation of the former governor.

The PTB internal contest proved to be more dramatic than the November 1963 election. As in 1959 the anti-PTB forces split and nominated two candidates—the MTR's Cândido Norberto dos Santos and the ADP's Sinval Guazzelli, both popular young state deputies. In contrast to 1959 neither candidate succeeded in identifying himself to the voters as the principal anti-PTB candidate. Despite lengthy negotiations the rival anti-PTB forces failed to reach a compromise to support a single candidate.[15]

By far the strongest unity candidate would have been Cândido Norberto. A matinee idol, he had used his popularity as a sportscaster and television soap-opera star to become one of Rio Grande's leading vote-getters. But the reformist Norberto was an individualist in the Jânio Quadros mold and one of the few politicians who had effectively defied the Gaúcho curse on turncoats. Relying on personal popularity rather than on party support, he had been elected state deputy successively on the Socialist, Liberator, and Labor Renovation tickets. After their unhappy experience with Quadros, the conservative forces preferred to lose with Guazzelli than win with the independent, unpredictable Norberto.

Lose they did. Blighted by the certainty of defeat, the anti-PTB forces failed to generate the enthusiasm or effectiveness of the Loureiro crusade. With the powerful Pôrto Alegre PTB machine behind him, Sereno Chaise obtained 100,075 votes, more than the combined total of Norberto's 55,725 and Guazzelli's 40,481.[16]

The PTB fared less well in the interior, where the ADP captured nearly two-thirds of the counties. Three factors took a toll of Labor candidates—ADP control of state government patronage and electoral machinery, increased PTB disorganization in the interior due to Brizola's concentration on national politics, and the continued backlash against Brizolism. This did not greatly upset Brizola, who had dedicated himself to gaining national leadership of the PTB and the radical left.

As in Rio Grande, Brizola employed radio as a primary weapon, using his personally controlled nationwide chain, Radio Mayrink Veiga. As parallel arms he established a weekly newspaper, *O Panfleto,* and a system of Groups of Eleven, small guerrilla reserve units theoretically prepared to move into action rapidly like the historical Gaúcho provisional corps. Moreover, Brizola was nominal leader of the Popular Mobilization Front, formed in April 1963 in an attempt to unite and coordinate diverse organizations of the radical left.[17]

As his political-military organization grew, Brizola increased his criticism of Jango's moderate reform program, becoming more extreme in his demands and threatening force if they were not fulfilled. These demands included the replacement of congress by a constituent assembly to draw up a new constitution, the right to vote for illiterates, a moratorium on the payment of the foreign debt, and federal control over the conservative Brazilian press.

Brizola's radicalism undermined Jango's left flank. Labor unions, increasingly dominated by Communists and extreme leftists, began to switch their allegiance from Jango to Brizola. Numerous PTB elements, particularly those more radically oriented, viewed Brizola as de facto party leader. They repudiated Jango, who was still trying to function on the basis of the outdated PSD-PTB alliance. Confident in their growing strength, Brizola and his followers rejected Jango's attempts to create a united front of moderate and radical leftists.

In contrast, the extreme right not only welcomed but even appealed to frightened moderates and centrists to join their antigovernment, antiradical revolutionary cause. Faced with an increasing lack of discipline in the lower ranks of the military, officers began to fear the loss of control in the command hierarchy. Faced with the spectre of growing labor militancy, officers also began to fear the loss of position in the national structure. [18]

Large landowners who had supported or allied with rancher Vargas because he had restricted reforms to the city now confronted a serious movement for agrarian reform led by his political heirs. Moreover, the increased activity of the Peasant Leagues and rural unions, including sporadic land seizures, terrified the landowners, who expanded their private armies and increased their supplies of arms and ammunition.

Since these landowners formed the base of the conservative PSD, their growing reaction had grave implications for the eternal PSD-PTB alliance, which began to collapse. Brizola accelerated this process by seizing from Jango much of the control over the PTB and thereby radicalizing the party image. Fearing the destruction of the nation's socioeconomic structure, the PSD found itself being forced into an alliance with the anti-Vargas UDN.

As the extreme right sucked moderates into its camp and the Brizola-led radicals undermined Jango's student, labor, and PTB support, the president found his moderate leftist base disappearing. He decided that there was no future in continued efforts to manipulate centrist elements. So Goulart opted to move toward the left, attracted by its verve, blatancy, claims of power, and sense of impending victory.

At first Jango moved with characteristic indecision. The first crisis occurred in September 1963, when six hundred military non-commissioned officers and enlisted men staged an abortive attempt to take over the federal government in Brasília. Their revolt quickly shattered, the rebels asserted that they had acted merely to express their grievances, particularly against a court decision barring them from running for elective office. Faced with this serious challenge to military discipline, Goulart chose neutrality, neither criticizing nor defending the rebels.[19]

The following month, in a move reminiscent of Getúlio, Jango tried to stampede congress into voting a thirty-day state of siege on the grounds of increased nationwide violence and strikes. When congressional leaders responded with suspicious hesitation, the uncertain president backed down. Simultaneously Goulart failed in an inept plot to arrest Carlos Lacerda, his most outspoken rightist antagonist, and Pernambuco governor Miguel Arraes, the northeastern equivalent of Leonel Brizola and a serious rival for Jango's control of the Labor Party in that region.[20]

Goulart's hesitant steps to the left had resulted in a series of fiascos. His extremist advisers convinced him that he would have to act more decisively to galvanize popular forces against his implacable enemies—the exploitive alliance of domestic elites and foreign interests. Against his moderate nature, Goulart allowed himself to be drawn into a radical stance in competition with his brother-in-law.

The "new" Goulart made his debut at a massive March 13, 1964, rally in Rio de Janeiro, with 150,000 present and millions more watching on nationwide television. Shedding his history of moderation, Jango announced plans to make illiterates and military enlisted men eligible to vote (only officers could vote), overhaul the tax structure, and institute other reforms. To dramatize his resolve, he publicly signed two decrees nationalizing private oil refineries and legalizing the expropriation of certain lands bordering federal irrigation and drainage projects, highways, railways, and dams.[21]

Radical activities increased. On March 26 more than one thousand sailors and marines staged a protest revolt. They barricaded themselves in the headquarters of the metallurgical workers' union in Rio in protest against the navy's attempt to repress the Sailors' Association, a new, radical, naval enlisted men's union. To resolve the crisis, Goulart selected a new naval minister from a list of candidates presented by the increasingly radical General Labor Command. The minister's first act was to grant full amnesty to the rebel sailors. Four nights later, as if to condone the destruction of military discipline, Goulart spoke to a meeting of army sergeants.[22]

The March 13 rally convinced the opposition that Goulart had cast his lot with the radicals. It also increased fears that Jango was planning to extend his presidency by antidemocratic means in the Vargas manner. A number of senior military officers who in October 1963 had formed a defensive conspiracy against a possible leftist coup now shifted to the offensive. Goulart's tacit sanction of the March 26 sailors' revolt solidified the movement by impelling military moderates toward revolution as the only solution. Frightened civilian moderates looked to the military for salvation. The governors of Brazil's four most important states—São Paulo, Minas Gerais, Rio Grande do Sul, and Guanabara—also joined the conspiracy, although state-level preparations had begun long before the military decided to act.[23]

In reality, from the moment Ildo Meneghetti became governor of Rio Grande following his 1962 electoral victory, the Gaúcho Popular Democratic Action forces had begun to make plans to transform Rio Grande into a new citadel of legality. But this time the aim was to block the suspected continuist coup of João Goulart.

To offset Brizola's Groups of Eleven, the ADP organized a series of counterinsurgency reserve units known as Groups of Twenty. Governor Meneghetti also met with General Olympio Mourão Filho, who commanded the army garrison in Santa Maria until transferred to São Paulo in February 1963. The two discussed what was to become known as Operation Farroupilha, a plan to resist in Rio Grande against any attempt of Jango to extend his stay in power. Operation Farroupilha rested on two basic premises: first, there would be close Third Army-Gaúcho government cooperation; second, strongholds of resistance would be established in the strategic railroad centers of Santa Maria and Passo Fundo, sites of large Gaúcho military brigade contingents.[24]

The Rio Grande government maintained constant communications with the other major anti-Jango governors via Treasury Secretary José Antônio Aranha and Interior Secretary Mário

Mondino. Except for São Paulo's governor Adhemar de Barros, who called for immediate action in late 1963, the other governors opted for a defensive alliance along the lines of Flôres da Cunha's state autonomy pact of 1937. They even contemplated establishing a provisional revolutionary government in the Paraná coastal forests as the heart of democratic resistance should a leftist coup occur and the military not oppose it. [25]

But the military did act, before any leftist coup could occur. Conspirators scheduled a revolt for April 2, but at dawn on March 31, 1964, General Mourão Filho, now commander of the Fourth Military Region in Minas Gerais, marched on Rio, precipitating events. João Goulart, then in Rio, sent troops from Guanabara to crush the revolt. However, it soon became apparent that these forces would not sacrifice themselves for his discredited government. When Jango rejected an appeal from General Amaury Kruel, commander of the Second Army in São Paulo, to renounce the support of the General Labor Command in order to save his presidency, Kruel also ordered his troops to move on Rio.

Realizing the futility of remaining in Rio, Jango flew to Brasília at noon on April 1. Finding the situation equally hopeless in the federal capital, the president flew to Pôrto Alegre that same night. Brizola had already returned to Pôrto Alegre and had begun to mobilize pro-Jango resistance.

In an expedient but flagrantly unconstitutional act, Senate president Auro Moura de Andrade ruled that the presidency was vacant. He then swore in chamber of deputies president Ranieri Mazzilli as acting president of the country, which he had been for a short time in 1961. [26] With Mazzilli as acting president, the anti-Goulart military in control of central Brazil, and Goulart and Brizola back in Pôrto Alegre to make a last stand, it appeared as if the Legality movement might be reenacted.

But three years had wrought a tremendous change in the Gaúcho polity. The strife-ridden state had become more reminiscent of the divided Rio Grande of October 1937 than the united Rio Grande of August 1961. The increased radicalism of Brizola and Goulart had deepened existent Gaúcho divisions by adding the threat of class warfare. Repeated, unpredictable strikes by Brizola-led unions had created perpetual turmoil, particularly in such labor centers as Pôrto Alegre, Santa Maria, and Rio Grande. The PTB-backed Landless Farmers' Movement and the Gaúcho

Agrarian Front had been invading and settling on large farms and ranches, with the support of the federal Superintendency of Agrarian Reform Policy. Finally, less than two weeks prior to the revolution, Pôrto Alegre's Radio Metropole had inaugurated the "Hour of Enlightenment," a daily noontime program featuring inflammatory speeches of Brizola and other PTB leaders.

In addition to the deep state divisions, there were other basic differences between the Rio Grandes of August 1961 and April 1964. Brizola did not control the Gaúcho government as in 1961, but rather the anti-Jango Ildo Meneghetti governed the state. The Third Army commander was not a strong legalist but rather a general with little commitment to the Goulart government. The Third Army did not operate with its previous cohesion and responsiveness to its commander but instead functioned as a collection of semiautonomous units under the direction of their individual commanders. Finally the major unit commanders were not pro-Jango but instead committed themselves to the revolution. [27]

Throughout late 1963 and early 1964, the anti-Goulart conspirators had subverted army garrisons in Rio Grande. In addition the Gaúcho government had made preliminary agreements for emergency action with the Third Army commander, General Benjamin Rodrigues Galhardo. The government even had prepared unsigned decrees requisitioning radio stations, fuel reserves, and vehicles. In case of revolution these would be issued with the joint signatures of Meneghetti and Galhardo. [28]

Nevertheless, General Mourão Filho's precipitated revolt caught the Gaúcho conspirators by surprise on March 31. So did the sudden, perplexing news that Goulart had removed Galhardo as Third Army commander and replaced him with General Ladário Pereira Telles, who would arrive from Rio the following morning with Brizola. Despite his previous commitments to Meneghetti, Galhardo accepted the orders and flew to Rio. Finding himself without the expected army support and fearing that resistance in Pôrto Alegre might make the capital the site of a devastating civil war, Meneghetti and some close advisers flew to Passo Fundo. Here Meneghetti reestablished his state government in the Turis Hotel, which became known as the Palace of Liberty.

Passo Fundo rested astride the single railroad line running north into Santa Catarina. Following the general concept of Operation Farroupilha, state government leaders planned to try to make that northeastern Gaúcho city a sort of screen between the rebels in the rest of Brazil and pro-Goulart forces in Rio Grande.[29] To do so, Meneghetti mobilized the local military brigade garrison and appealed for volunteer units throughout northeastern Rio Grande. Among those who answered the call was octogenarian Colonel Victor Dumoncel Filho, Flôres da Cunha's main northern caudilho, who had fallen with his chief in 1937. Dumoncel organized a unit on his Santa Barbara ranch to renew the anti-Vargas fight he had lost nearly thirty years earlier.

Meneghetti's assumption was that Brizola would try to rally the Gaúchos to Jango's defense as he had in 1961, and Brizola did try. He and his aides resurrected the Legality network on April 1 in the Pôrto Alegre city hall, where Brizola's protégé, Sereno Chaise, was mayor. General Ladário Pereira Telles, who had come with Brizola to take over the Third Army, had his troops occupy all Pôrto Alegre radio and television stations. He also federalized and requisitioned the state military brigade as Dutra had done in 1937.

But General Ladário quickly learned that he held no more than nominal military control. Brigade commander Colonel Otávio Frota and Interior Secretary Mário Mondino rejected the requisition order on the grounds that it could be issued only by Governor Meneghetti. Most of the interior army garrisons sided with the revolution, and troops began to converge on Pôrto Alegre, practically the only Jangist "stronghold" in Rio Grande. Brizola's radio pleas to the sergeants in the interior units to revolt and overpower their officers brought no response.

Euphoric memories of 1961 soon gave way to harsh realities as reports arrived of rebel successes throughout Brazil and pro-revolutionary defections in interior Rio Grande. The six thousand people around the city hall began to disperse. Even the "faithful" inside city hall left, choosing discretion over valor.[30]

The most important defector was Jango himself. On April 2, the morning after his arrival in Pôrto Alegre, Goulart met with Brizola and three leading generals. Brizola and General Ladário called on the president to establish his national government in the Piratini Palace, with Brizola as justice minister and Ladário as war minister. General Floriano Machado countered by informing Jango of the desperate military situation and the impossibility of successful resistance. Still Brizola appealed to his brother-in-law to fight to the finish.[31] According to Brizola, the lack of a heroic, bloody tradition lay at the heart of Brazil's national weakness. A last stand in Pôrto Alegre could give the country the tempering of blood and spiritual strength it lacked.[32]

But Jango wanted no bloodshed. Sparing the Gaúcho capital, he flew to São Borja. On April 4, just four days after the beginning of the revolution, Goulart and his family escaped to Uruguay, traditional home of Gaúcho exiles.[33]

With the symbol of resistance gone, Brizola's incantations from the city hall balcony evoked little enthusiasm. As a final gesture of disdain for the revolution and show of bravado, Brizola refused to go immediately into exile. Instead he traversed the sprawling ranches of the Gaúcho frontier zone for a few weeks, eluding army pursuers. Having proven his bravery to his own satisfaction, Brizola followed his brother-in-law into Uruguayan exile.

In 1937 the exile of Gaúcho chieftain Flôres da Cunha had solidified the Vargas era in Brazilian politics. Twenty-seven years later the exile of two more Gaúchos brought the Vargas era to an end. In the words of Rio Grande historian Moysés Vellinho, "Getúlio Vargas killed himself on August 24, 1954, but it can be said that he has just been buried, almost ten years after that pathetic day."

PART FOUR

Epilogue

11

Elections of 1966

For the fifth time in twenty-five years the military had deposed a president (1930, 1945, 1954, 1955, and 1964). After each previous episode it had permitted a civilian to take over the vacant office.* This time the military decided that the ravaged nation could no longer be left to the politicians, who had created turmoil with their ineptitude, opportunism, and corruption. Like the 1930 tenentes, the 1964 military revolutionaries, including such old tenentes as Eduardo Gomes, Juarez Távora, and Juracy Magalhães, sought national moral regeneration, political cleansing, and economic reform.

Despite Mazzilli's presence as interim president, de facto power lay with the Supreme Revolutionary Command, composed of the three military ministers. After vainly waiting a few days for congress to pass the recommended housecleaning measures, the Revolutionary Command issued an institutional act on April 9.[1] The act ordered congress to elect a new national president immediately, drastically altered the 1946 constitution, and assured the new government "the means indispensable to the work of economic, financial, political, and moral reconstruction of Brazil." The act also gave the new president power to ram constitutional amendments and other legislation through congress, to dismiss public employees with job tenure, to cancel the mandates of congressmen, and to suspend the political rights of any citizen for ten years. Governors, too, were empowered to dismiss employees

---

*In 1945 the military permitted the scheduled presidential election. Although the eventual winner was a general, Eurico Gaspar Dutra, he was elected directly by the people as candidate of a political party and served as a civilian rather than as a military president.

and cancel mandates of state assemblymen and county councilmen.

Two days later congress dutifully elected the new president, Marshal Humberto Castelo Branco, former army chief of staff. To give "balance" to the ticket it also elected a civilian vice-president, Minas Gerais PSD federal deputy José Maria Alkmin, formerly Kubitschek's finance minister.

Armed with the new, extraordinary governmental powers, the military declared war on Communism, corruption, and the legacy of the Vargas heirs. It initiated an austerity program to stem Brazil's dazzling inflation and reduce government corruption and bureaucratic ineptitude, instituted nearly six hundred investigations of the Goulart era, and purged labor unions and student organizations. Furthermore, it discharged or retired hundreds of military officers, removed thousands of government employees, and canceled the mandates of more than one hundred governors, senators, congressmen, state assemblymen, and other elected officials, including Goulart, Brizola, and Senator Kubitschek. These three, plus Jânio Quadros and hundreds of others, lost their political rights.[2]

The axe fell hardest on the PTB and, by extension, on Rio Grande do Sul. Within the first month the federal government removed from office and suspended the political rights of Goulart, Brizola, three of the state's fourteen congressmen, three of the twenty-three Gaúcho PTB state assemblymen, the mayors of Pôrto Alegre, Santa Maria, and Rio Grande, and twenty-nine other elected officials.[3] Over the more than two years that the government retained such drastic powers, twenty-two Gaúcho assemblymen lost their mandates and political rights, more than in any other state.

In addition to purging much of the opposition leadership, the military also mobilized civilian political support. It helped form the Revolutionary Parliamentary Bloc, led by Gaúcho UDN senator Daniel Krieger, who considered himself heir to the Pinheiro Machado-Flôres da Cunha national political boss role. Although based on the anti-Vargas UDN, the bloc included one-third of the PSD delegation and more than one-fifth of the PTB congressmen, who rejected the doomed attempt of Goulart and Brizola to maintain party control from Montevideo. Finally, to assure continuity and reduce electoral agitation, the government postponed the presidential election from 1965 to 1966 and extended President Castelo Branco's term until March 15, 1967.[4]

Despite government purges the 1965 gubernatorial elections, which were held in eleven states, reflected a partial repudiation of the 1964 revolution and the unpopularity of the government's deflationary policies. The opposition scored major triumphs in Guanabara and Minas Gerais, defeating the UDN gubernatorial candidates.[5] Perceiving this warning signal, the government issued a series of major electoral reforms prior to the 1966 election. These were intended to strengthen the government politically, assure the election of a pro-1964 revolution president, and prevent the loss of other major state governorships, primarily in São Paulo and Rio Grande do Sul.

To give itself closer "supervision" over the choice of federal and state executives, the revolutionary government canceled direct popular elections for president and governors, decreeing instead that congress would elect the president and that state legislatures would elect the governors. In addition, indirect gubernatorial elections were scheduled to be held prior to the direct congressional and state legislative contests. This would give the party of the newly elected governor a tremendous advantage in the direct elections, because it could appeal to the electorate with the promise of assured gubernatorial power and patronage.

The government also established a new system for senatorial elections. Each party could nominate as many as three candidates for a senatorial seat, and their votes would be totaled. Victory would go to the party with the highest vote total; then the candidate with the most votes on the winning party's ticket would be declared the victor. A "linked vote" system was instituted, making it mandatory for the elector to vote for federal and state deputy candidates of the same party.

Finally, in federal and state deputy elections, the government restricted the use of the single ballot to state capitals and cities of at least one hundred thousand people. In cities of less than one hundred thousand, candidates would have to distribute their own individual ballots. This increased the power of the interior political bosses, who could influence and restrict the distribution of the ballots.[6]

By these measures the government changed the rules of the game. It also changed the names of the players by decreeing the extinction of the old political parties and establishing legal conditions for the creation in their place of two electoral alliances, one progovernment and one antigovernment.[7] Like Raul Pilla and the PL, who saw presidentialism as the source of Brazil's evils and parliamentarism as the national panacea, another group felt the multiparty system's fragmenting effect was the basis of Brazil's ills. This group believed that a two-party system in the U.S. mold would lead to more effective democracy. The 1961 Legality movement had brought an unsuccesful parliamentarist experiment; the 1964 revolution now brought an unexpected two-party system (although officially termed electoral alliances, the two new aggregations functioned as political parties).

The government forces chose the name National Renovation Alliance (ARENA—Aliança Renovadora Nacional), while the opposition united as the Brazilian Democratic Movement (MDB—Movimento Democrático Brasileiro). As the thirteen congressional parties contracted into two new aggregations, ARENA emerged with a 43-to-21 lead in the senate and a 254-to-150 majority in the chamber of deputies.

In most states the now partyless politicians engaged in a wild scramble to form ad hoc progovernment and antigovernment alliances; but in Rio Grande do Sul the official decrees had little impact. Rio Grande had long been a polarized, de facto two-party state, calcified through years of struggle and elections. The federal decrees merely brought a name change and the institutionalization of an existing state of affairs.

In Rio Grande the PSP and the five Popular Democratic Action parties maintained their 1962 electoral alliance, merely adopting the ARENA name. The MDB became basically an expanded PTB. Since Fernando Ferrari's MTR had begun as a dissident movement within the PTB, it naturally selected the MDB as the most acceptable alternative. In addition, a small part of the PSD, a minority wing of the PDC, and the weak Socialist Republican Alliance (ARS—Aliança Republicana Socialista) entered the MDB. These Social Democrats were mainly the personal followers of former president Kubitschek, whom the revolutionary government had stripped of his political rights. The MDB Christian Democrats generally were members of Christian Democratic Youth and other radical supporters of Paulo de Tarso, a national PDC leader and Goulart's education minister. The Socialist

Republican Alliance was a fusion of the Brazilian Socialist Party and the Rio Grande do Sul section of the Minas-based Republican Party. Although nationally the Republican Party was a core of Brazilian conservatism, the Gaúcho PR merely served as an electoral front for Communist candidates.

By sheer mathematics the uniting of the one ARS, four MTR, and twenty-three PTB deputies within the MDB should have given the latter a twenty-eight-to-twenty-seven margin over ARENA, composed of eleven PSD, six PL, four PDC, three PRP, and three UDN deputies. But, as during the Vargas-Flôres struggle, state deputies became objects of great government attention. In contrast to the 1936-37 contest, when there were offsetting pressures by federal and state authorities, the 1965-66 reorganization found ARENA in control of both the presidency and the governorship. Through this combined pressure ARENA obtained the adhesion of a single MTR state deputy, Heitor Campos. With this lone addition ARENA erected a single-vote majority, of utmost importance in the upcoming assembly election of the new governor.

The 1962 struggle over the selection of a gubernatorial candidate had almost destroyed the Popular Democratic Action alliance. Another gubernatorial conflict threatened to shatter ARENA in 1966. Two major factions formed behind Labor Minister Walter Peracchi Barcellos and Federal Deputy Tarso Dutra, both veteran Social Democrats who had failed in previous gubernatorial bids.

As President Castelo Branco's "man in Rio Grande," Peracchi based his strength on his own PSD minority wing and most of the alliance's former National Democratic Unionists, Liberators, and Christian Democrats. Dutra's power rested on the bulk of the Gaúcho Social Democrats and the cohesive former PRP. He also had close political ties with War Minister Marshal Arthur da Costa e Silva, a Gaúcho and odds-on favorite to succeed Castelo Branco as president.

Unhappy with the ex-PSD's apparent domination of ARENA, a minor third force emerged within the government alliance, led by PL federal deputy Carlos de Britto Velho, three PL state deputies, and two PDC state deputies. This movement reflected both the historical Liberator oppositionist tradition and the anti-Getulist supermorality of these dissidents, who still considered the

PSD to be tainted with the original sin of having been founded by Vargas.

To counter PSDism, the dissidents proposed that ARENA nominate Dr. Ruy Cirne Lima, an eminent Pôrto Alegre lawyer. Although he had never participated actively in politics, Cirne Lima had served with distinction for a short period as finance secretary in the postrevolution Meneghetti government. The dissidents argued that by being both prorevolution and nonpolitical, Cirne Lima would be an ideal unifying symbol for the state. Mathematically the Cirne Lima candidacy would assure a twenty-eight-to-twenty-seven ARENA gubernatorial victory in the assembly. This was not the case with Peracchi or Dutra, since the five dissident state deputies refused to support either ex-Social Democrat. But neither PSD contender would permit an outsider to preempt his holy grail.

Repeated statements by revolutionary leaders, like ARENA national president Daniel Krieger, had made it clear that the federal government would not permit the opposition to elect any governors.[8] So the Gaúcho MDB tried a clever gambit. Rather than nominate one of its own members, the MDB took advantage of the ARENA division and gave its official, if not spiritual, support to Ruy Cirne Lima.

One week before the ARENA convention, the twenty-seven MDB and four of the ARENA dissident state deputies, with the pledge of support from still another ARENA deputy then in the United States, invited Cirne Lima to be their candidate in the name of the assembly majority.[9] When he accepted, the MDB officially nominated him.[10] As in the cases of the United Front of 1929-30, the modus vivendi of January 1936, and the Gaúcho parliamentarist constitution of 1947, Liberators had made a pact with their enemies to secure what they considered to be worthy ends.

Meanwhile the major ARENA contestants struggled to the finish. In a bitter convention battle Peracchi defeated Dutra by 252 to 236, with 15 votes going to Cirne Lima.[11] Castelo Branco's presidential leverage had conquered Tarso Dutra's state-girdling machine. The president then turned his attention to the MDB challenge.

Faced with a potential thirty-two-to-twenty-three Cirne Lima triumph, Castelo Branco used his presidential powers to secure victory for his protégé, Peracchi Barcellos. First he canceled the mandates of seven MDB deputies; then he issued the bizarre Complementary Act No. 16, known as the Act of Party Fidelity. This made it illegal for legislators of one party to vote for the presidential, vice-presidential, or gubernatorial candidates of the other party.[12] Since Cirne Lima was officially the MDB candidate, the decree prevented the five ARENA dissidents from voting for him.

With his candidacy dead, Cirne Lima withdrew. The fifty-five-seat Rio Grande do Sul assembly then "elected" Peracchi Barcellos governor by twenty-three votes to zero.[13] In a historical sense Castelo Branco had resurrected the role of Getúlio Vargas by making himself Rio Grande's Great Elector. Peracchi Barcellos was less a state-elected governor than a presidentially anointed interventor in the tradition of Daltro Filho, Cordeiro de Farias, and Ernesto Dornelles.

As in 1945, 1954, and 1961, reaction from all sectors exploded against this new federal assault on Gaúcho rights, providing the MDB with an emotional electoral appeal–a vote for the MDB would be a vote against this federal attack on Gaúcho autonomy, a traditional Rio Grande political theme. This MDB emotional advantage was offset by a number of negative factors. For the first time the legislative election came after rather than simultaneously with the gubernatorial election. This greatly favored ARENA, which already had captured the statehouse and could use its clientelist, municipal-level approach much more effectively. In contrast, the MDB already had lost the governorship, preventing a campaign based on the potential linkage of local interests to the state executive. It could not offer the hope of the immediate conquest of power, but could only criticize the government and attempt to turn the election into a plebiscite on the revolution.[14]

The Gaúcho MDB also suffered from the destruction of most of its leadership. The two-year government purge had decimated the Gaúcho PTB. With the exile of Goulart and Brizola and the loss of rights of most of the other major Gaúcho PTB figures, state PTB leadership had fallen to State Deputy Siegfried Emanuel Heuser, a moderate of the Egydio Michaelsen type. When the new political aggregations were created, the determined, efficient, but uninspiring Heuser naturally assumed the MDB presidency.

Government pressure also hampered the MDB's electoral activities. Many ranchers, industrialists, and businessmen who normally supported the PTB refrained in 1966 out of fear of government reprisal. To avoid losing their political rights, most PTB candidates conducted moderate campaigns of tepid criticism. Finally, the military in the interior harassed the opposition with such acts as confiscating pro-MDB newspapers and impeding the distribution of MDB ballots.[15]

A serious tactical error in the senatorial contest also hurt the MDB. ARENA took full advantage of the new electoral system by nominating three senatorial candidates—PRP senator Guido Mondim, PDC state deputy Mario Mondino, and UDN state deputy Synval Guazzelli. The MDB nominated only state party president Siegfried Heuser, who chose to conduct a campaign of moderation of the type used by PTB gubernatorial candidate Michaelsen in 1962. He courted independent centrist voters by presenting himself as a candidate of moderate opposition to the revolution.

There was a movement among Brizolists for the nomination of a second MDB senatorial candidate, Mariano Beck, who had been Brizola's former education secretary and the losing PTB senatorial candidate in 1962. In contrast to Heuser, who was a moderate Lutheran, Beck was both a practicing Catholic and a Brizola-style populist. But Heuser feared that Beck might obtain more votes, defeat him, and oust him from party leadership. Confident of victory on the basis of Gaúcho wounded pride and antirevolutionary sentiment, Heuser blocked Beck's nomination.

Heuser's strategy failed. Although the MDB triumphed in the chamber and assembly contests and although Heuser obtained the largest vote of any individual senatorial candidate, his 638,140 votes fell short of the 672,480 total of the three ARENA candidates.[16] MDB superiority in the proportional elections did not transfer to the senatorial contest, mainly because the more radical Brizolists defected out of anger at Heuser's moderate campaign. Had Mariano Beck run with Heuser, they undoubtedly would have defeated the ARENA trio. Instead many of the more radical MDB supporters expressed their disenchantment with Heuser by the traditional Brazilian protest act of incorrectly marking and thereby nullifying their senatorial ballots.

Other defecting MDB votes went to the ex-UDN's Synval Guazzelli, whom some considered more liberal than Heuser, and the ex-PRP's Guido Mondim.[17] The latter, the most conservative candidate, received votes from some Laborites who had supported him in 1958 as Brizola's running mate and still identified him with the exiled populist. This MDB failure to "reeducate" the Labor voter in the interior reflected both the inadequacy of MDB electoral publicity and the government's success in restricting the MDB campaign.

MDB defections gave a gift victory to Mondim, the PRP land-scape painter. Although little more than half of Heuser's total, Mondim's 322,901 votes topped Guazzelli's 206,917 and Mondino's 142,662. It was an ironic turn of events. Elected in 1958 on Brizola's coattails, Mondim rode to victory in 1966 on the strength of the electoral error of Siegfried Heuser and the political machine of Tarso Dutra, who backed Mondim in exchange for the PRP's support of his gubernatorial bid.

In the proportional elections, the MDB won by 693,998 to 658,760 in the chamber balloting and by 694,970 to 675,957 in the assembly voting.* As a result, the MDB gained a twenty-eight-to-twenty-seven edge in the state assembly, reversing the one-vote margin which ARENA had acquired in a nonelectoral manner by corralling MTR deputy Heitor Campos. In the chamber contest the MDB captured fifteen seats, the same number that the PTB and MTR had obtained in 1962, while ARENA won fourteen seats, equal to the 1962 ADP total. Since Paulo Brossard de Souza Pinto, one of the ARENA dissidents, captured a congressional seat on the MDB ticket, it could be argued that ARENA actually deserved the fifteen-to-fourteen bulge. However, had Brossard run on the ARENA ticket and taken most of his votes with him, the MDB might still have won the election and maintained its fifteen-to-fourteen edge.

The 1966 elections provided a fitting epilogue for the turbu-lent Gaúcho political era which had begun with one revolution in 1930 and ended with another in 1964. In one sense the elections confirmed the continuity of Gaúcho political traditions. However,

---

*The true difference between MDB and ARENA electoral strength was even smaller than that reflected by their ticket totals. As a result of preelection maneuvering, some ARENA dissidents ran on the MDB ticket. Their votes were, in effect, traditional anti-PTB votes being cast against the revolution rather than for the MDB. If ARENA dissident votes were deducted from the MDB total and added to the ARENA vote, a virtual dead heat would be created. The MDB won the chamber elections in only two other states—Guanabara and Rio de Janeiro.

at the same time, they gave indications that the essence of Gaúcho politics might be undergoing a basic transformation.

Traditions remained. Gaúchos continued to view elections as confrontations between the forces of Vargas and those who opposed the Vargas heritage. Rio Grande voters also retained their scorn for those they considered political turncoats. Except for the powerful Paulo Brossard de Souza Pinto, who narrowly won a chamber of deputies seat, all of the ARENA dissidents suffered defeat in their 1966 electoral bids. And the widespread Gaúcho outcry–"he can't do that to Rio Grande"–which erupted when President Castelo Branco mangled the Gaúcho assembly to "elect" his gubernatorial candidate, showed that, at least in the minds of some, the belief in Rio Grande autonomy had survived the buffetings of time and the realities of increasing federal power.

And yet there was something uncharacteristically hollow about the 1966 elections. Gone was the vibrancy that had marked past clashes between the Vargas and anti-Vargas armies. For the most part candidates ran low-key, moderate campaigns, partially out of fear of possible federal government nullification of overly critical antigovernment candidates.

Even Castelo Branco's single-handed defeat of Gaúcho majority gubernatorial candidate Ruy Cirne Lima took place in an almost matter-of-fact atmosphere–a far cry from the explosive tensions of past Gaúcho-federal confrontations. Angry but obviously ineffective Gaúcho protests against Castelo Branco's actions were but a faint echo of past protests of Vargas, Aranha, Flôres da Cunha, and Brizola. Rio Grande's days as a national political-military threat seemed to have ended.

12

Rio Grande in Retrospect

Although Rio Grande as a state had ceased to be a political-military threat, individual Gaúchos continued to be politically successful nationally and Gaúcho federal-level influence reached new heights. In October 1966, functioning under military supervision, congress elected War Minister Marshal Arthur da Costa e Silva, a Gaúcho, to the Brazilian presidency. Following Costa e Silva's death in 1969, another Gaúcho, General Emílio Garrastazú Médici, was chosen to succeed him. Of Italian and Basque ancestry, Garrastazú Médici became the first Gaúcho ethnic to reach the presidency. Garrastazú Médici selected still another Gaúcho—General Ernesto Geisel (a Lutheran of German descent)—as his successor in the presidency. Ratified by the obedient congress, Geisel was inaugurated in 1974.

As never before, Gaúchos obtained important decision-making posts in the federal government. In terms of Gaúchos in national power, 1967 more than reincarnated post-1930 revolutionary Brazil. As in 1930 there was a Gaúcho president—Costa e Silva. As in 1930 the major federal government political coordinator was a Gaúcho—Senator Daniel Krieger, president of ARENA. As in 1930 there were important Gaúcho ministers—Tarso Dutra of education and Colonel Mário Andreazza of transportation. Even more than in 1930 there were Gaúchos in important posts in the federal financial structure—the president of the Bank of Brazil, a director of the National Housing Bank, a director of the National Bank of Economic Development, and a director of the Central Bank of the Republic.

Costa e Silva's death and Garrastazú Médici's ascension to the presidency in 1969 increased Gaúcho federal power. Under Garrastazú Médici, Gaúcho military men held such posts as war minister, chief of the armed forces general staff, and governor of the Federal District. Riograndense João Leitão de Abreu became chief of the civil cabinet, the president's main civilian adviser. Colonel Andreazza continued as minister of transportation, and Gaúchos were named to the heads of other ministries—Luis Fernando Cirne Lima of agriculture, Marcos Vinicius Pratini de Morais of commerce and industry, and Colonel Higínio Corsetti of communications.[1]

Ary Burger, former Gaúcho finance secretary who became a director of the Central Bank of the Republic under Costa e Silva, summed up the significance of the many, broad-scale appointments for Rio Grande:

> I feel that these are unique conditions and that Rio Grande do Sul never had such possibilities. We must call attention to the following: ministries are not enough. It is necessary for Rio Grande do Sul to be represented in the key posts where finances are granted and funds are allocated. We have had previous experiences in which, with no scheme established as now, it was not enough to have several ministers, since we did not do much for our state. We hope that, with the aid of the state government in the elaboration of good plans for the solution of our problems, we in the federal government will be able to offer the maximum possible resources to transform these projects into reality.[2]

And the federal government has supplied considerable resources for Rio Grande. Transportation Minister Andreazza initiated a program for restructuring the outdated Rio Grande transportation system, including extensive highway building. Federal expansion of hydroelectric power in Rio Grande struck at another weakness of the Gaúcho economic infrastructure. Agriculture Minister Cirne Lima strongly supported Gaúcho agricultural and pastoral development, including experimentation with new strains of wheat capable of thriving in Rio Grande and the acceleration of the mass vaccination campaign inaugurated in 1965 to wipe out hoof-and-mouth disease.[3]

The result has been the beginning of what may be a Gaúcho economic renaissance. Wheat production, which had been suffering for decades, has risen dramatically as Rio Grande spearheads Brazil's struggle for self-sufficiency in that essential food product. With Rio Grande leading the way, Brazil has climbed to fifth in world tobacco production. The successful war on hoof-and-mouth disease has led to a meat export boom, while the Gaúcho shoe industry, one of the state's most prosperous, has vigorously expanded its production and exports. Rio Grande still faces major socioeconomic problems, but events of the last nine years indicate that the state may have turned the corner economically.[4]

At the same time, Gaúcho politics has become even less autonomous and more dominated from the federal level by the military government. In the 1970 Rio Grande gubernatorial election, President Garrastazú Médici rejected the candidates of the Peracchi Barcellos and Tarso Dutra factions of Gaúcho ARENA (including Dutra himself). Instead he saw to the election of Congressman Euclides Triches, former governor Ildo Meneghetti's secretary of public works and loser (to Leonel Brizola) in the 1955 Pôrto Alegre mayoralty election.[5]

With Rio Grande possibly entering a new, calmer political age, far less intense than the 1930-64 years, it is appropriate to ask the retrospective question—just what was the essence of Gaúcho politics during that turbulent era? Seven main factors formed the spine of Gaúcho political behavior during those years.

Basic was Rio Grande's apparently irresistible impulse to divide into two political camps, with historically durable political parties and alliances. In contrast, prior to 1937 the rest of Brazil was characterized by a series of unstable, transitory political alliances (three notable exceptions being the Paulista Republican Party, the Mineiro Republican Party, and the illegal Brazilian Communist Party). For six years beginning in 1945, Gaúchos experimented with a multiparty system as part of the new national multiparty system; but by 1951 Rio Grande had returned to its traditional duality. Following the 1964 revolution the military government decreed the extinction of existing parties and the establishment of a national two-party system. This set off a realignment scramble throughout the rest of Brazil, but in Rio Grande it merely institutionalized a long extant state of affairs.

Second, the two-party struggle generally took precedence over other Gaúcho political proclivities. Gaúchos normally elevated the quest for party victory over the advisability of state unity, the defense of state autonomy, or even the support of state political and economic interests. Only in rare moments did Gaúcho unity prevail over party divisiveness, as during the 1930 election and the 1930 and 1961 Rio Grande armed movements. The virulence of the conflict consistently undermined the state's national political position and economic well-being. In addition, the general refusal of Gaúcho parties to cooperate prevented Rio Grande from making best use of its potential strength and wealth. When the two-party struggle took the form of a clash between the Rio Grande government and Gaúchos in national government, the state as a whole usually became the loser. Such federal-state Gaúcho conflicts often restricted Rio Grande's ability to obtain federal benefits and sometimes caused the state to suffer federal recriminations.

Third, in the post-1950 era a delicate electoral equilibrium developed between the two political camps. Seldom did the governor have a solid assembly majority on which he could depend to implement his program. This equilibrium led to an alternation in power, with no party able to win the governorship twice in succession between 1947 and 1962. The absence of governmental continuity resulted in a concentration on short-range, stopgap programs. Even worse, incumbent politicians had to hasten to reap governmental benefits while they concentrated on fortifying their parties against the inevitable ensuing four years of opposition control.[6]

The two-camp struggle also modified the impact of the fourth Gaúcho political characteristic—the tendency to use Rio Grande military force to resolve national problems. Five times from 1930 to 1964 during national confrontations, Rio Grande proved the decisive element in Brazil's internal military balance of power. Three times Rio Grande functioned as a positive factor—twice installing a Gaúcho in the presidency (the 1930 revolution and 1961 Legality movement) and once enabling a Riograndense president to survive the military challenge of another state (the 1932 São Paulo revolution). Twice Rio Grande played an essentially negative role in the balance of power, permitting national military forces to carry the day. During these two other crises—the 1936-37 Flôres-Vargas struggle and the 1964 revolution—Rio Grande internal political strife negated potential military power.

A fifth element of Gaúcho politics was the belief in state

autonomy, a useful weapon brandished by politicians when it suited their purposes. However, when internal victory depended on federal support, Gaúcho leaders often forgot about state autonomy. At times they even appealed to the central government to intervene in Rio Grande.

Sixth, Gaúchos often seemed anxious to cleanse themselves of the historical taint of Gaúcho provincialism. Although they used Rio Grande as a base for personal projection on the national scene, once in power they tended to loosen ties with their home state, reject their "regional" pasts, and become "national" politicians. Although Gaúchos held the presidency for more than twenty-two of the thirty-four years between 1930 and 1964, this can not be viewed as Rio Grande's domination over Brazil. Only from 1930 to 1937 was the state of Rio Grande the prime force in Brazilian politics.

Finally, despite a modification of the traditional Gaúcho chieftain system during the Third Republic, personalism remained a major factor in Rio Grande politics. The post-1945 state political division was between the forces supporting and those opposing Vargas and his heirs, João Goulart and Leonel Brizola. The powerful national Brazilian Labor Party, whose leadership was composed heavily of Gaúchos and whose power base lay in Rio Grande, developed organizationally in the Gaúcho chieftain tradition under the autocratic leadership of Vargas, Goulart, and Brizola. In contrast, the Social Democratic Party and National Democratic Union developed as national alliances of state leaders, reminiscent of the First Republic's coalition of major states, the "Politics of the Governors."

Such were the principal characteristics of Gaúcho political behavior from 1930 to 1964. Not all of these traits were uniquely Gaúcho. In varying combinations and degrees, they may have provided part of the political patterns of other Brazilian states. However, it was this particular blend of characteristics which made Gaúcho politics special and distinctive.

For all of the harm that the old Gaúcho politics has caused for the state, it is still a cherished part of the Rio Grande heritage. Gaúchos are a proud people. They are proud of being different from other Brazilians. They are proud of their state's military history. They are proud of their party fidelity and political conflicts. They are proud of their heroes and leaders, even those against whom they have fought. They are proud of their state autonomy, even though it is more mythological than real and Gaúchos themselves have done damage to that myth when it suited their political purposes.

As well as pride, Gaúchos have *saudades* for their political past. A beautiful, nearly untranslatable Portuguese word, *saudade* approximates longing, remembrance, yearning, nostalgia . . . and more. Gaúchos look back on their political history with *saudades*–the knowledge that the old Gaúcho politics is gone. And as much as the deeply romantic Gaúcho might wish, it will never return.

Notes

Abbreviations Used in Notes

Archives
  ABA — Joaquim Francisco de Assis Brasil Archive
  ADS — Archives of the U.S. Department of State
  AMA — Francisco Antunes Maciel Junior Archive
  APR — Arquivo da Presidência da República
  BMA — Antônio Augusto Borges de Medeiros Archive
  GVA — Getúlio Vargas Archive
  LAA — Rony Lopes de Almeida Archive
  LCA — Lindolfo Collor Archive
  MFA — Afrânio de Melo Franco Archive
  OAA — Oswaldo Aranha Archive
  SSA — Sinval Saldanha Archive

Names in Correspondence Cited in Footnotes
  Alencastro — Napoleão de Alencastro Guimarães
  A. Aranha — Adalberto Aranha
  J. Aranha — José Antônio Aranha
  O. Aranha (Aranha) — Oswaldo Aranha
  Assis — Joaquim Francisco de Assis Brasil
  Borges — Antônio Augusto Borges de Medeiros
  Bueno — Lucillo Bueno
  Canto — José Bernardino de Camara Canto
  Cardoso — Maurício Cardoso
  Castleman — Reginald S. Castleman
  Collor — Lindolfo Collor
  Cordeiro — Oswaldo Cordeiro de Farias
  Daltro — Manoel de Cerqueira Daltro Filho

215

Diogo – José Diogo Brochado da Rocha
Dornelles – Ernesto Dornelles
E. Dutra (Dutra) – Eurico Gaspar Dutra
V. Dutra – Viriato Dutra
Esteves – Emílio Lúcio Esteves
Fernandes – Aguinaldo Fernandes
Flôres – José Antônio Flôres da Cunha
Góes – Pedro Aurélio Góes Monteiro
Lima – Bruno de Mendonça Lima
Lopes – Rony Lopes de Almeida
Loureiro – José Loureiro da Silva
Luzardo – João Baptista Luzardo
Maciel – Francisco Antunes Maciel Junior
Matta – Mário da Matta
Melo – Afrânio de Melo Franco
Morato – Francisco Morato
Neves – João Neves da Fontoura
Paim – Firmino Paim Filho
Pasqualini – Alberto Pasqualini
Pilla – Raul Pilla
Saldanha – Sinval Saldanha
Sarmanho – Walder Sarmanho
Tostes – Miguel Tostes
Valadares – Benedito Valadares
B. Vargas – Benjamin Vargas
G. Vargas (Vargas) – Getúlio Vargas
P. Vargas – Protásio Vargas
S. Vargas – Serafim Vargas
V. Vargas – Viriato Vargas

Miscellaneous Abbreviations
Brazil, CNE – Brazil, Conselho Nacional de Economia
Brazil, IBGE – Brazil, Instituto Brasileiro de Geografia e Estatística
Brazil, TSE – Brazil, Tribunal Superior Eleitoral
RGS – Rio Grande do Sul
RGS, TRE – Rio Grande do Sul, Tribunal Regional Eleitoral

Chapter 1: A Military Heritage

1. Geographical data drawn from Amyr Borges Fortes, *Panorama Econômico do Rio Grande do Sul* (Pôrto Alegre: Livraria Sulina, 1959), pp. 28-68.

2. Moysés Vellinho, *Capitania d'El-Rei. Aspectos Polémicos da Formação Rio-Grandense* (Pôrto Alegre: Editôra Globo, 1964), pp. 30-34.

3. José Honório Rodrigues, *O Continente do Rio Grande* (Rio de Janeiro: Edições S. José, 1954), pp. 55-60.

4. Alcides Lima, *História Popular do Rio Grande do Sul* (Pôrto Alegre: Edição da Livraria do Globo, 1935), pp. 190-91.

5. Among the major works on the Farroupilha era are Alfredo Varela, *História da Grande Revolução. O Ciclo Farroupilha no Brasil*, 6 vols. (Pôrto Alegre: Editôra Globo, 1933); Dante de Laytano, *História da República Riograndense, 1835-1845* (Pôrto Alegre: Editôra Globo, 1936); Walter Spalding, *A Revolução Farroupilha* (São Paulo: Editôra Nacional, 1939).

6. E.F. de Souza Docca, *História do Rio Grande do Sul* (Rio de Janeiro: Organização Simões, 1954), pp. 218-20, 230-37.

7. Ibid., pp. 377-79.

8. The material in this section is largely based on Richard Kornweibel, "Júlio de Castilhos and the Republican Party of Rio Grande do Sul" (Ph.D. diss., University of California, Santa Barbara, 1971).

9. Sérgio da Costa Franco, *Júlio de Castilhos e Sua Época* (Pôrto Alegre: Editôra Globo, 1967), pp. 62-65; idem, "O Sentido Histórico da Revolução de 1893," *Fundamentos da Cultura Rio-Grandense*, 5th ser. (1962), pp. 195-99.

10. Rio Grande do Sul, *Constituições Sul-Riograndenses, 1843-1947* (Pôrto Alegre: Imprensa Oficial, 1963), pp. 54-71.

11. Costa Franco, *Júlio de Castilhos*, pp. 145-52.

12. Miguel José Pereira, *Esboço Histórico da Brigada Militar do Rio Grande do Sul*, vol. 1, *Janeiro de 1890 a Julho de 1918*, 2d ed. (Pôrto Alegre: Oficinas Gráficas da Brigada Militar, 1950), pp. 60-333.

13. Joseph L. Love, *Rio Grande do Sul and Brazilian Regionalism, 1882-1930* (Stanford, Calif.: Stanford University Press, 1971), p. 72.

14. My concepts of Gaúcho history are the result not only of documentary research but also of many stimulating conversations with native and "naturalized" Gaúchos. Among those who gave me special insights into the Rio Grande phenomenon were José Fernando Carneiro, José Antônio Aranha, Erico Verissimo, Maurício Rosenblatt, Moysés Vellinho, and Leônidas Xausa.

Chapter 2: The Old Republic

1. Costa Franco, *Júlio de Castilhos*, p. 204.

2. Author's interviews with Raul Pilla, Pôrto Alegre, May 9, 1967, and José Diogo Brochado de Rocha, Pôrto Alegre, Jan. 10, 1967.

3. The best sources on the Borges de Medeiros era are João Neves da Fontoura, *Memórias*, 2 vols. (Pôrto Alegre: Editôra Globo, 1958-63); Love, *Rio Grande do Sul*.

4. Othelo Rosa, *Pinheiro Machado* (Pôrto Alegre, 1951), pp. 17-38; Love, *Rio Grande do Sul*, pp. 137-72.

5. Love, *Rio Grande do Sul*, pp. 188-96.

6. Glauco Carneiro, *História das Revoluções Brasileiras*, vol. 1, *Da Revolução da República à Coluna Prestes (1889/1927)* (Rio de Janeiro: Edições o Cruzeiro, 1965), pp. 227-37.

7. A discussion of the tenente phenomenon can be found in Virginia Santa Rosa, *Que Foi o Tenentismo?*, 2d ed. (Rio de Janeiro: Editôra Civilização Brasileira, 1963); Octavio

Malta, *Os Tenentes na Revolução Brasileira* (Rio de Janeiro: Editôra Civilização Brasileira, 1969).

8. Cited in Hélio Silva, *O Ciclo de Vargas*, vol. 1, *1922: Sangue na Areia de Copacabana* (Rio de Janeiro: Editôra Civilização Brasileira, 1964), p. 289.

9. The best picture of the 1923 revolution can be found in José Antônio Flôres da Cunha, *A Campanha de 1923* (Rio de Janeiro: Livraria-Editôra Zelio Valverde, [1942]).

10. Cited in Silva, *Sangue na Areia*, pp. 353-57.

11. Edgard Carone, *Revoluções do Brasil Contemporâneo, 1922/1938* (São Paulo: Coleção Buriti, 1965), pp. 49-57.

12. Arthur Ferreira Filho, *História Geral do Rio Grande do Sul, 1503-1964*, 3d ed. (Pôrto Alegre: Editôra Globo, 1965), pp. 167-69.

13. Hélio Silva, *O Ciclo de Vargas*, vol. 2, *1926: A Grande Marcha* (Rio de Janeiro: Editôra Civilização Brasileira, 1965), pp. 52-107.

14. Arthur Ferreira Filho, *Revoluções e Caudilhos*, 2d ed. (Pôrto Alegre: Editôra Querência, n.d.), p. 134.

15. Carone, *Revoluções do Brasil*, pp. 62-64.

16. Joaquim Luis Osorio, *Partidos Políticos no Rio Grande do Sul. Período Republicano* (Pôrto Alegre: Livraria do Globo, 1930), pp. 235-70.

17. Author's interview with Raul Pilla, Pôrto Alegre, May 9, 1967.

18. Author's interview with José Antônio Aranha, Pôrto Alegre, Aug. 4, 1966.

19. Jordan M. Young, *The Brazilian Revolution of 1930 and the Aftermath* (New Brunswick, N.J.: Rutgers University Press, 1967), pp. 29, 37-38; Love, *Rio Grande do Sul*, pp. 221-25.

20. [Alexandre José] Barbosa Lima Sobrinho, *A Verdade sôbre a Revolução de Outubro* (São Paulo: Gráfica-Editôra Unitas, 1933), pp. 34-35; Neves da Fontoura, *Memórias*, vol. 2, p. 25.

21. Virgílio A. de Melo Franco, *Outubro, 1930*, 4th ed. (Rio de Janeiro: Schmidt, 1931), pp. 151-54; author's interview with Raul Pilla, Pôrto Alegre, May 9, 1967.

22. Cited in Paulo Nogueira Filho, *Ideais e Lutas de um Burguês Progressista. O Partido Democrático e a Revolução de 1930*, 2d ed., vol. 2 (Rio de Janeiro: Livraria José Olympio Editôra, 1965), pp. 702-6.

23. José Antônio Aranha, unpublished manuscript on Brazilian political history, pp. 68-69.

24. Ann Quiggins Tiller, "The Igniting Spark—Brazil, 1930," *Hispanic American Historical Review* 45 (Aug. 1965): 384-92.

25. Author's interview with Sinval Saldanha, Pôrto Alegre, July 30, 1966.

26. Gil de Almeida, *Homens e Factos de uma Revolução* (Rio de Janeiro: Calvino Filho, 1934), pp. 179-221.

27. *Correio do Povo* (Pôrto Alegre), Nov. 2, 1930, p. 16.

28. Among the important recent books on the 1930 revolution are Young, *Brazilian Revolution;* Hélio Silva, *O Ciclo de Vargas, vol. 3, 1930: A Revolução Traída* (Rio de Janeiro: Editôra Civilização Brasileira, 1966). The Rio Grande do Sul aspects can be found in Love, *Rio Grande do Sul;* Neves da Fontoura, *Memórias, 2; Revolução de Outubro de 1930: Imagens e Documentos* (Pôrto Alegre: Barcellos, Bertaso & Cia., 1931); Almeida, *Homens e Factos de uma Revolução.*

29. For an analysis of Oswaldo Aranha see Theodore Michael Berson, "A Political Biography of Dr. Oswaldo Aranha of Brazil, 1930-1937" (Ph.D. diss., New York University, 1971).

30. Author's interview with Alzira Vargas do Amaral Peixoto, Rio de Janeiro, Oct. 12, 1967.

31. Aranha, manuscript, p. 186.

32. Ibid., pp. 465-68.

Chapter 3: Revolution to Revolution

1. Decree Law No. 19,398 of November 11, 1930, in Nogueira Filho, *Partido Democrático*, 2, 741-43.
2. Almeida, *Homens e Factos,* p. 316; Renato Jardim, *A Aventura de Outubro e a Invasão de São Paulo,* 3d ed. (Rio de Janeiro: Civilização Brasileira Editôra, 1932), pp. 109-14; author's interview with Sinval Saldanha, Pôrto Alegre, Oct. 28, 1966.
3. Author's interview with Leda Collor de Melo, Rio de Janeiro, Sept. 9, 1967.
4. Author's interview with Moysés Vellinho, Pôrto Alegre, May 3, 1966.
5. See J. F. de Assis Brasil, *Atitude do Partido Democrático Nacional na Crise da Renovação Presidencial para 1930-1934* (Pôrto Alegre: Oficinas Gráficas da Livraria do Globo, 1929).
6. See Santa Rosa, *Tenentismo;* John D. Wirth, "Tenentismo in the Brazilian Revolution of 1930," *Hispanic American Historical Review* 44 (May 1964): 161-79.
7. Neves da Fontoura, *Memórias,* 2, 439-40; author's interview with Raul Pilla, Pôrto Alegre, May 9, 1967.
8. *Estado do Rio Grande* (Pôrto Alegre), Nov. 26, 1930, p. 3; Dec. 8, 1930, p. 5; Jan. 8, 1931, p. 3.
9. Raul Pilla to Getúlio Vargas, Pôrto Alegre, Jan. 2, 1931, Joaquim Francisco de Assis Brasil Archive (ABA).
10. Young, *Brazilian Revolution,* pp. 84-85.
11. Manifesto of Partido Democrático Paulista, São Paulo, Apr. 5, 1931, cited partially in Paulo Nogueira Filho, *Ideais e Lutas de um Burguês Progressista. A Guerra Cívica. 1932,* vol. 1, *Ocupação Militar* (Rio de Janeiro: Livraria José Olympio Editôra, 1965), pp. 73-75.
12. *Correio do Povo,* Apr. 16, 1931, pp. 5, 12; Apr. 17, 1931, pp. 5, 12; Apr. 18, 1931, pp. 5, 7; Apr. 19, 1931, pp. 8-9; Apr. 21, 1931, pp. 8, 14.
13. *Correio do Povo,* Mar. 6, 1931, p. 1.
14. Conflicting interpretations of the Pelotense Bank crisis can be found in Pedro Luis Osorio, *O Banco Pelotense. A Conduta da Ditadura. Advertência às Casas de Crédito. Documentos e Fatos. Apreciação sôbre Bancos* (Pelotas: A Universal–Echenique & Comp. Editores, 1935); Alcibiades de Oliveira, *Um Drama Bancário. O Esplendôr e a Quéda do Banco Pelotense* (Pôrto Alegre: Oficinas Gráficas da Livraria do Globo, 1936).
15. Author's interview with Renato Costa, Pôrto Alegre, Apr. 9, 1967.
16. P. L. Osorio, *Banco Pelotense,* pp. 47-139.
17. José Antônio Flôres da Cunha to Oswaldo Aranha, Pôrto Alegre, Dec. 2, 1930, Oswaldo Aranha Archive (OAA).
18. Francisco Antunes Maciel Junior to João Neves da Fontoura, Pôrto Alegre, Dec. 18, 1930, in Neves da Fontoura, *Memórias,* 2, 475-76.
19. *Estado do Rio Grande,* July 9, 1931, p. 1.
20. *Correio do Povo,* Aug. 28, 1931, p. 1.
21. *Correio do Povo,* Sept. 12, 1931, p. 1; Sept. 13, 1931, p. 20.
22. Antônio Augusto Borges de Medeiros and Pilla to Vargas, Cachoeira do Sul, Nov. 15, 1931, Sinval Saldanha Archive (SSA).
23. Jardim, *Aventura de Outubro,* pp. 109-14.
24. Vargas to Joaquim Francisco de Assis Brasil, Rio de Janeiro, Mar. 4, 1932, ABA.
25. Aureliano Leite, *Martírio e Glória de São Paulo* (São Paulo: Emprêsa Gráfica da *Revista dos Tribunais,* 1934), pp. 35-38.
26. Vargas to Assis, Rio de Janeiro, Mar. 17, 1932, ABA.
27. Cited in *Correio do Povo,* Mar. 20, 1932, p. 9.
28. Vargas to Flôres, Rio de Janeiro, undated, in Hélio Silva, *O Ciclo de Vargas,* vol. 4, *1931: Os Tenentes no Poder* (Rio de Janeiro: Editôra Civilização Brasileira, 1966), pp. 319-20.
29. Leite, *Martírio e Glória,* pp. 39-40.
30. Correspondence between Aranha and Flôres, Rio de Janeiro and Pôrto Alegre, Mar.-June 1932, OAA.

31. Walter Spalding, "Dinheiro Emitido no Rio Grande do Sul," *Revista do Globo,* May 11, 1963, p. 8.

32. Aranha, manuscript, p. 198.

33. Maciel to Assis, Pôrto Alegre, Mar. 31, 1932, Francisco Antunes Maciel Junior Archive (AMA).

34. Neves to Borges, Pilla, and Flôres, Rio de Janeiro, May 6, 1932, Antônio Augusto Borges de Medeiros Archive (BMA).

35. Neves to Flôres, Borges, and Pilla, Rio de Janeiro, June 7, 1932; Neves to Pilla, Rio de Janeiro, June 15, 1932, BMA.

36. Neves to Flôres, Rio de Janeiro, June 29, 1932, SSA.

37. Pilla to Francisco Morato, Pôrto Alegre, July 5, 1932, Lindolfo Collor Archive (LCA): Manifesto of Pilla, Neves, Lindolfo Collor, and João Baptista Luzardo, Buenos Aires, Oct. 15, 1932, SSA.

38. Deposition of Laudelino Barcellos, Rony Lopes de Almeida Archive (LAA); "Depoimento do dr. Glycério Alves" in *O General Flôres da Cunha e a Revolução Paulista (Decisão do Tribunal de Honra e Outros Documentos)* (Pôrto Alegre: Oficinas Gráficas d'*A Federação,* 1933), pp. 91-106; João Neves da Fontoura, *Accuso!* (Rio de Janeiro, 1933), pp. 149-84.

39. *General Flôres,* pp. 104-5; author's interviews with José Diogo Brochado da Rocha, Pôrto Alegre, Jan. 10, 1967, and Sinval Saldanha, Pôrto Alegre, Oct. 28, 1966.

40. Glauco Carneiro, *História das Revoluções Brasileiras,* vol. 2, *Da Revolução Liberal à Revolução de 31 de Março (1930/1964)* (Rio de Janeiro: Edições o Cruzeiro, 1965)·pp. 402-3; Bertoldo Klinger, "O Alto Comando," in idem et al., *Nós e a Dictadura. A Jornada Revolucionária de 1932* (n.p., 1933), p. 13; Euclydes de Figueiredo, "O Plano de Operações," in ibid., pp. 41-42.

41. Othelo Franco, "Porque Não Fui contra S. Paulo (Depoimento de um Exilado Político)," in Klinger et al., *Nós e a Dictadura,* pp. 106-13; author's interview with Celestino Prunes, Pôrto Alegre, Sept. 29, 1966.

42. Hélio Silva, *O Ciclo de Vargas,* vol. 5, *1932: A Guerra Paulista* (Rio de Janeiro: Editôra Civilização Brasileira, 1967), p. 132.

43. Borges to Flôres, Cachoeira, July 9, 1932, in *General Flôres,* p. 52.

44. Flôres to Borges, Pôrto Alegre, July 10, 1932, in *General Flôres,* p. 53; Flôres to Vargas, Pôrto Alegre, July 10, 1932, in ibid.

45. Vargas to Flôres, Rio de Janeiro, July 10, 1932, in ibid., p. 54.

46. Flôres to Vargas, Pôrto Alegre, July 10, 1932, in ibid.

47. Author's interviews with José Antônio Aranha, Pôrto Alegre, Aug. 4, 1966, Daniel Krieger, Pôrto Alegre, Feb. 21, 1967, and Dário Crespo, Rio de Janeiro, Sept. 29, 1967.

48. Deposition of Alfredo Rodrigues da Silva, LAA.

49. Aldo Ladeira Ribeiro, manuscript of a forthcoming book, *Esboço Histórico da Brigada Militar do Rio Grande do Sul,* vol. 3, *Outubro de 1930 a Dezembro de 1961,* p. 73.

50. Manifesto of Borges and Pilla, Pôrto Alegre, July 13, 1932, in *Estado do Rio Grande,* July 13, 1932, p. 1.

51. Borges and Pilla to Morato and Altino Arantes, Pôrto Alegre, undated, in Silva, *1932,* p. 101.

52. Flôres to Vargas, Pôrto Alegre, July 19, 1932, AMA.

53. Borges to Vargas, Pôrto Alegre, July 19, 1932, in Silva, *1932,* pp. 121-22; deposition of Luzardo, LAA.

54. Ladeira Ribeiro, manuscript, p. 201; *Correio do Povo,* July 26, 1932, p. 14.

55. Peace Agreement, Vacaria, July 24, 1932, SSA.

56. Walder Sarmanho to Flôres, Rio de Janeiro, undated, in Silva, *1932,* p. 122.

57. Aureliano Leite, *Páginas de uma Longa Vida* (São Paulo: Livraria Martins Editôra, 1968), pp. 75-76.

58. Neves to Borges, São Paulo, July 20, 1932, in Silva, *1932,* p. 132.

59. Author's interviews with Walter Peracchi Barcellos, Pôrto Alegre, July 13, 1967, and Rony Lopes de Almeida, Pôrto Alegre, May 11, 1967.

60. Deposition of Luzardo, LAA.

61. Glycério Alves, "A Revolução de 1932," *Correio do Povo*, July 11, 1958, pp. 4, 19; depositions of Legendre Chagas Pereira and Glycério Alves, LAA.

62. S. Faria Corrêa, *Serro Alegre (Revolução Riograndense de 1932)* (n.p., 1933), pp. 24-25; deposition of Luzardo, LAA.

63. Ladeira Ribeiro, manuscript, p. 203; manifesto of Borges, Pilla, Luzardo, and Collor, Santa Maria, Aug. 1932, in *General Flôres,* pp. 85-87; author's interview with Raul Pilla, Pôrto Alegre, May 9, 1967.

64. Flôres to Sinval Saldanha and Francisco Flôres da Cunha, Pôrto Alegre, Aug. 26, 1932, SSA; Maciel to Aranha, Pôrto Alegre, Aug. 30, 1932; deposition of Luzardo, LAA.

65. Deposition of José R. Sobral, LAA; deposition of Urbana B. dos Santos, SSA; Ladeira Ribeiro, manuscript, pp. 213-17; Maciel to Vargas, Pôrto Alegre, Sept. 6, 1932; Sept. 15, 1932, AMA.

66. Depositions of Marcial Terra and Turíbio Gomes, LAA.

67. Ladeira Ribeiro, manuscript, pp. 217-18.

68. Deposition of Alfredo Rodrigues da Silva, LAA; Herculano de Carvalho e Silva, *A Revolução Constitucionalista. Subsídios para a Sua História, Organizados pelo Estado Maior da Força Pública de S. Paulo* (Rio de Janeiro: Civilização Brasileira Editôra, 1932), pp. 106-10.

69. Maciel to Assis, Pôrto Alegre, July 14, 1932; André Carrazzoni to Assis, Pôrto Alegre, July 14, 1932; Pericles da Silveira to Assis, Rio de Janeiro, July 15, 1932, ABA.

70. Deposition of Armando Borges, LAA.

71. Faria Corrêa, *Serro Alegre,* pp. 79-87; A. A. Borges de Medeiros, "Borges de Medeiros," in *A Campanha Revolucionária de 1932 (Depoimentos Prestados no Rio de Janeiro, às Autoridades da Ditadura) (Subsídios para a História)* (São Paulo: Editorial Bandeirante, 1934), pp. 33-34; deposition of Martim Cavalcanti, LAA.

72. Author's interview with Daniel Krieger, Pôrto Alegre, Feb. 21, 1967.

73. Aranha, manuscript, p. 167.

Chapter 4: Uneasy Alliance

1. Manifesto of the PRR Central Commission, Pôrto Alegre, Nov. 29, 1936, in *Correio do Povo*, Nov. 29, 1936, p. 17.

2. Partido Republicano Liberal, *Partido Republicano Liberal, 15 de Novembro de 1932* (n.p., n.d.), pp. 7-14.

3. *Correio do Povo,* July 8, 1934, p. 10.

4. Urbano Garcia and Bruno de Mendonça Lima to Assis, Pelotas, Oct. 19, 1932, ABA.

5. Flôres to Vargas, Pôrto Alegre, Oct. 19, 1932, Getúlio Vargas Archive (GVA).

6. *Correio do Povo,* Apr. 19, 1933, p. 5.

7. Raul Azambuja to Aranha, Pôrto Alegre, Jan. 4, 1933, OAA; U.S. Consul Reginald S. Castleman to Edwin V. Morgan, U.S. ambassador to Brazil, Pôrto Alegre, Jan. 18, 1933, Archives of the United States Department of State (ADS).

8. *Correio do Povo,* May 5, 1933, p. 7.

9. *Correio do Povo,* July 6, 1933, p. 9.

10. Aranha, manuscript, pp. 57, 172.

11. Alzira Vargas do Amaral Peixoto, *Getúlio Vargas, Meu Pai* (Pôrto Alegre: Editôra Globo, 1960), pp. 93-94.

12. Lourival Coutinho, *O General Góes Depõe . . . ,* 3d ed. (Rio de Janeiro: Livraria Editôra Coelho Branco, 1956), pp. 249-50.

13. The most complete discussion of the 1933-34 constituent assembly is Hélio Silva, *O Ciclo de Vargas,* vol. 7, *1934: A Constituinte* (Rio de Janeiro: Editôra Civilização Brasileira, 1969).

14. Love, *Rio Grande do Sul,* p. 27.

15. Amaral Peixoto, *Getúlio Vargas,* p. 249.

16. Cited in *Correio do Povo,* Apr. 24, 1934, p. 9.

17. Cited in *Correio do Povo,* Apr. 26, 1934, p. 18.

18. Luiz Prates to Luzardo, Pôrto Alegre, Apr. 19, 1934, LCA; Vargas to Flôres, Rio de Janeiro, Apr. 30, 1934, GVA.

19. Paul Frischauer, *Presidente Vargas* (São Paulo: Companhia Editôra Nacional, 1943), p. 315; author's interview with Moysés Vellinho, Pôrto Alegre, May 27, 1966.

20. Mário da Matta to Collor, Buenos Aires, June 25, 1934, LCA.

21. Collor to Pilla, Lima, Mar. 27, 1934; Pilla to Collor, Montevideo, Apr. 18, 1934; Rony Lopes de Almeida to Collor, Buenos Aires, Apr. 20, 1934, LCA.

22. Coutinho, *General Góes,* p. 256.

23. A. A. Borges de Medeiros, *O Poder Moderador na República Presidencial. (Um Ante-projecto da Constituição Brasileira)* ([Recife], 1933).

24. Unsigned letter to Collor, Rio de Janeiro, Aug. 3, 1934, LCA; Adroaldo Mesquita da Costa, "Recordando," *Correio do Povo,* June 4, 1957, p. 4.

25. *Correio do Povo,* July 22, 1934, p. 28; July 24, 1934, p. 1.

26. Protásio Vargas to G. Vargas, São Borja, May 25, 1934; Viriato Vargas to G. Vargas, São Borja, July 21, 1934, GVA.

27. A. G. de Araujo Jorge to Afrânio de Melo Franco, Montevideo, Sept. 25, 1932, Afrânio de Melo Franco Archive (MFA).

28. Lucillo Bueno to Melo, Asunción, Jan. 7, 1933; Bueno to Melo, Asunción, Jan. 11, 1933, MFA; Hélio Silva, *O Ciclo de Vargas,* vol. 6, *1933: A Crise do Tenentismo* (Rio de Janeiro: Editôra Civilização Brasileira, 1968), pp. 76-86.

29. Series of letters of Gaúcho exiles, Feb. 14, 1934-June 25, 1934, LCA; K. P. Ribeiro, *Porque Morreu Waldemar Ripoll* (Rio de Janeiro: A. Coelho Branco Filho, 1936), pp. 65-132.

30. Antonio Amoros (Hijo), *Caudillismo salvaje. La verdad sobre el crimen del dr. Ripoll. El periodismo al servicio de la justicia* (Montevideo: Talleres Gráficos Prometeo, 1939), pp. 70-76.

31. Ibid., pp. 83-105; author's interview with Dário Crespo, Rio de Janeiro, Sept. 29, 1967.

32. *Correio do Povo,* Nov. 25, 1934, p. 19.

33. Robert M. Levine, *The Vargas Regime: The Critical Years, 1934-1938* (New York: Columbia University Press, 1970), pp. 81-99.

34. Fifty-five percent of the Gaúcho Integralist leaders were of German extraction. Reinhard Maack. "The Germans in South Brazil: A German View," *Inter-American Quarterly* 1 (July 1939): p.19.

35. Castleman to U.S. Embassy in Rio, Pôrto Alegre, June 21, 1934, ADS; *Correio do Povo,* Aug. 2, 1934, p. 18.

36. Castleman to U.S. Embassy in Rio, Pôrto Alegre, Aug. 28, 1934; Sept. 4, 1934; Sept. 11, 1934; Sept. 18, 1934; Sept. 25, 1934; Oct. 9, 1934, ADS.

37. *Correio do Povo,* Dec. 16, 1934, p. 16.

38. Amyr Borges Fortes and João Baptista Santiago Wagner, *História Administrativa, Judiciária e Eclesiástica do Rio Grande do Sul* (Pôrto Alegre: Oficinas Gráficas da Livraria do Globo, 1963), pp. 159-60, 234-35, 250-51.

39. *Correio do Povo,* Dec. 16, 1934, p. 16; Dec. 18, 1934, p. 12; Jan. 6, 1935, p. 14.

40. *Correio do Povo,* Nov. 25, 1934, p. 17.

41. Pilla and Oswaldo Vergara to Flôres, Pôrto Alegre, Apr. 11, 1935, LCA.

42. Rio Grande do Sul, *Constituições Sul-Riograndenses,* pp. 125-58.

43. Flôres to Vargas, Pôrto Alegre, Apr. 18, 1935, GVA.

44. Flôres to Vargas, Pôrto Alegre, Apr. 20, 1935, GVA.

45. *Correio do Povo,* May 14, 1935, p. 9.

46. Coutinho, *General Góes,* p. 265.

47. *Correio do Povo,* Feb. 15, 1935, p. 1; July 30, 1935, p. 1.

48. For details on the various state conflicts, see Hélio Silva, *O Ciclo de Vargas,* vol. 8, *1935: A Revolta Vermelha* (Rio de Janeiro: Editôra Civilização Brasileira, 1969), pp. 47-49,

85-94, 107-13, 121-24, 132-34, 158, 209-55.
49. Aranha, manuscript, p. 208.
50. G. Vargas to P. Vargas, Rio de Janeiro, Oct. 8, 1935, GVA.
51. Moysés Vellinho to Aranha, Pôrto Alegre, Oct. 5, 1935, GVA; Brazil, *Diário do Congresso Nacional,* Apr. 11, 1953, pp. 2642-43.
52. Author's interview with Luiz Francisco Guerra Blessmann, Pôrto Alegre, Oct. 5, 1966.
53. *Correio do Povo,* Oct. 10, 1953, p. 18.

Chapter 5: Open Struggle

1. *Correio do Povo,* Dec. 25, 1935, p. 20.
2. Collor and Luzardo to Pilla and Maurício Cardoso, Rio de Janeiro, Nov. 19, 1935, LCA.
3. Levine, *The Vargas Regime,* pp. 104-22; Silva, *1935,* pp. 279-400.
4. José Maria dos Santos, *Notas à História Recente* (São Paulo: Editôra Brasiliense, 1944), pp. 163-78.
5. José Loureiro da Silva to Miguel Tostes, Pôrto Alegre, Jan. 24, 1936, GVA; *Correio do Povo,* Oct. 18, 1936, p. 1.
6. Benjamin Vargas to G. Vargas, Pôrto Alegre, Dec. 22, 1935, GVA.
7. Cardoso to Vargas, Pôrto Alegre, Feb. 15, 1936, GVA; *Correio do Povo,* Apr. 7, 1936, p. 10.
8. Rio Grande do Sul Modus Vivendi, Pôrto Alegre, Jan. 17, 1936, BMA.
9. Ladeira Ribeiro, manuscript, pp. 56, 273.
10. Alberto Pasqualini to Vargas, Pôrto Alegre, Mar. 12, 1936; secret plan of PRL Dissidency, Pôrto Alegre, Apr. 1936, GVA.
11. Press release of Benedito Valadares, Rio de Janeiro, Aug. 30, 1936, in *Correio do Povo,* Sept. 1, 1936, p. 10.
12. *Correio do Povo,* Sept. 16, 1936, pp. 1, 3.
13. This is based on numerous interviews conducted by the author and voluminous correspondence in the Getúlio Vargas Archive.
14. Author's interviews with Daniel Krieger, Pôrto Alegre, Feb. 21, 1967, and Antônio Guerra Flôres da Cunha, Pôrto Alegre, Aug. 24, 1966.
15. Rio Grande do Sul, *Anais da Assembléia Legislativa do Estado do Rio Grande do Sul, 1936,* vol. 3, *1 de Outubro de 1936 a 30 de Novembro de 1936,* pp. 93-94; author's interview with Moysés Vellinho, Pôrto Alegre, May 27, 1966.
16. *Folha da Tarde* (Pôrto Alegre), Oct. 16, 1936, p. 2.
17. G. Vargas to P. Vargas, Rio de Janeiro, Oct. 17, 1936, GVA.
18. Press release of PRL Central Directory Commission, Pôrto Alegre, Oct. 20, 1936, in *Correio do Povo,* Oct. 21, 1936, p. 1.
19. Pilla and Collor to Neves and Luzardo, Pôrto Alegre, undated, LCA.
20. B. Vargas to G. Vargas, Pôrto Alegre, Nov. 23, 1936; Serafim Vargas to G. Vargas, Pôrto Alegre, Nov. 25, 1936; B. Vargas to Sarmanho, Pôrto Alegre, Nov. 26, 1936, GVA.
21. G. Vargas to P. Vargas, Rio de Janeiro, Oct. 23, 1936, GVA.
22. G. Vargas to B. Vargas, Rio de Janeiro, Nov. 26, 1936, GVA.
23. B. Vargas to G. Vargas, Pôrto Alegre, Dec. 23, 1936, GVA; Viriato Dutra to Flôres, Pôrto Alegre, Jan. 2, 1937, in *Correio do Povo,* Jan. 3, 1937, p. 28.
24. Aranha to Flodoardo Silva, Washington, undated, OAA.
25. Loureiro to Tostes, Pôrto Alegre, Jan. 17, 1937, GVA; Aranha to Liberal Dissidents, Rio de Janeiro, Apr. 8, 1937, OAA.
26. *O Globo* (Rio de Janeiro), Jan. 12, 1937, p. 1; Jan. 13, 1937, p. 1; *A Nota* (Rio de Janeiro), Jan. 16, 1937, p. 1.
27. Loureiro to Tostes, Pôrto Alegre, Feb. 3, 1937, GVA.
28. Loureiro to Tostes, Pôrto Alegre, Mar. 20, 1937, GVA.
29. *Correio do Povo,* Apr. 14, 1937, p. 1.

30. P. Vargas and B. Vargas to Sarmanho, Pôrto Alegre, Apr. 14, 1937, GVA; *Correio do Povo,* Apr. 10, 1937, p. 1.

31. G. Vargas to B. Vargas, Rio de Janeiro, Apr. 7, 1937, GVA.

32. Aranha to Liberal Dissidents, Rio de Janeiro, Apr. 8, 1937, OAA.

33. Author's interview with José Antônio Aranha, Pôrto Alegre, Jan. 23, 1967.

34. Coutinho, *General Góes,* pp. 281-82; Aranha, manuscript, pp. 441-44.

35. Coutinho, *General Góes,* pp. 283-86.

36. Maciel to Flôres, Rio de Janeiro, Dec. 7, 1936, AMA; Leite, *Páginas de Uma Longa Vida,* pp. 266-68; author's interview with Juracy Magalhães, Rio de Janeiro, Sept. 19, 1967.

37. Rio Grande do Sul, *Anais da Assembléia Legislativa, 1937,* vol. 1, *12 de Abril de 1937 a 26 de Maio de 1937,* pp. 10-12.

38. *Correio do Povo,* Mar. 5, 1937, p. 10; Mar. 6, 1937, p. 9; Mar. 7, 1937, p. 15; Mar. 9, 1937, p. 10.

39. Lima to Pilla, Pelotas, Nov. 20, 1936, ABA; Manifesto of Lima, Pelotas, Dec. 30, 1936, in *Correio do Povo,* Dec. 31, 1936, p. 20.

40. *Correio do Povo,* June 24, 1937, p. 9.

41. Benedito Valadares, *Tempos Idos e Vividos. Memórias* (Rio de Janeiro: Editôra Civilização Brasileira, 1966), pp. 120-33.

42. Manifesto of Ação Libertadora, Pôrto Alegre, June 7, 1937, in *Correio do Povo,* June 8, 1937, p. 11; Manifesto of the PL Central Directory, Pôrto Alegre, June 8, 1937, in *Correio do Povo,* June 9, 1937, p. 16.

43. G. Vargas to B. Vargas, Petropolis, Apr. 11, 1937; G. Vargas to B. Vargas, Petropolis, Apr. 14, 1937, GVA.

44. Twenty Rio Grande do Sul state deputies to Vargas, Pôrto Alegre, Apr. 24, 1937, GVA.

45. B. Vargas to G. Vargas, Pôrto Alegre, undated, GVA.

46. Correspondence and telegraphic conferences between Eurico Gaspar Dutra and Emílio Lúcio Esteves, Rio de Janeiro and Pôrto Alegre, Apr. 28, 1937; May 4, 1937; May 10, 1937; Pedro Aurélio Góes Monteiro to E. Dutra, Curitiba, May 25, 1937, GVA.

47. B. Vargas to G. Vargas, Pôrto Alegre, May 3, 1937; B. Vargas and Luzardo to G. Vargas, Pôrto Alegre, May 3, 1937, GVA.

48. Coutinho, *General Góes,* p. 292.

49. Valadares, *Tempos Idos e Vividos,* p. 84.

50. Góes to Esteves, Rio de Janeiro, May 18, 1937, in *Correio do Povo,* May 19, 1937, p. 1.

51. Góes to E. Dutra, Curitiba, May 27, 1937, GVA.

52. Góes to E. Dutra, Curitiba, May 25, 1937, GVA; *Diário da Noite* (Rio de Janeiro), Mar. 17, 1945, p. 2.

53. B. Vargas to Aguinaldo Fernandes, Pôrto Alegre, Sept. 1, 1937, GVA.

54. Author's interviews with Camillo Martins Costa, Pôrto Alegre, July 24, 1967, and Moysés Vellinho, Pôrto Alegre, June 29, 1967.

55. Raul Pilla, *Oração Proferida pelo Sr. Raul Pilla na Sessão Inaugural do Congresso do Partido Libertador em Bagé a 10 de Agôsto de 1945* (Pôrto Alegre: Oficinas Gráficas da Livraria do Globo, n.d.), pp. 5-6; author's interviews with Raul Pilla, Pôrto Alegre, June 29, 1967, and José Antônio Aranha, Pôrto Alegre, Oct. 12, 1966.

56. Léa Brenner, "Um Homem de Vanguarda," *Revista do Globo,* Nov. 24-Dec. 7, 1962, p. 25; author's interview with José Antônio Aranha, Pôrto Alegre, June 29, 1967.

57. Author's interview with Raul Pilla, Pôrto Alegre, May 11, 1967.

58. *Correio do Povo,* Aug. 26, 1937, p. 3; author's interview with Camillo Martins Costa, Pôrto Alegre, July 24, 1967.

59. Adalberto Aranha to O. Aranha, Rio de Janeiro, Sept. 4, 1937, OAA; *Correio do Povo,* Sept. 17, 1937, p. 5; author's interviews with Carlos Santos, Pôrto Alegre, May 17, 1967, and José Antônio Aranha, Pôrto Alegre, Jan. 23, 1967.

60. G. Vargas to B. Vargas, Rio de Janeiro, Oct. 1, 1937, GVA.

61. Report of Manoel de Cerqueira Daltro Filho, Rio de Janeiro, Nov. 3, 1937, in *Correio do Povo,* Nov. 5, 1937, p. 3.

62. Aranha, manuscript, p. 225.
63. Author's interview with Walter Peracchi Barcellos, Pôrto Alegre, July 13, 1967.
64. Coutinho, *General Góes,* pp. 298-99; Affonso Henriques, *Ascensão e Queda de Getúlio Vargas,* vol. 1, *Vargas o Maquiavélico* (Rio de Janeiro: Distribuidora Record, 1966), pp. 453-63.
65. Information on the events of October 16 and 17, 1937, was drawn from a variety of sources. Among these were: Proclamation of Daltro, Pôrto Alegre, Oct. 16, 1937, in *Correio do Povo,* Oct. 17, 1937, p. 1; report of Daltro, Rio de Janeiro, Nov. 3, 1937, in *Correio do Povo,* Nov. 5, 1937, p. 3; Matta to Oscar Carneiro da Fontoura, Pôrto Alegre, Nov. 16, 1937, in *Correio do Povo,* Nov. 21, 1937, p. 28; Ladeira Ribeiro, manuscript, pp. 274-75; Aranha, manuscript, pp. 225-26. In addition, the author interviewed numerous participants in the events of those dramatic two days.
66. *Correio do Povo,* Oct. 19, 1937, p. 1.
67. Author's interview with Oswaldo Cordeiro de Farias, Pôrto Alegre, July 15, 1967.

Chapter 6: The Estado Nôvo

1. Coutinho, *General Góes,* p. 292.
2. G. Vargas to B. Vargas, Rio de Janeiro, Oct. 17, 1937, GVA.
3. José Antônio Aranha to O. Aranha, Pôrto Alegre, undated, OAA.
4. Daltro to Dutra, Pôrto Alegre, undated, GVA.
5. *Correio do Povo,* Oct. 20, 1937, p. 1.
6. Valadares to Vargas, Belo Horizonte, Oct. 29, 1937; Oct. 30, 1937; Nov. 3, 1937; Nov. 5, 1937, GVA.
7. Coutinho, *General Góes,* p. 315; Pilla, *Oração Proferida,* p. 7.
8. Cited in Virgílio A. de Melo Franco, *A Campanha da U.D.N. (1944-1945)* (Rio de Janeiro: Livraria Editôra Zelio Valverde, 1946), pp. 95-100.
9. A detailed documentary recounting of the 1936-37 events which culminated with the overthrow of the Second Republic and establishment of the Estado Nôvo is Hélio Silva, *O Ciclo de Vargas,* vol. 9, *Todos os Golpes Se Parecem* (Rio de Janeiro: Editôra Civilização Brasileira, 1970), pp. 225-469.
10. PRL Central Directory Commission to Daltro, Pôrto Alegre, Nov. 11, 1937, in *Correio do Povo,* Nov. 14, 1937, p. 3.
11. *Correio do Povo,* Nov. 17, 1937, p. 14; Nov. 18, 1937, p. 5; Mar. 8, 1945, p. 8; author's interview with Raul Pilla, Pôrto Alegre, June 29, 1967.
12. Press release of the PRR, PL, and PRL Dissidency, Pôrto Alegre, Nov.19, 1937, in *Correio do Povo,* Nov. 20, 1937, p. 6.
13. P. Vargas to G. Vargas, Pôrto Alegre, Nov. 25, 1937; Interparty Mixed Commission to Daltro, Pôrto Alegre, Nov. 27, 1937, GVA.
14. Nelson Werneck Sodré, *História Militar do Brasil* (Rio de Janeiro: Editôra Civilização Brasileira,1965), pp. 276-80; Lima Figueiredo, *Eurico G. Dutra.Trajos Biográficos* (n.p., n.d.), pp. 17-26; Theodorico Lopes and Gentil Torres, *Ministros da Guerra do Brasil, 1808-1946* (Rio de Janeiro, 1947), pp. 249-59, 280-319, 333-39.
15. Karl Loewenstein, *Brazil under Vargas* (New York: The Macmillan Company, 1944), pp. 59-75; Aranha, manuscript, p. 286.
16. Mário Wagner Vieira da Cunha, *O Sistema Administrativo Brasileiro, 1930-1950* (Rio de Janeiro: Centro Brasileiro de Pesquisas Educacionais, 1963), pp. 70-94; Hélio Jaguaribe, *Economic & Political Development: A Theoretical Approach & a Brazilian Case Study* (Cambridge, Mass.: Harvard University Press, 1968), p. 144.
17. Aranha, manuscript, p. 186.
18. *Correio do Povo,* Dec. 4, 1937, p. 14.
19. Amaral Peixoto, *Getúlio Vargas,* pp. 231-33.
20. P. Vargas to G. Vargas, Pôrto Alegre, Feb. 25, 1938; Oswaldo Cordeiro de Farias to G. Vargas, Pôrto Alegre, Mar. 5, 1938, GVA.
21. Aranha to Vargas, Washington, Oct. 27, 1937, GVA.
22. Aranha to Vargas, Washington, Nov. 24, 1937, GVA.
23. Author's interview with João Baptista Luzardo, Pôrto Alegre, Aug. 14, 1966.

24. Correspondence from Luzardo, Cordeiro, José Bernardino de Camara Canto, and Adolfo de Alencastre Guimarães to Vargas, Montevideo, Pôrto Alegre, and Buenos Aires, Nov. 17, 1937- Jan. 31, 1941, GVA.

25. Among the numerous accounts of the Integralist assault of May 11, 1938, are Amaral Peixoto, *Getúlio Vargas,* pp. 117-33; G. Carneiro, *Revoluções Brasileiras,* 2, 437-57; David Nasser, *A Revolução dos Covardes,* 2d ed. (Rio de Janeiro: Edições o Cruzeiro, 1966); John W. F. Dulles, *Vargas of Brazil: A Political Biography* (Austin: University of Texas Press, 1967), pp. 181-88; Hélio Silva, *O Ciclo de Vargas,* vol. 10, *1938: Terrorismo em Campo Verde* (Rio de Janeiro: Editôra Civilização Brasileira, 1971), pp. 161-273.

26. Luzardo to Vargas, Montevideo, May 13, 1938; Canto to Vargas, Montevideo, May 21, 1938, GVA; author's interview with Antônio Guerra Flôres da Cunha, Pôrto Alegre, Aug. 24, 1966.

27. Luzardo to Vargas, Montevideo, Feb. 26, 1938, GVA.

28. Luzardo to Vargas, Montevideo, June 26, 1938-May 10, 1939, GVA.

29. Flôres to Dutra, Montevideo, July 21, 1939; Luzardo to Vargas, Montevideo, Aug. 7, 1939, GVA.

30. Manifesto of Flôres, Montevideo, Dec. 19, 1941, in U.S. Consul Daniel M. Braddock to Jefferson Caffery, U.S. ambassador to Brazil, Pôrto Alegre, Dec. 23, 1941, ADS 832.00/1469.

31. Among the studies of Estado Nôvo economic development are Jaguaribe, *Economic & Political Development;* Stanley E. Hilton, "Brazil and the Great Power Trade Rivalry in South America, 1934-1939" (Ph.D. diss., University of Texas, 1969); John D. Wirth, *The Politics of Brazilian Development, 1930-1954* (Stanford, Calif.: Stanford University Press, 1970); George Wythe, "Brazil: Trends in Industrial Development," in *Economic Growth: Brazil, India, Japan,* ed. Simon Kuznets, Wilbert E. Moore, and Joseph J. Spengler (Durham, N.C.: Duke University Press, 1955), pp. 29-77.

32. Thomas Pompeu Accioly Borges, "Relationships between Economic Development, Industrialization and the Growth of Urban Population in Brazil," in *Urbanization in Latin America,* ed. Philip M. Hauser (New York: Columbia University Press, 1961), p. 155.

33. Paulo Schilling, *Crise Econômica no Rio Grande do Sul,* vol. 1, *A Crise Agro-Pecuária* (Pôrto Alegre: Difusão de Cultura Técnica, 1961), pp. 27-29.

34. *Correio do Povo,* Dec. 17, 1938, p. 12.

35. Ney Ulrich Caldas, *A Conjuntura Nacional e os Problemas do Rio Grande do Sul (Necessidade de Planejamento Regional)* (Pôrto Alegre: Livraria Sulina, 1963), pp. 78-83; "Panorama Econômico-Social do Rio Grande do Sul," *Conjuntura Social* 6 (December 1952): 58-59; Paulo César Delayti Mota, "Considerações sôbre a 'Economia do Estado do Rio Grande do Sul' " (study prepared at the Rio Grande do Sul Conselho de Desenvolvimento do Estado, Pôrto Alegre, 1967), p. 1.

36. Rio Grande do Sul, Assembléia Legislativa, Comissão de Desenvolvimento Econômico, *Análise do Insuficiente Desenvolvimento Econômico do Rio Grande do Sul,* 1965, *Boletim,* no. 16, p. 53; Aranha, manuscript, pp. 321-22.

37. Caldas, *Conjuntura Nacional,* p. 42; "Panorama Econômico-Social do Rio Grande do Sul," p. 59; Mota, "Considerações sôbre a 'Economia,' " p. 1.

38. J. P. Santos, "Levantamento Censitário e Análise Sociográfica de um Município Pastoril," pt. 1, "Famílias Necessitadas," *Província de São Pedro* 3 (December 1935): 125-28; Rubens Vidal, "O Êxodo no Sul do País," *Revista do Globo,* Oct. 13, 1951, pp. 43-44.

39. José Fernando Carneiro, *Imigração e Colonização no Brasil* (Rio de Janeiro: Cadeira de Geografia do Brasil da Faculdade Nacional de Filosofia, 1950), pp. 53-54; Brazil, Instituto Brasileiro de Geografia e Estatística, *Recenseamento Geral do Brasil (1.º de Setembro de 1940),* Série Regional 20, *Rio Grande do Sul,* vol. 1, *Censo Demográfico. População e Habitação,* 1950, p. 8; Brazil, IBGE, *Estado do Rio Grande do Sul, 1950,* 1, 10; "Panorama Econômico-Social do Rio Grande do Sul," p. 59.

40. Computed from Stuart Clark Rothwell, *The Old Italian Colonial Zone of Rio Grande do Sul* (Pôrto Alegre: Edições da Faculdade de Filosofia, Universidade do Rio Grande do Sul, 1959), p. 7.

41. Maack, "Germans in South Brazil," pp. 14-16; Alton Frye, *Nazi Germany and the American Hemisphere, 1933-41* (New Haven, Conn.: Yale University Press, 1967), pp. 67-68.

42. Jean Roche, *La Colonisation Allemande et le Rio Grande do Sul* (Paris: Institut des Hautes Études de L'Amérique Latine, 1959), pp. 552-57; Aranha, manuscript, p. 13; author's interview with Mario Gardelin, Caxias do Sul, RGS, Apr. 27, 1967.

43. *Correio de Povo*, Dec. 16, 1934, p. 16; Dec. 18, 1934, p. 12; Jan. 6, 1935, p. 14.

44. Loewenstein, *Brazil under Vargas*, pp. 155-204; Maack, "Germans in South Brazil," pp. 19-20; Ferreira Filho, *História Geral*, p. 178.

45. Paulo Pinheiro Chagas, *O Brigadeiro da Libertação*, 3d ed. (Rio de Janeiro: Livraria-Editôra Zelio Valverde, 1945), pp. 197-99.

46. Oswaldo Aranha, *Carta do Dr. Oswaldo Aranha ao Gal. Góes Explicando os Motivos de Sua Demissão do Ministério da Relação Exterior* (Pôrto Alegre: Of. Gráf. da Livraria do Globo, 1945), pp. 4-10

47. Bulletin of the Federal Department of Public Security, Rio de Janeiro, Oct. 17, 1944; Bulletin of the Federal District Police Department, Rio de Janeiro, Nov. 6, 1944, GVA; Nelson de Assis, "A Juventude na Política," *Revista do Globo*, Jan. 11, 1947, pp. 47-48; author's interview with Raul Pilla, Pôrto Alegre, May 11, 1967.

48. G. Vargas to P. Vargas, Rio de Janeiro, Aug. 30, 1943; P. Vargas to G. Vargas, Pôrto Alegre, Sept. 15, 1943, GVA.

49. Ernesto Dornelles to G. Vargas, Pôrto Alegre, Sept. 15, 1943, GVA.

50. Dornelles to Vargas, Pôrto Alegre, July 15, 1944, GVA; Justino Martins, "Pasqualini de Corpo Inteiro," *Revista do Globo*, Dec. 7, 1946, pp. 23-27, 75.

51. Coutinho, *General Góes*, pp. 404-5; José Caó, *Dutra. O Presidente e a Restauração Democrática* (São Paulo: Progresso Editorial, 1949), pp. 214-17.

52. For an interesting brief analysis of the PSD see "O Eterno PSD" in José Fernando Carneiro, *Conversa Amarga* (Rio de Janeiro: Organização Simões Editôra, 1958), pp. 35-49.

53. Loewenstein, *Brazil under Vargas*, pp. 285-314; Robert J. Alexander, *Labor Relations in Argentina, Brazil, and Chile* (New York: McGraw-Hill Book Company, 1962), pp. 60-62.

54. Phyllis Jane Peterson, "Brazilian Political Parties: Formation, Organization, and Leadership, 1945-1959" (Ph.D. diss., University of Michigan, 1962), pp. 68-69.

55. Manifesto of the Rio Grande do Sul Democratic Left, Pôrto Alegre, undated, in *Correio do Povo*, Sept. 2, 1945, p. 3.

56. P. Vargas to G. Vargas, Pôrto Alegre, May 31, 1945, GVA; Partido Social Democrático, *Anais da Convenção do Partido Social Democrático* (Pôrto Alegre: Tipografia Esperança, 1945), pp. 75-79.

57. Author's interviews with José Diogo Brochado da Rocha, Pôrto Alegre, Jan. 10, 1967, and José Mariano de Freitas Beck, Pôrto Alegre, Jan. 28, 1967.

58. Manifesto and Program of the Brazilian Social Union, Pôrto Alegre, Sept. 15, 1945, in *Correio do Povo*, Sept. 16, 1945, p. 11; author's interview with Milton Dutra, Santiago de Boqueirão, RGS, Apr. 13, 1967.

59. Pact of the Brazilian Labor Party and the Brazilian Social Union, Pôrto Alegre, undated, in *Correio do Povo*, Nov. 4, 1945, p. 20.

60. Maack, "Germans in South Brazil," p. 19.

61. Getúlio Vargas, *A Nova Política do Brasil*, vol. 11, *O Brasil na Guerra. 1 de Julho de 1944 a 30 de Outubro de 1945* (Rio de Janeiro: Livraria José Olympio Editôra, 1947), pp. 198-99.

62. Coutinho, *General Góes*, pp. 440-67; Luiz Vergara, *Fui Secretário de Getúlio Vargas. Memórias dos Anos de 1926-1954* (Pôrto Alegre: Editôra Globo, 1960), pp. 173-89.

Chapter 7: Return of Vargas

1. Napoleão de Alencastro Guimarães to Vargas, Rio de Janeiro, Nov. 8, 1945; Neves to Vargas, Rio de Janeiro, Nov. 24, 1945, GVA.

2. Coutinho, *General Góes*, pp. 478-79.

3. P. Vargas to G. Vargas, Pôrto Alegre, Nov. 13, 1945; G. Vargas to P. Vargas, São Borja, undated, GVA.

4. Neves to G. Vargas, Rio de Janeiro, Nov. 14, 1945; Neves to P. Vargas, Rio de Janeiro, Nov. 14, 1945; G. Vargas to Neves, São Borja, Nov. 18, 1945; G. Vargas to P. Vargas, São Borja, Nov. 19, 1945, GVA; Diário de Notícias (Pôrto Alegre), Nov. 10, 1949, p. 14.

5. Neves to Vargas, Rio de Janeiro, Nov. 24, 1945, GVA.

6. Dutra to the PTB, Rio de Janeiro, Nov. 22, 1945, GVA.

7. Icaro Sydow and J. C. Pedroso to Vargas, São Paulo, undated, GVA; J. Aranha, manuscript, p. 307.

8. Alencastro to Vargas, Rio de Janeiro, Nov. 19, 1945, GVA.

9. Neves to Vargas, Rio de Janeiro, Nov. 24, 1945, GVA; Diário de Notícias, Nov. 10, 1945, p. 14.

10. Cited in Getúlio Vargas, A Política Trabalhista no Brasil (Rio de Janeiro: Livraria José Olympio Editôra, 1950), pp. 15-16.

11. Statistics for the December 2, 1945, election were taken from Brazil, Tribunal Superior Eleitoral (TSE), Dados Estatísticos, vol. 1, Eleições Federal, Estadual e Municipal Realizadas no Brasil a partir de 1945, 1964; Rio Grande do Sul, Tribunal Regional Eleitoral (RGS, TRE), unpublished official electoral statistics bound as "Eleição de 2 de Dezembro de 1945."

12. Jaguaribe, Economic & Political Development, p. 145; Thomas E. Skidmore, Politics in Brazil, 1930-1964. An Experiment in Democracy (New York: Oxford University Press, 1967), pp. 69-70.

13. Vargas, Política Trabalhista, pp. 193-307; Dulles, Vargas of Brazil, pp. 283-85.

14. Lopes to Pasqualini, Rivera, Dec. 15, 1933, LAA; author's interview with Rony Lopes de Almeida, Pôrto Alegre, June 2, 1967.

15. P. Vargas to G. Vargas, Pôrto Alegre, Oct. 21, 1936, GVA.

16. See Alberto Pasqualini, Bases e Sugestões para uma Política Social (Pôrto Alegre: Editôra Globo, 1948).

17. Author's interview with José Diogo Brochado da Rocha, Pôrto Alegre, Jan. 10, 1967.

18. Partido Social Democrático, Anais da Convenção, pp.75-79.

19. Author's interview with José Diogo Brochado da Rocha, Pôrto Alegre, Jan. 10, 1967.

20. Armando Fay de Azevedo, "Pelos Caminhos da Política," Revista do Globo, June 20, 1964, p. 78; author's interview with Walter Spalding, Pôrto Alegre, Jan. 23, 1967.

21. Author's interview with Leônidas Xausa, Pôrto Alegre, May 9, 1967.

22. A. Fay de Azevedo in idem and F. Contreiras Rodrigues, "Os Partidos Políticos no Rio Grande do Sul. Dois Pontos de Vista," Revista Brasileira de Estudos Políticos, no. 2 (July 1957), pp. 86-87.

23. Vargas, Política Trabalhista, pp. 117-71.

24. Justino Martins, "O Gaúcho Jobim," Revista do Globo, Jan. 11, 1947, pp. 21-23.

25. Rubens Vidal, Subsídios para as Memórias de Getúlio Vargas. Suplemento da Revista do Globo (Pôrto Alegre, 1950), p. 80.

26. G. Vargas to P. Vargas, São Borja, Nov. 19, 1945, GVA.

27. Vargas, Política Trabalhista, p. 46.

28. Ibid., p. 52.

29. José Diogo Brochado da Rocha, Discurso Proferido pelo Deputado José Diogo Brochado da Rocha na Sessão no Dia 31-3-1947 (Pôrto Alegre: Imprensa Oficial, 1947), p. 4; author's interview with Carlos de Britto Velho, Tôrres, RGS, Feb. 13, 1967.

30. Ibid., pp. 6-8.

31. Statistics for the January 19, 1947, election were taken from Brazil, TSE, Dados Estatísticos, vol. 1; RGS, TSE, Votação por Distrito dos Candidatos ao Govêrno do Estado e Legendas Partidárias, Eleições de 19 de Janeiro de 1947, 1947; RGS, TRE, unpublished official electoral statistics bound as "Eleição de 19 de Janeiro de 1947," vols. 1 and 2.

32. Author's interview with Raul Pilla, Pôrto Alegre, June 29, 1967.

33. Rio Grande do Sul UDN Circular No. 16, Pôrto Alegre, June 26, 1947, BMA; Clio Fiori Druck, *Os Invioláveis* (Pôrto Alegre: Oficinas Gráficas da Livraria do Globo, 1947), pp. 42-43.

34. Rio Grande do Sul, *Constituições Sul-Riograndenses,* pp. 236-37.

35. Ibid., pp. 331-55.

36. Ibid., pp. 355-93.

37. Rio Grande do Sul, Secretária da Educação e Cultura, Divisão de Estatística Educacional, *Anuário de Estatísticas Educacionais e Culturais, 1961,* 1961, p. 39; Arthur Ferreira Filho, "Crônica dos Tempos Presentes (1928 a 1957), *Enciclopédia Rio-grandense,* 3, 65-66; Franklin de Oliveira, *Rio Grande do Sul: Um Nôvo Nordeste. O Desenvolvimento Econômico e as Disparidades Regionais,* 2d ed. rev. (Rio de Janeiro: Editôra Civilização Brasileira, 1961), pp. 183-84. Highway construction statistics were furnished by the Rio Grande do Sul Departamento Autônomo de Estradas de Rodagem.

38. Joel Bergsman, *Brazil: Industrialization and Trade Policies* (London: Oxford University Press, 1970), pp. 27-29.

39. Hélio Jaguaribe, "Que É o Adhemarismo? ," *Cadernos do Nosso Tempo,* January-June 1954, pp. 139-49.

40. Alceu Barbedo, *O Fechamento do Partido Comunista do Brasil (os Pareceres Barbedo)* (Rio de Janeiro: Imprensa Nacional, 1947), pp. 9-63.

41. Tarso Dutra, *Autonomismo e Fidelidade à Bandeira Partidária. Discurso Pronunciado na Assembléia Legislativa a 16 de Junho de 1950* (Pôrto Alegre, n.d.), pp. 22-87.

42. Coutinho, *General Góes,* pp. 494-500.

43. João Café Filho, *Do Sindicato ao Catete. Memórias Políticas e Confissões Humanas,* vol. 1, *Do Sindicato ao Catete* (Rio de Janeiro: Livraria José Olympio Editôra, 1966), pp. 85-99.

44. Author's interviews with Arthur Ferreira Filho, Pôrto Alegre, Apr. 10, 1967, and Adroaldo Mesquita da Costa, Pôrto Alegre, Jan. 2, 1967.

45. Author's interview with Hugo Berta, Pôrto Alegre, July 31, 1967.

46. Author's interview with José Antônio Aranha, Pôrto Alegre, Oct. 12, 1966.

47. Author's interview with José Mariano de Freitas Beck, Pôrto Alegre, Jan. 28, 1967.

48. Statistics for the October 3, 1950, election were taken from Brazil, TSE, *Dados Estatísticos,* vol. 2, *Eleições Federais e Estaduais Realizadas no Brasil em 1950,* 1964; RGS, TRE, unpublished official electoral statistics bound as "Eleição de 3 de Outubro de 1950," vols. 1 and 2.

49. Rio Grande do Sul, *Plano de Investimentos e Serviços Públicos, 1964-1966 (Síntese),* 1963, pp. 155-57.

50. Brazil, IBGE, *Estado do Rio Grande do Sul, 1950,* 1, 1; T. Lynn Smith, *Brazil: People and Institutions* (Baton Rouge: Louisiana State University Press, 1963), p. 492.

51. A. Gaylord Obern, *Métodos de Mudança em Duas Subculturas Brasileiras. Um Estudo Micro-comparativo de Govêrno* (Pôrto Alegre: Centro de Estudos Sociais da Faculdade de Filosofia da Universidade Federal do Rio Grande do Sul, 1966), p. 20.

52. "Panorama Econômico-Social do Rio Grande do Sul," p. 60.

Chapter 8: Fall of a Titan

1. Author's interview with Milton Dutra, Santiago de Boqueirão, RGS, Apr. 13, 1967.

2. Skidmore, *Politics in Brazil,* pp. 91-92, 99.

3. Nelson de Souza Sampaio, *Do Inquerito Parlamentar* (Rio de Janeiro: Fundação Getúlio Vargas, 1964), pp. 109-44; Affonso Henriques, *Ascensão e Queda de Getúlio Vargas,* vol. 3, *Declínio e Morte* (Rio de Janeiro: Distribuidora Record, 1966), pp. 23-93.

4. Skidmore, *Politics in Brazil,* pp. 103-5.

5. Dulles, *Vargas of Brazil,* p. 314.

6. Limeira Tejo, *Jango. Debate sôbre a Crise dos Nossos Tempos* (Rio de Janeiro: Editorial Andes, 1957), p. 88; author's interview with Horácio Silva, São Borja, RGS, Apr. 16, 1967.

7. Henriques, *Declínio e Morte*, pp. 118-73.

8. Cited in Oliveiros S. Ferreira, *As Fôrças Armadas e o Desafio da Revolução* (Rio de Janeiro: Edições GRD, 1964), pp. 122-29.

9. Ferreira Filho, "Crônica dos Tempos Presentes," p. 66; author's interview with Arthur Ferreira Filho, Pôrto Alegre, Apr. 10, 1967.

10. Lucídio Castelo Branco, "Agora É Governar," *Revista do Globo*, Oct. 30-Nov. 12, 1954, p. 39.

11. *Correio do Povo*, Nov. 8, 1959, pp. 35, 56.

12. Joseph Zukauskas, "Assim Falou Meneghetti: A Mim Compete Governar; aos Partidos Politicar," *Revista do Globo*, Feb. 5-18, 1955, p. 35; J. Aranha, manuscript, p. 2 of introduction to chapter 21; author's interview with José Antônio Aranha, Pôrto Alegre, Oct. 12, 1966.

13. *Correio do Povo*, Nov. 11, 1951, p. 32.

14. Author's interview with José Fernando Carneiro, Pôrto Alegre, Aug. 8, 1966.

15. Author's interview with José Diogo Brochado da Rocha, Pôrto Alegre, Jan. 16, 1967.

16. Castelo Branco, "Agora É Governar," p. 43; author's interview with Hugo Berta, July 31, 1967.

17. Henriques, *Declínio e Morte*, pp. 143-44.

18. João Neves da Fontoura, *Depoimentos de um Ex-Ministro* (Rio de Janeiro: Organização Simões, 1957), pp. 9-63.

19. Skidmore, *Politics in Brazil*, pp. 133-34.

20. Affonso Henriques' three-volume *Ascensão e Queda de Getúlio Vargas* presents a less charitable view of Vargas. This bible of anti-Getulism consists of nearly fifteen hundred pages of scandals surrounding Vargas.

21. Vergara, *Fui Secretário de Getúlio Vargas*, pp. 246-48.

22. Hugo Baldessarini, *Crônica de uma Epoca (de 1850 ao Atentado contra Carlos Lacerda). Getúlio Vargas e o Crime de Toneleros* (São Paulo: Companhia Editôra Nacional, 1957), pp. 169-99.

23. F. Zenha Machado, *Os Últimos Dias do Govêrno de Vargas (A Crise Política de Agôsto de 1954)* (Rio de Janeiro: Editôra Lux, 1955), pp. 177-94.

24. Café Filho, *Do Sindicato ao Catete*, pp. 321-34.

25. John V. D. Saunders, "A Revolution of Agreement among Friends: The End of the Vargas Era," *Hispanic American Historical Review* 44 (May 1964), 208-10.

26. Cited in Afonso César, *Política, Cifrão e Sangue: Documentação do 24 de Agôsto* (Rio de Janeiro: Editorial Andes, 1955), pp. 219-20.

27. Ferreira Filho, "Crônica dos Tempos Presentes," p. 67; author's interview with Antônio Guerra Flôres da Cunha, Pôrto Alegre, Aug. 24, 1966.

28. "Lágrimas de Dor e de Fumaça" *Revista do Globo*, Sept. 18-Oct. 1, 1954, pp. 57, 64, 71.

29. Castelo Branco, "Agora É Governar," p. 43; author's interview with Paulo Brossard de Souza Pinto, Pôrto Alegre, Jan. 6, 1967.

30. Author's interviews with José Diogo Brochado da Rocha, Pôrto Alegre, Jan. 16, 1967, and Pedro Chaves Barcellos, Pôrto Alegre, Jan. 14, 1967.

31. Castelo Branco, "Agora É Governar," p. 42; author's interview with Celestino Prunes, Pôrto Alegre, Sept. 29, 1966.

32. Author's interview with Fernando Gay de Fonseca, Pôrto Alegre, July 13, 1967.

33. Statistics for the October 3, 1954, election were taken from Brazil, TSE, *Dados Estatísticos*, vol. 3, pt. 1, *Eleições Federais, Estaduais e Municipais Realizadas no Brasil em 1952, 1954 e 1955, e em Confronto com Anteriores;* pt. 2, *Eleições Federais e Estaduais Realizadas em 1954 e 1955*, 1964; RGS, TRE, *Relatório Apresentado pela Comissão Apuradora das Eleições de 3 de Outubro de 1954*, 1954; RGS, TRE, unpublished official electoral statistics bound as "Eleições de 3 de Outubro de 1954."

34. José Diogo Brochado da Rocha to Salus Laks, Pôrto Alegre, Sept. 4, 1954; Adhemar de Barros to J. Diogo, São Paulo, Sept. 9, 1954, shown during author's interview with José Diogo Brochado da Rocha, Pôrto Alegre, Jan. 16, 1967.

35. Author's interview with Mário Gardelin, Caxias do Sul, RGS, Apr. 27, 1967.

Chapter 9: Triumph of the Vargas Heirs

1. J. Aranha, manuscript, pp. 402-3.
2. Tejo, *Jango*, pp. 139-41.
3. Ibid.
4. Fernando Ferrari, *Minha Campanha* (Pôrto Alegre: Editôra Globo, 1961), pp. 6-7.
5. Skidmore, *Politics in Brazil*, p. 158.
6. Statistics for the October 3, 1955, election were taken from Brazil, TSE, *Dados Estatísticos*, vol. 3; RGS, TRE, *Eleições Presidenciais de 1955*, 1956.
7. *Correio do Povo*, Oct. 11, 1955, p. 22.
8. J. Aranha to O. Aranha, Pôrto Alegre, Nov. 11, 1955, OAA.
9. Two important document collections on the October-November 1955 crisis are Loureiro Junior, *O Golpe de Novembro e Outros Discursos* (Rio de Janeiro: Livraria Clássica Brasileira, 1957); Bento Munhoz da Rocha Netto, *Radiografia de Novembro*, 2d ed. (Rio de Janeiro: Editôra Civilização Brasileira, 1961).
10. Dorival Teixeira Vieira, *O Desenvolvimento Econômico do Brasil e a Inflação* (São Paulo: Faculdade de Ciências Econômicas e Administrativas da Universidade de São Paulo, 1962), pp. 21-27; *Juscelino Kubitschek, el hombre e su obra* (Montevideo: Instituto de Cultura Uruguayo-Brasileño, 1958), pp. 47-108.
11. Rio Grande do Sul, *Plano de Investimentos*, pp. 4-8; Rio Grande do Sul, Assembléia Legislativa, *Análise do Insuficiente Desenvolvimento Econômico,* p. 41; Mota, "Considerações sôbre a 'Economia,' " p. 2.
12. Emil Farhat, *O País dos Coitadinhos (Algumas Idéias sôbre o Brasil)* (São Paulo: Companhia Editôra Nacional, 1966), pp. 162-68.
13. Rio Grande do Sul, *Plano de Investimentos*, pp. 221, 239-40; Rio Grande do Sul, Assembléia Legislativa, *Análise do Insuficiente Desenvolvimento Econômico*, p. 17; Schilling, *Crise Agro-Pecuária*, p. 29.
14. Brazil, Conselho Nacional de Economia (Brazil, CNE), *Exposição Geral da Situação Econômica do Brasil, 1962*, 1963, pp. 285-86; F. Oliveira, *Rio Grande do Sul*, pp. 102-3.
15. Werner Baer, *Industrialization and Economic Development in Brazil* (Homewood, Ill.: Richard D. Irwin, Inc., 1965), p. 56; Brazil, CNE, *Exposição Geral . . . 1962*, pp. 68, 271; Bergsman, *Brazil: Industrialization and Trade Policies*, pp. 74-78.
16. Brazil, CNE, *Exposição Geral . . . 1962*, pp. 144-47, 286, 290.
17. Ferreira Filho, *História Geral*, pp. 183-84; F. Oliveira, *Rio Grande do Sul*, pp. 23-25.
18. J. Aranha to O. Aranha, Pôrto Alegre, May 19, 1958, OAA.
19. A. Fay de Azevedo, "Balanço das Eleições de 1958 no Rio Grande do Sul," *Revista Brasileira de Estudos Políticos*, no. 8 (Apr. 1960), pp. 259-60.
20. Ibid., p. 261; Brazil, CNE, *Exposição Geral . . . 1962*, p. 142; author's interview with José Diogo Brochado da Rocha, Pôrto Alegre, Jan. 16, 1967.
21. Author's interviews with Carlos de Britto Velho, Tôrres, RGS, Feb. 13, 1967, José Antônio Aranha, Pôrto Alegre, Nov. 22, 1966, and Fernando Gay de Fonseca, Pôrto Alegre, July 13, 1967.
22. Statistics for the October 3, 1958, election were taken from Brazil, TSE, *Dados Estatísticos*, vol. 4, *Eleições Federais, Estaduais, Realizadas no Brasil em 1958, e em Confronto com Anteriores*, 1964; RGS, Departamento Estadual de Estatística, Serviço de Estatística Política e Social, *Estatística Eleitoral. Resultado das Eleições Realizadas em 1958 no Estado do Rio Grande do Sul*, 1959; RGS, TRE, unpublished official electoral statistics bound as "Eleições de 3 de Outubro de 1958."
23. Peterson, "Brazilian Political Parties," p. 205.

24. Ferrari, *Minha Campanha*, pp. 5-6.

25. Ibid., pp. 6-7.

26. Enéas de Souza, "PTB Rebelde Ganha com Loureiro," *Revista do Globo*, Nov. 28-Dec. 11, 1959, p. 6; author's interview with Leônidas Xausa, Pôrto Alegre, May 9, 1967.

27. Idem, "Pôrto Alegre: Escolhe Seu Prefeito," *Revista do Globo*, Oct. 31-Nov. 14, 1959, pp. 76-77; Ferrari, *Minha Campanha*, p. 73.

28. See page 132.

29. Ferrari, *Minha Campanha*, pp. 67-74.

30. *Correio do Povo*, Nov. 14, 1959, p. 16.

31. Timothy F. Harding, "Revolution Tomorrow: The Failure of the Left in Brazil," *Studies on the Left* 4 (Fall 1964): 36.

32. Ferrari, *Minha Campanha*, pp. 132, 176.

33. Statistics for the October 3, 1960, election were taken from Brazil, TSE, *Dados Estatísticos*, vol. 5, *Eleições Federais, Estaduais, Realizadas no Brasil em 1960, e em Confronto com Anteriores*, 1964.

34. Milton Senna, *Como Não Se Faz um Presidente* (Rio de Janeiro: Edições Gernasa, 1968), pp. 42-43, 54-55, 80-82.

35. Caldas, *Conjuntura Nacional*, p. 40.

36. Rio Grande do Sul, Assembléia Legislativa, *Análise do Insuficiente Desenvolvimento Econômico*, pp. 31-33. For a thorough analysis of Rio Grande do Sul's agricultural problems, see Peter T. Knight, *Brazilian Agricultural Technology and Trade. A Study of Five Commodities* (New York: Praeger Publishers, 1971).

37. Rio Grande do Sul, *Plano de Investimentos*, p. 358; F. Oliveira, *Rio Grande do Sul*, pp. 153-54.

38. F. Oliveira, *Rio Grande do Sul*, pp. 148-49.

39. Ibid., pp. 43-49, 130; Rio Grande do Sul, Assembléia Legislativa, *Análise do Insuficiente Desenvolvimento Econômico*, pp. 66-69.

40. Brazil, IBGE, *Estado do Rio Grande do Sul, 1950*, vol. 2, *Censos Econômicos*, p. 151; Brazil, IBGE, *Censo Industrial de 1960. Paraná-Santa Catarina-Rio Grande do Sul*, p. 72; Rio Grande do Sul, *Plano de Investimentos*, pp. 3-4; Rio Grande do Sul, Assembléia Legislativa, *Análise do Insuficiente Desenvolvimento Econômico*, p. 20.

41. Plínio Cabral, *Política sem Cartola* (Rio de Janeiro: Gráfica Record Editôra, 1967), pp. 44-45.

42. Rio Grande do Sul, *Plano de Investimentos*, p. 11; Rio Grande do Sul, Assembléia Legislativa, *Análise do Insuficiente Desenvolvimento Econômico*, pp. 34-35.

43. Gileno dé Carli, *Anatomia da Renúncia* (Rio de Janeiro: Edições o Cruzeiro, 1962), pp. 122-74; [Luis Alberto] Moniz Bandeira, *O 24 de Agôsto de Jânio Quadros*(Rio de Janeiro: Editôra Melso, 1961), pp. 25-51.

44. Cited in Mário Victor, *Cinco Anos Que Abalaram o Brasil (de Jânio Quadros ao Marechal Castelo Branco* (Rio de Janeiro: Editôra Civilização Brasileira, 1965), pp. 347-48.

45. The account of the Legality movement is based primarily on the following sources: Victor, *Cinco Anos Que Abalaram o Brasil;* Josimar Leite, *Brizola, o Homem de Agôsto* (Rio de Janeiro: Editôra Gráfica Lagunilla, 1963); Werneck Sodré, *História Militar do Brasil*; João Aldo Danesi, "10 Dias Que Abalaram o Brasil: Retrospecto de uma Epopéia," *Militia*, September-October 1961, pp. 9-16; "Os Doze Dias Que Abalaram o País," *Revista do Globo*, Sept. 16-29, 1961, pp. 2-15. In addition, the author interviewed numerous people who were involved in the Legality movement, including Leonel Brizola, Montevideo, Uruguay, Mar. 17, 1967.

46. Leite, *Brizola*, p. 27.

47. "Os Doze Dias Que Abalaram o País," p. 9.

48. Ibid., p. 12.

49. Victor, *Cinco Anos Que Abalaram o Brasil*, pp. 390-405.

Chapter 10: The Goulart-Brizola Era

1. Author's interview with João Cândido Maia Neto, Montevideo, Uruguay, Mar. 19, 1967.

2. Leonel Brizola to Franklin de Oliveira, Pôrto Alegre, Sept. 20, 1960, in F. Oliveira, *Rio Grande do Sul,* pp. xxxix-xlv; Mota, "Considerações sôbre a 'Economia,' " p. 7.

3. Rio Grande do Sul, Secretária da Educação e Cultura, Divisão de Estatística Educacional, *Anuário de Estatísticas Educacionais e Culturais, 1964,* 1964, p. 74.

4. Cabral, *Política sem Cartola,* p. 73; Ferreira Filho, *História Geral,* p. 186.

5. Cited in Victor, *Cinco Anos Que Abalaram o Brasil,* pp. 442-43.

6. Ibid., p. 444; Paula Beiguelman, *Pequenos Estudos de Ciência Política* (São Paulo: Editôra Centro Universitário, 1967), p. 96.

7. A. Fay de Azevedo, "Balanço das Eleições de 62 no Rio Grande do Sul," *Revista Brasileira de Estudos Políticos,* no. 16 (January 1964), p. 264.

8. Léa Brenner, "Michaelsen, um Trabalhista Conservador," *Revista do Globo,* Sept. 15-28, 1962, pp. 9-10.

9. Author's interviews with José Antônio Aranha, Pôrto Alegre, Nov. 22, 1966, and Leônidas Xausa, Pôrto Alegre, May 9, 1967.

10. Statistics for the October 7, 1962, election were taken from Brazil, TSE, *Dados Estatísticos,* vol. 6, *Eleições Federais, Estaduais, Realizadas no Brasil em 1962 e em Confronto com Anteriores. Referendum 6.163,* 1964; Rio Grande do Sul, Departamento Estadual de Estatística, *Estatística Eleitoral. Eleições Realizadas em 1962,* n.d.

11. Eduardo Pinto, "A Morte Rouba um Líder ao Rio Grande: Ferrari," *Revista do Globo,* June 8-21, 1963, pp. 2-5.

12. Statistics for the January 6, 1963, referendum were taken from Brazil, TSE, *Dados Estatísticos,* vol. 6; RGS, TRE, unpublished official electoral statistics bound as "Referendum de 6 de Janeiro de 1963."

13. John W. F. Dulles, *Unrest in Brazil: Political-Military Crises, 1955-1964* (Austin: University of Texas Press, 1970), pp. 202-5.

14. João Cândido Maia Neto, *Brasil. Guerra Quente na América Latina* (Rio de Janeiro: Editôra Civilização Brasileira, 1965), pp. 3-7; Edmar Morel, *O Golpe Começou Washington* (Rio de Janeiro: Editôra Civilização Brasileira, 1965), pp. 63-65; Harding, "Revolution Tomorrow," pp. 43-52.

15. Author's interview with Cândido Norberto dos Santos, Pôrto Alegre, July 7, 1967.

16. *Correio do Povo,* Nov. 20, 1963, p. 1.

17. Robert T. Daland, *Brazilian Planning: Development Politics and Administration* (Chapel Hill: University of North Carolina Press, 1967), pp. 159-60; Dulles, *Unrest in Brazil,* p. 246.

18. Skidmore, *Politics in Brazil,* pp. 260-64.

19. Dulles, *Unrest in Brazil,* pp. 230-32.

20. Skidmore, *Politics in Brazil,* pp. 261-63.

21. Morel. *O Golpe Começou em Washington,* pp. 76-77; Abelardo Jurema, *Sexta-Feira, 13. Os Últimos Dias do Govêrno João Goulart,* 3d ed. (Rio de Janeiro: Edições o Cruzeiro, 1964), pp. 139-49.

22. Werneck Sodré, *História Militar do Brasil,* pp. 391-94.

23. Skidmore, *Politics in Brazil,* pp. 294-99.

24. Eduardo Pinto, "A Revolução Vista do Rio Grande," *Revista do Globo,* May 9-22, 1964, pp. 37-38.

25. Ibid., p. 39.

26. Victor, *Cinco Anos Que Abalaram o Brasil,* p. 534.

27. Ronald M. Schneider, *The Political System of Brazil: Emergence of a "Modernizing" Authoritarian Regime, 1964-1970* (New York: Columbia University Press, 1971), pp. 101-2.

28. Pinto, "A Revolução Vista do Rio Grande," p. 43.

29. Author's interviews with José Antônio Aranha, Pôrto Alegre, Oct. 12, 1966, Plínio Cabral, Pôrto Alegre, May 14, 1967, and Túlio Fontoura, Passo Fundo, RGS, Apr. 23, 1967.

30. Pinto, "A Revolução Vista do Rio Grande," pp. 47-48.

31. Assis Brasil, "Brizola Queria Sangue," *O Cruzeiro* (Rio de Janeiro), May 16, 1964, pp. 43-44.

32. Author's interview with Leonel Brizola, Montevideo, Uruguay, Mar. 17, 1967.

33. G. Carneiro, *História das Revoluçoes Brasileiras,* 2,590-91.

34. Moysés Vellinho, "Encerra-se o Ciclo Getuliano," *Revista do Globo,* May 23-June 5, 1964, p. 8.

Chapter 11: Elections of 1966

1. Cited in Victor, *Cinco Anos Que Abalaram o Brasil,* pp. 597-600.

2. Charles Daugherty, James Rowe, and Ronald Schneider, eds., *Brazil. Election Factbook,* no. 2 (Washington: Institute for the Comparative Study of Political Systems, 1965), p. 15.

3. Victor, *Cinco Anos Que Abalaram o Brasil,* pp. 548-54.

4. Daugherty, Rowe, and Schneider, *Brazil. Election Factbook,* p. 15.

5. Ibid., pp. 90-91.

6. Aderson de Menezes, "As Eleições Federais de 1966: A Legislação Eleitoral e o Bi-partidarismo Nacional," *Revista Brasileira de Estudos Políticos,* nos. 23 and 24 (July 1967-January 1968), pp. 11-15; Schneider, *Political System of Brazil,* pp. 170-75.

7. Ibid.; Daland, *Brazilian Planning,* pp. 194-95.

8. *Zero Hora* (Pôrto Alegre), June 4, 1966, p. 2.

9. Opposition deputies to Ruy Cirne Lima, Pôrto Alegre, June 25, 1966, in *Correio do Povo,* June 26, 1966, p. 56.

10. *Zero Hora,* July 13, 1966, p. 6

11. *Correio do Povo,* July 3, 1966, p. 1.

12. *Zero Hora,* July 5, 1966, p. 8; July 20, 1966, p. 8.

13. *Correio do Povo,* Sept. 4, 1966, p. 1.

14. Leônidas Xausa and Francisco Ferraz, "As Eleições de 1966 no Rio Grande do Sul," *Revista Brasileira de Estudos Políticos,* nos. 23 and 24 (July 1967-January 1968), pp. 246-47.

15. This discussion of the 1966 elections is based primarily on numerous interviews and on my observations as a resident of Pôrto Alegre during the 1966 electoral struggle.

16. Statistics for the November 15, 1966, election were taken from RGS, TRE, unpublished official electoral statistics bound as "Eleições de 15 de Novembro de 1966. Apuração das Eleições Federais e Estaduais," vols. 1 and 2.

17. There are no figures available at this time from which to ascertain how many normally MDB votes went to Guazzelli and Mondim. However, during the counting of the Pôrto Alegre ballots there was considerable radio and press commentary as to the large number of ballots containing votes for MDB deputy candidates and Guazzelli rather than Heuser.

Chapter 12: Rio Grande in Retrospect

1. *New York Times,* Apr. 2, 1972, p. 3.

2. *Diário de Notícias,* Feb. 18, 1967, p. 1.

3. Inter-American Development Bank, *IDB Newsletter,* October 1969, p. 1; Brazilian Government Trade Bureau, *Brazilian Bulletin* (New York), Mar. 1968, p. 1; Brazilian Embassy, *Boletim Especial* (Washington, D.C.), Mar. 5, 1970, p. 2.

4. *Times of the Americas,* July 12, 1972, p. 5; *Brazilian Bulletin,* June 1969, p. 3; Nov. 1970, p. 3.

5. Schneider, *Political System of Brazil,* p. 320.

6. For a stinging indictment of the Gaúcho political process by one of its participants see Cabral, *Política sem Cartola.*

Glossary of
Brazilian Portuguese Terms

Bahiano. One from the state of Bahia.

Banda Oriental. East Bank of the Rio de la Plata across the estuary from Buenos Aires; modern Uruguay.

banha. Lard.

Carioca. One from the city of Rio de Janeiro.

Catarinense. One from the state of Santa Catarina.

Catete. Former Brazilian presidential palace in Rio de Janeiro.

caudilho. Political chieftain, often charismatic, autocratic, or militaristic (in Spanish, *caudillo*).

Chimango. Vulturelike bird; member of the Riograndense Republican Party during the Old Republic.

colono. Colonist; non-Portuguese European immigrant (mainly German and Italian) and descendants.

compadrio. Extended family.

conto. Unit of Brazilian currency.

coronel. Traditional Brazilian county political chieftain, often a wealthy landowner (plural, *coronéis*).

coronelismo. System of coronel control of rural and small town politics, particularly through electoral domination and manipulation.

cristianizar. To nominate a candidate but support and vote for the opposition.

Estado Nôvo. New State; Brazilian dictatorship of Getúlio Vargas, 1937-45.

estância. Ranch.

estancieiro. Owner of an estância.

235

Farroupilha. 1835-45 war between Rio Grande do Sul and the Brazilian Empire.

fazenda. Ranch, plantation, or large farm.

fazendeiro. Owner of a fazenda.

Gaúcho. Riograndense; one from the state of Rio Grande do Sul.

Lloyd Brasileiro. Brazilian national merchant fleet.

Luso. Portuguese.

Maragato. Member of the Federalist Party of Rio Grande do Sul during the Old Republic.

Mineiro. One from the state of Minas Gerais.

município. Administrative division roughly equivalent to a county.

Paulista. One from the state of São Paulo.

pelego. Sheep hide; agent who represented labor ministry officials or Brazilian Labor Party politicians in relations with unions.

Pernambucano. One from the state of Pernambuco.

Piratini. Rio Grande do Sul governor's palace in Pôrto Alegre.

prefeito. Mayor; chief government official of a município.

provisório. Rapidly mobilizable state military ready reserve.

queremismo. 1945 pro-Vargas movement which favored his remaining as president during the national constituent assembly.

queremista. Adherent of queremismo.

Riograndense. Gaúcho; one from the state of Rio Grande do Sul.

saudade. Longing; remembrance; yearning; nostalgia.

tenente. Lieutenant; nationalistic, reform-minded military man involved in a movement for Brazilian political, economic, and social regeneration, beginning in the 1920s.

tenentismo. Movement of Brazilian political, economic, and social regeneration, begun in the 1920s by nationalistic, reform-minded military men known as tenentes.

trabalhismo. Laborism; Vargas' basic political program, which blended social welfare paternalism, governmental centralism, economic nationalism, and expanded presidentialism.

Note on Sources

The most important sources for this book, particularly chapters three through seven, were the personal archives of eight leading Gaúcho politicians: Getúlio Vargas, governor of Rio Grande do Sul (1928-30), president of Brazil (1930-45, 1951-54), and founder of the Brazilian Labor and Social Democratic parties; Oswaldo Aranha, Gaúcho interior secretary (1928-30), Brazilian justice, finance, and foreign minister for various periods from 1930 to 1954, and ambassador to the United States (1934-37); Antônio Augusto Borges de Medeiros, governor of Rio Grande do Sul (1898-1907, 1913-27) and chief of the Riograndense Republican Party (1903-37); Joaquim Francisco de Assis Brasil, agriculture minister (1930-32) and founder of the Liberator Party; Lindolfo Collor, labor minister (1930-32), Gaúcho finance secretary (1936), and founder of the Castilhist Republican Party; Francisco Antunes Maciel Junior, Gaúcho finance secretary (1930-32) and Brazilian justice minister (1932-34); Sinval Saldanha, Rio Grande interior secretary (1930-32); and Rony Lopes de Almeida, active Republican and later Castilhist Republican politician and jounalist.

In addition to using the archives of these Gaúcho leaders, I also worked with the papers of Minas Gerais' Afrânio de Melo Franco, Brazilian foreign minister (1930-33), in the Biblioteca Nacional in Rio de Janeiro and with the Arquivo da Presidência da República in Rio's Arquivo Nacional. Background information and commentary on Brazilian politics were obtained from the records of the U.S. Embassy in Rio, which are housed in the U.S. National Archives in Washington, and the reports of the U.S. Consulate in Pôrto Alegre, which were stored in the U.S. Department of State.

237

Since considerable attention was devoted to the various Gaúcho and national elections, much of my analysis was based on electoral statistics. The basic source for these figures was the Rio Grande do Sul Tribunal Regional Eleitoral, which has the official statistics for all state and national elections in Rio Grande since 1945. To supplement these statistics I used the Brazilian Tribunal Superior Eleitoral's six-volume set of *Dados Estatísticos* (Imprensa Nacional, 1964).

In addition, I worked extensively in a number of other Brazilian libraries and government offices. I found useful collections of books and documents on Rio Grande do Sul in Pôrto Alegre in the Biblioteca da Assembléia Legislativa, the Biblioteca Pública, the Arquivo Histórico do Estado, the Biblioteca da Faculdade de Filosofia da Universidade Federal do Rio Grande do Sul, and particularly the Instituto Histórico e Geográfico do Rio Grande do Sul, which has the important Borges de Medeiros papers. Basic sources for Gaúcho economic statistics were the Conselho de Desenvolvimento do Estado and the Departamento Estadual de Estatística, both in Pôrto Alegre. Finally, in Rio de Janeiro I supplemented my Rio Grande work with research in the Biblioteca Nacional, Arquivo Nacional, and Biblioteca do Instituto Brasileiro de Geografia e Estatística.

Brazilian newspapers and magazines also were basic sources for this study. Most important was Pôrto Alegre's leading newspaper, *Correio do Povo.* Although it has severely reduced the scope of its political coverage in recent years, *Correio do Povo* was of inestimable value in the study of Gaúcho politics during the 1930s, particularly because it published complete documents such as party manifestoes, political correspondence, and speeches.

In addition, throughout Gaúcho history, political parties and politicians have spawned a number of newspapers to serve as their official voices. Most famous were *A Federação,* the official Rio-grandense Republican and later Liberal Republican newspaper, and *O Estado do Rio Grande,* the Liberator daily. Finally, at various periods in its uneven history, Pôrto Alegre's *Revista do Globo* carried articles on Gaúcho politicians, historical figures, elections, revolutions, and other important events.

Interviews with nearly one hundred politicians, historians, and other analysts and observers also formed an essential part of my research. Although most of my interviewing occurred in Pôrto

Alegre and Rio de Janeiro, I also talked with a number of Gaúcho political leaders and historians during two months which my wife and I spent in the state's interior. In addition we visited Montevideo, where I interviewed Gaúcho and other Brazilian exiles.

To supplement my basic research in archives, government offices, newspapers, and interviews, I consulted a large number of books and unpublished manuscript sources. Three principal unpublished manuscripts stand out. José Antônio Aranha, a veteran Gaúcho leader, kindly permitted me to read the preliminary manuscript of a major study of twentieth-century Brazilian political history on which he was working at the time of his death. Colonel Aldo Ladeira Ribeiro, former chief of staff of the Gaúcho military brigade, allowed me to read his manuscript for the third volume of the *Esboço Histórico da Brigada Militar do Rio Grande do Sul.* For the first chapter of my book I made considerable use of Richard Kornweibel's fine Ph.D. dissertation, "Júlio de Castilhos and the Republican Party of Rio Grande do Sul" (Department of History, University of California, Santa Barbara).

As for books, a basic list of works on Rio Grande do Sul since the fall of the Empire in 1889 is *Bibliografia da História do Rio Grande do Sul (Período Republicano)* (Pôrto Alegre: Faculdade de Filosofia da Universidade Federal do Rio Grande do Sul, 1967), compiled by Richard Kornweibel and Carlos Cortés. Although the quantity of books on Rio Grande is impressive, the quality is uneven. There is no really outstanding general history of the state. In partial compensation we have Erico Verissimo's seven-volume historical novel, *O Tempo e o Vento,* 3d ed. (Pôrto Alegre: Editôra Globo, 1962). The first two volumes have been published in English as *Time and the Wind* (New York: The Macmillan Company, 1951). This epic story of Rio Grande from its origins through World War II is one of the finest, most sweeping historical novels on any subnational political unit in the world. Less impressive are the general histories of the state, the best being E. F. de Souza Docca's detailed *História do Rio Grande do Sul* (Rio de Janeiro: Organização Simões, 1954) and Arthur Ferreira Filho's shorter, more readable *História Geral do Rio Grande do Sul,* 3d ed. (Pôrto Alegre: Editôra Globo, 1965).

Most period histories of Rio Grande focus on the years through the 1930 revolution, paying only minimal attention to the post-1930 epoch. Like U.S. Revolutionary War and Civil War historians, Gaúcho authors enjoy resurrecting Rio Grande's days of military glory. The most popular topics have been the patriotism-inspiring Farroupilha War (1835-45), the less glorious but bloodier Federalist Revolution (1893-95), and the 1930 overthrow of the Old Republic. The latter can be relived by reading the second volume of João Neves da Fontoura's *Memórias* (Pôrto Alegre: Editôra Globo, 1963) and the exhaustive, 486-page special edition of the *Revista do Globo* entitled *Revolução de Outubro de 1930: Imagens e Documentos* (Pôrto Alegre: Barcellos, Bertaso & Cia., 1931). The most important study of Rio Grande during the Old Republic is Joseph L. Love's *Rio Grande do Sul and Brazilian Regionalism, 1882-1930* (Stanford, Calif.: Stanford University Press, 1971).

The post-1930 period of Rio Grande history generally has been ignored, although there are limited studies of a few leading Riograndenses (Oswaldo Aranha, João Goulart, and Leonel Brizola) and a plethora of books on the major Gaúcho figure, Getúlio Vargas, including John W. F. Dulles' *Vargas of Brazil: A Political Biography* (Austin: University of Texas Press, 1967). There is no overall history of Rio Grande do Sul since 1930, the present book excepted. The most useful single work on the 1930-37 era is João Neves da Fontoura's *Accuso!* (Rio de Janeiro, 1933), which suffers from the author's obvious aim of venting his wrath against Gaúcho interventor José Antônio Flôres da Cunha. The Estado Nôvo era is almost totally ignored in Gaúcho historical literature, except for a few contemporary discussions of the problem of German and Italian colonists.

The post-1945 period has received slightly better treatment, including a group of critical studies on selected aspects of Rio Grande politics and economics. In the former category are: A. Gaylord Obern's *Métodos de Mudança em Duas Subculturas Brasileiras* (Pôrto Alegre: Centro de Estudos Sociais da Faculdade de Filosofia da Universidade Federal do Rio Grande do Sul, 1966), a comparison of two Gaúcho counties; Clio Fiori Druck's *Os Invioláveis* (Pôrto Alegre: Oficinas Gráficas da Livraria do Globo, 1947), a snide collection of articles on the 1947 Rio Grande constitutional convention; and Plínio Cabral's *Política sem Cartola* (Rio de Janeiro: Gráfica Record Editôra, 1967), a bitter, penetrating series of essays on the post-Estado Nôvo Gaúcho political process.

Most of the economic studies concentrate on the search for the causes of Rio Grande's economic problems. The best are two publications of the Rio Grande government—*Plano de Investimentos e Serviços Públicos, 1964-1966 (Síntese)* (São Leopoldo: Oficinas Gráficas de Rotermund & Cia., 1963) and *Análise do Insuficiente Desenvolvimento Econômico do Rio Grande do Sul* (Assembléia Legislativa, Comissão de Desenvolvimento Econômico, *Boletim,* no. 16, 1965). Franklin de Oliveira gives a more emotional analysis in *Rio Grande do Sul. Um Nôvo Nordeste. O Desenvolvimento Econômico e as Disparidades Regionais,* 2d ed. rev. (Rio de Janeiro: Editôra Civilização Brasileira, 1961).

In addition to these regional studies, I made use of a number of works on Brazil in general. The outstanding general history of 1930-64 Brazil is Thomas E. Skidmore's *Politics in Brazil, 1930-1964: An Experiment in Democracy* (New York: Oxford University Press, 1967). Among other broad-scope works on that era are Glauco Carneiro's two-volume *História das Revoluções Brasileiras* (Rio de Janeiro: Edições o Cruzeiro, 1965), Edgard Carone's *Revoluções do Brasil Contemporâneo, 1922/1938* (São Paulo: Coleção Buriti, 1965), John D. Wirth's *The Politics of Brazilian Development, 1930-1954* (Stanford, Calif.: Stanford University Press, 1970), Werner Baer's *Industrialization and Economic Development in Brazil* (Homewood, Ill.: Richard D. Irwin, 1965), Affonso Henriques' three-volume *Ascensão e Queda de Getúlio Vargas* (Rio de Janeiro: Distribuidora Record, 1966), John W. F. Dulles' *Unrest in Brazil: Political-Military Crises, 1955-1964* (Austin: University of Texas Press, 1970), Mário Victor's *Cinco Anos Que Abalaram o Brasil (de Jânio Quadros ao Marechal Castelo Branco)* (Rio de Janeiro: Editôra Civilização Brasileira, 1965), and Alfred Stepan's *The Military in Politics: Changing Patterns in Brazil* (Princeton, N.J.: Princeton University Press, 1971). Shockingly, the best study of the Estado Nôvo is still Karl Loewenstein's *Brazil under Vargas* (New York: The Macmillan Company, 1944).

Memoirs provide personalistic if somewhat distorted insights into the Gaúcho political phenomenon. Of particular interest are the memoirs of six Gaúchos. José Antônio Flôres da Cunha's *A*

Campanha de 1923 (Rio de Janeiro: Livraria-Editôra Zelio Valverde, [1942]) vividly re-creates the 1923 Liberator-Republican struggle in Rio Grande. On the 1930 revolution, the best Gaúcho account is the second volume of João Neves da Fontoura's *Memórias*, while S. Faria Corrêa's *Serro Alegre (Revolução Rio-grandense de 1932)* (n.p., 1933) presents the 1932 revolution from the perspective of the Borges de Medeiros column. Two laudatory views of Getúlio Vargas are *Getúlio Vargas, Meu Pai* (Rio de Janeiro: Editôra Globo, 1960), the memoirs of his daughter, Alzira Vargas do Amaral Peixoto, and *Fui Secretário de Getúlio Vargas. Memórias dos Anos de 1926-1954* (Pôrto Alegre: Editôra Globo, 1960), the memoirs of his secretary, Luiz Vergara. Finally, Fernando Ferrari has documented his 1959-60 struggle with João Goulart in his *Minha Campanha* (Pôrto Alegre: Editôra Globo, 1961).

Memoirs by non-Gaúchos also shed some light on Rio Grande do Sul. Most important is Lourival Coutinho's *O General Góes Depôe . . .* , in which Pedro Aurélio Góes Monteiro justifies his political career, often at the expense of such people as Vargas and Flôres da Cunha. Other useful memoirs are former Minas Gerais governor Benedito Valadares' *Tempos Idos e Vividos. Memórias* (Rio de Janeiro: Editôra Civilização Brasileira, 1966), former president João Café Filho's two-volume *Do Sindicato ao Catete. Memórias Políticas e Confissões Humanas* (Rio de Janeiro: Livraria José Olympio Editôra, 1966), and a number of works by Paulistas, whose attention is directed particularly to the 1930 and 1932 revolutions.

Finally, mention should be made of two published document collections. *O General Flôres da Cunha e a Revolução Paulista (Decisão do Tribunal de Honra e Outros Documentos* (Pôrto Alegre: Oficinas Gráficas d'*A Federação*, 1933) is a valuable book of documents published soon after the 1932 revolution by a Rio Grande Tribunal of Honor appointed by Flôres to establish for posterity the legitimacy of his position during the 1932 conflict. Even more comprehensive is Hélio Silva's multivolume *O Ciclo de Vargas* (Rio de Janeiro: Editôra Civilização Brasileira, 1964-72). Currently twelve volumes covering the period from 1922 through 1942, it is projected to grow to include the years through Vargas' suicide in 1954. A structured series of selections from previously unpublished documents tied together by textual commentary, *O Ciclo de Vargas* is one of the most ambitious historical projects currently in progress on twentieth-century Brazil and a prime source for anyone planning to do research on Brazil since 1922.

Index

ABC pact, 144–45
Act of Party Fidelity (Complementary Act No. 16), 205
ADP. *See* Popular Democratic Action
Agrarian Front, 192–93
agriculture, 2, 37, 97–99, 158–60, 170, 210–11
Alcântara Monteiro, Alfeu de, 175
Alkmin, José Maria, 200
Almeida, José Américo de, 80, 81, 90, 91
Amazonas, 16
Andrada, Antônio Carlos de, 18–19, 21, 71
Andrade, Auro Moura de, 192
Andreazza, Mário, 209, 210
Aranha, José Antônio, 143, 191
Aranha, Oswaldo, 24–25, 57, 80, 83, 90, 107–8, 117, 123, 147, 153–54, 176, 185, 208; death of, 164; Flôres and, 25, 39, 50, 51, 54, 107; in National Democratic Union, 107, 116; in 1923 revolution, 15; in 1930 revolution, 20–21, 22; as Octobrist, 31, 32; as presidential candidate, 74–77, 79; Vargas, split with, 94–95, 103; in Vargas government, 30–31, 35, 36, 37, 38, 50, 51, 54, 77, 94–95, 138–39
ARENA. *See* National Renovation Alliance
Argentina, 4, 5, 8, 51, 59, 98, 111, 144–45, 161
Arraes, Miguel, 190
ARS. *See* Socialist Republican Alliance
Assis Brasil, Joaquim Francisco de, 13, 17, 19, 23, 45, 47; as gubernatorial candidate, 13–14; in 1923 revolution, 15; in Vargas government, 29, 32, 34, 36, 51
Assis Brasil, Ptolomeu de, 29
Autonomous Social Democratic Party (PSDA), 131, 132, 135, 141, 142
Azores Islands, 3

Bahia, 12, 19, 56, 76, 78
Banda Oriental, 3, 4
Barcellos, Christóvão, 65, 66
Barros, Adhemar de, 135, 148, 149, 163; as governor, 128–29; as presidential candidate, 137, 144, 153, 155, 156, 169, 173; Vargas, alliance with, 129–30
Barros Cassal, Annibal de, 29, 36
Beck, José Mariano de Freitas, 181, 206
Bernardes, Arthur da Silva, 12, 31, 43, 71, 129, 146
Bittencourt, Lúcio, 165
Borges de Medeiros, Antônio Augusto, 16, 18–19, 23, 25–26, 34, 35, 36, 37, 50, 51, 55, 69, 70, 107, 108, 118, 122, 138, 185; death of, 164; as governor, 11–15, 18, 162; in 1930 revolution, 21, 31; in 1932 revolution, 40–47, 50; as presidential candidate, 58; as Riograndense Republican Party chief, 10, 12
Brasília, 158, 181, 192
Brazilian Communist Party (PCB), 110, 111, 116–18, 124–25, 126, 128, 132, 133, 137, 140, 168, 186–87, 211. *See also* Communism